SECRET LIVES OF
GREAT AUTHORS

SECRET LIVES

OF

GREAT AUTHORS

WHAT YOUR TEACHERS NEVER TOLD YOU ABOUT FAMOUS NOVELISTS, POETS, AND PLAYWRIGHTS

QUIRK BOOKS
PHILADELPHIA

BY ROBERT SCHNAKENBERG

ILLUSTRATED BY MARIO ZUCCA

Library of Congress Cataloging in Publication Number: 2007937187
ISBN: 978-1-59474-211-8
Printed in China
Typeset in Gill Sans, Helvetica, and Trade Gothic

The author would like to acknowledge Jean Kim, Jure Fiorillo, and Karen Lurie
for their help in researching this book.

Cover designed by Doogie Horner
Interior designed by Joshua McDonnell
Illustrations by Mario Zucca

Distributed in North America by Chronicle Books
680 Second Street
San Francisco, CA 94107

10 9 8 7 6 5 4 3 2 1

Quirk Books
215 Church Street
Philadelphia, PA 19106
www.quirkbooks.com

CONTENTS

INTRODUCTION

IS IT JUST ME, or do we expect great authors to lead sedate, contemplative, uninteresting lives? Granted, some of them do—I'm looking at *you*, Jane Austen—but you won't find any of them in this book. The vast majority of literary legends live more like debauched Hollywood actors than shy, retiring bookworms. They're drug addicts and pee drinkers, womanizers and wannabe movie stars, more likely to be seen with a half-empty bottle of gin in hand than a feathered quill.

We can probably thank our teachers for this misperception. They were trying so hard to encourage us to slog through *Ulysses*, they forgot to tell us about James Joyce's weird sex life—which, come to think of it, might have made it easier to slog through *Ulysses* (or at least understand it). Just as knowing how much Ayn Rand enjoyed the 1970s TV jigglefest *Charlie's Angels* might have made us more inclined to read all 1,100 pages of *Atlas Shrugged*. Well, okay, maybe not so much.

But you get the point. Great writers put their underwear on one leg at a time just like the rest of us (although in Hemingway's case, it might be ladies' underwear). They freak out, feud with each other, get slammed in the press, and join obscure religious cults just like anyone else in the public eye. This book fills you in on all the flaws, foibles, and human frailties that you may not have heard about the first time you encountered these literary giants, and hopefully you will be intrigued enough to read, or reread, their works. Along the way, you may just learn a few useful facts that could help you fill out that skimpy term paper or keep up with that cocktail party blowhard who somehow found the time to read every one of Faulkner's novels—in French. One well-placed "Did you know?" from the tidbits compiled here could be the room-clearing rim shot you need at the next campus bull session.

A note about the contents. A book like this one is bound to be subjective, and it is not meant to offer a comprehensive survey of the world's great writers. I struggled with leaving out a figure as colorful as Truman Capote. But the opportunity to discuss his mesmerizing performance in Neil Simon's *Murder by Death* will have to wait for another day. Norman Mailer was another late scratch. His bizarre 1969 vanity campaign for mayor of New York City merits a volume all its own. What I have tried to do is narrow the list of subjects down to a fair, representative sampling of history's most accomplished, most iconic, and most interesting authors. Your high school English teacher may have wanted to keep all this stuff secret, but, to borrow another line from Shakespeare, the truth will out.

WILLIAM SHAKESPEARE

APRIL 23, 1564–APRIL 23, 1616

NATIONALITY:
ENGLISH

ASTROLOGICAL SIGN:
TAURUS

MAJOR WORKS:
THE MERCHANT OF VENICE (1596),
ROMEO AND JULIET (1599), *HAMLET* (1602)

CONTEMPORARIES & RIVALS:
CHRISTOPHER MARLOWE, BEN JONSON

LITERARY STYLE:
RICHLY POETIC AND LACED WITH
SALACIOUS AND WITTY PUNS

WORDS OF WISDOM ➤ *"THE WEB OF OUR LIFE IS OF A MINGLED YARN, GOOD AND ILL TOGETHER."*

April 23 is one of the most joyous—and saddest—days in literary history. That's the day, in 1564, that William Shakespeare was born (if you subscribe to the reasonable supposition that his delivery predated his baptism by three days) as well as the day he died, fifty-two years later. April 23, 1616, is also the day Miguel de Cervantes died, but surely even the author of *Don Quixote* would have graciously accepted being upstaged by a man considered to be the greatest writer ever.

Shakespeare wasn't exactly born into a distinguished family. His father, John, was a prosperous glove maker who sometimes ran afoul of the law. He was fined for maintaining a dunghill in front of the family's home and prosecuted for selling wool on the black market. Once a respected alderman, the elder Shakespeare saw his social status gradually decline to the point where his application for a family coat of arms was rejected by the College of Heralds. William Shakespeare would later succeed where his father had failed, selecting the motto *Non sanz droit* ("Not without right") that suggests he was still steamed at the way the old man had been treated.

Details on the Bard's early life are sketchy. At age eighteen, he was married to twenty-six-year-old Anne Hathaway, who was at least three months pregnant on their wedding day. By 1585 the Shakespeares had added a set of twins to the family. About this time, Shakespeare drops off the map, so to speak. Speculation abounds concerning his activities during the next seven years. Some say he worked as a scrivener, a gardener, a coachman, a sailor, a printer, or a moneylender. One fanciful Bardolater even posits that he spent some time as a Franciscan monk. We'll likely never know the real story.

Shakespeare returns to historical records in 1592, when a fellow playwright denounces him in print as an "upstart crow, beautified with our feathers." The cattiness of the remark indicates that young Will had already achieved some measure of success in London. Although his early plays may seem a bit raw today, they were huge hits at the time. The gate receipts for bawdy comedies such as *The Comedy of Errors* and gory tragedies like *Titus Andronicus* enabled Shakespeare to live the life of a country gentleman, a goal to which he had always aspired. He wheeled and dealed in real estate, lent money at interest and sued to get it back, and bought an equity stake in the Globe Theater that helped make him a wealthy man. He also cheated on his wife with impunity, flipped the taxman the bird, and generally acted like a man untouchable by both the law and bourgeois morality. Is it any wonder why we love this guy?

Life was good for Shakespeare when he retired to his estate at Stratford in 1613, and it's been good for him, literary-reputation-wise, ever since. Sure, there are still those who charge that someone from such humble origins and with less-than-stellar education could not possibly have written such brilliant plays, but they're mostly crackpots like Samuel Taylor Coleridge, Henry James, Charles Dickens, James Joyce, and Sir John Gielgud, to name just a few. Some even claim that Queen Elizabeth I wrote Shakespeare's plays, though how she continued writing them after her death in 1603 remains a mystery. The real Shakespeare lived on until 1616, when he became ill—possibly after a bout of hard drinking—and passed away at the (then) ripe-old age of fifty-two.

!

WHAT'S IN A NAME?

As anyone who's ever tried to plough through a trough can tell you, English spelling is notoriously irregular. In Shakespeare's time it was even more chaotic. As a result, there are more than eighty-three equally valid ways to spell Shakespeare. Shagspere and Shaxberd are just a couple of the more exotic. Even the Bard himself had trouble keeping his surname straight. He signed it at least six different ways, and in increasingly erratic handwriting: Shackper (on a 1612 deposition), Shakspear (on a 1612 deed), Shakspea (on a 1612 mortgage), Shackspere (on the first page of his 1616 will), Shakspere (on page 2 of that same document), and, finally, Shakspeare (on page 3 of, you guessed it, his last will and testament). At least he got a little closer every time.

OH, DEER!

Was England's most beloved poet and playwright a low-down dirty thief? Popular legend has it that sometime in the 1580s the young Shakespeare was busted for poaching deer on the estate of a powerful magistrate named Sir Thomas Lucy. Shortly after Shakespeare's death, a Gloucestershire clergyman named Richard Davies wrote that, as a young man, the playwright "was much given to all unluckiness in stealing venison and rabbit" and that Lucy "oft had him whipped and sometimes imprisoned and at last made him fly his native country to his great advancement." Whatever the reason, Shakespeare did flee Stratford for London around that time. He may have even gotten some measure of revenge against his tormentor. The character of Justice Shallow in *The Merry Wives of Windsor* and *Henry VI, Part 2* is said to be a thinly veiled caricature of Lucy.

TAX THIS!

By 1597 Shakespeare was already well-to-do by the standards of his day. And apparently he had discovered the traditional rich man's strategy for maintaining one's wealth: cheating on your taxes. The Bard is listed as a tax defaulter in the King's Remembrancer Subsidy Roll for that year. Three years later, his debt apparently remained unpaid. A 1600 tax record notes that a "tax bill of 13s.4d. is still outstanding" and refers the playwright's arrears to the Bishop of Winchester, whose jurisdiction included London's most notorious debtor's prison. Subsequent documents indicate that Shakespeare—or someone acting on his behalf—eventually coughed up the dough.

THE ORIGINAL SHYLOCK

Shakespeare may not have always paid his own debts, but he insisted on other people settling theirs. A tight-fisted moneylender, the Bard was known to provide capital to needy friends "at a price." "If you bargain with Mr. Shakespeare," the father of his prospective son-in-law once remarked, "bring your money home if you may." Shakespeare was well known for taking his borrowers to court to collect on unpaid debts, no matter how small. Even worse, he was a miser of Scrooge-like proportions. He never spent a penny on the poor folks of Stratford and was notorious for hoarding grain and malt during times of famine. Scholars are still debating whether the provision in Shakespeare's will that leaves to his widow only their "second best bed" was an affectionate gesture or one final turn of the screw from a dying tightwad.

SON OF WILL?

Bastard sons play critical roles in several of Shakespeare's plays, so it's no surprise he may have sired one himself. The playwright spent most of his time in London, leaving wife Anne Hathaway in Stratford to raise their children. When journeying home for visits, he passed through the town of Oxford, where he often stayed at a tavern owned by John Davenant, a wealthy vintner. Davenant had a comely wife of his own, Jane, and, well, rumor has it she and Billy Shakes made the beast with two backs together. Her son, named—ahem—William Davenant, was born in February 1606. Shakespeare was godfather to the child. As the boy grew, he developed several striking similarities to his putative progenitor. Will Davenant became a respected playwright, theater manager, and poet who was named England's poet laureate in 1637. He even collaborated with John Dryden on a new version of *The Tempest* in 1667. Of Davenant, Samuel Butler once observed, "It seemed to him that he writ with the very same spirit that Shakespeare [did], and seemed content enough to be called his son." Absent a DNA test, we may never know the validity of the claim.

SHAKESPEARE'S WIFE WAS ALREADY SEVERAL MONTHS PREGNANT ON THEIR WEDDING DAY—AND SHE WASN'T THE LAST WOMAN TO BEAR A CHILD OF THE BARD.

TOP BILLING

A randy Shakespeare once snookered his friend and fellow actor Richard Burbage out of a romantic rendezvous with a young lady who lived near the theater. The Bard overheard the two making plans for a secret assignation. "Announce yourself as Richard III," she told the actor. Thinking quickly, Shakespeare hustled off to the woman's home, gave the agreed-upon codename at the door, and was admitted to her boudoir for a spirited rogering session. When Burbage showed up a few minutes later, Shakespeare sent down a note: William the Conqueror came before Richard III.

BI ANY OTHER NAME

That Shakespeare was a bit of a rake is indisputable. After all, he did address twenty-six erotically charged love sonnets to an unnamed married woman known as the Dark Lady. But did the world's most revered romantic versifier occasionally go to bat for the other team? Scholars continue to debate whether Shakespeare was bisexual. Supporters of the idea point to the 126 *other* sonnets he wrote to a man, known as the Fair Youth or Fair Lord. The only edition of the sonnets published during his lifetime is dedicated to the mysterious "Mr. W. H." And, in his will, Shakespeare bequeathed money to his male friends John Heminges, Richard Burbage, and Henry Condell expressly for buying memorial rings to commemorate their close kinship. That kind of evidence has fueled academic ruminations for decades.

EMBARRASSING RELATIVES

Like most prominent public figures, Shakespeare was saddled with his share of embarrassing relatives—none more so than his lowlife son-in-law Thomas Quiney. A foul-mouthed tavern owner who was once nearly prosecuted for selling bad wine, Quiney was a poor match for Shakespeare's daughter Judith. Yet Shakespeare did not stand in the way of their union, and the two were married on February 10, 1616, just two months before the Bard's death. The wedding cake was barely stale when Judith discovered that Quiney had been sleeping with another woman. Stratford was scandalized. Shakespeare himself hurriedly modified his will to cut out Quiney entirely. On March 26, the philandering saloonkeeper was convicted of performing "carnal copulation." He was ordered to perform public penance, though the sentence was later commuted to a small fine and private penance. The sordid incident fueled speculation that Shakespeare was murdered by Quiney's own hand, as retribution for depriving him of an inheritance. However, no compelling evidence has yet been offered to support the theory.

BARD STIFF

To dissuade gravediggers from digging up and dumping his remains in a charnel house (a common practice at the time), Shakespeare put a curse on his tomb. It is inscribed with the following epitaph:

> Good friend for Jesus' sake forbear
> To dig the dust enclosed here!
> Blest be the man that spares these stones,
> And curst be he that moves my bones.

Some scholars have suggested exhuming Shakespeare's remains, either to study his skull to better determine what he looked like or to confirm the rumor that he was buried with a cache of unpublished masterpieces. Until now, however, no one has worked up enough courage to defy the Bard's malediction.

MYTHCONCEPTIONS

Along with the never-ending controversy over who "really" wrote Shakespeare's plays, several colorful myths have sprouted up regarding the playwright's life and career. One persistent legend holds that Shakespeare contributed to writing the King James Bible. Supposedly, if you take Psalm 46 and count 46 words from the beginning and 46 words from the end, you arrive at the words *shake* and *spear*. (What this proves is anyone's guess.) Another legend states that Shakespeare was in fact an Italian nobleman named Michelangelo Crollalanzo (the name translates as "shake spear") who fled to England at age twenty-four to escape the Spanish Inquisition.

BARNUM AND THE BARD

Each year, millions flock to Stratford-upon-Avon to visit Shakespeare's birthplace. If American circus impresario P. T. Barnum had gotten his way, the cottage in which Shakespeare was born might have been situated in the third ring, right next to the dancing elephant and the dog-faced boy. In the 1850s, Barnum was so appalled by the sorry state of the structure (part of it was being used as a butcher shop) that he tried to buy it, intending to ship it off to America for display. But before he could complete the acquisition, a justifiably shamed English government stepped in and designated the property as a national monument.

LORD BYRON

JANUARY 22, 1788–APRIL 19, 1824

NATIONALITY:
BRITISH

ASTROLOGICAL SIGN:
AQUARIUS

MAJOR WORKS:
CHILDE HAROLD'S PILGRIMAGE (1818),
DON JUAN (UNCOMPLETED)

CONTEMPORARIES & RIVALS:
PERCY BYSSHE SHELLEY,
JOHN KEATS, SAMUEL TAYLOR COLERIDGE

LITERARY STYLE:
BOLD, FLORID, AND ROMANTIC WITH A CAPITAL "R"

WORDS OF WISDOM

"GIN AND WATER IS THE SOURCE OF ALL MY INSPIRATION."

*T*ruth is always strange," George Gordon Noel Byron once wrote. "Stranger than fiction." In one line of verse he gave us both a truism still heard today and the perfect tagline for his brief, scandalous, hedonistic life.

When you're the son of a guy known as "Mad Jack," chances are you're in for a wild ride. Little George didn't get to know his father very well, for dear old dad drank himself to death when the boy was only three. But Mad Jack's legacy of excess seeped into his offspring's consciousness, if not his genes. In any case, Byron had little choice but to be his father's son, since his mother hated him. She called him her "lame little brat," on account of his clubfoot, and once tried to beat him to death with a set of fire tongs. Even worse, Byron's governess, May Gray, reportedly molested him at the age of nine. About the only good thing to happen in his childhood was that he inherited his uncle's wealth along with his title: Baron Byron of Rochedale. From then on, George Gordon was known as Lord Byron.

He grew into a strikingly handsome man. Other than his lame foot, for which he compensated through displays of athletic prowess, Byron's only imperfection was a tendency to put on weight. In typical nineteenth-century fashion, he overcame this predisposition by starving himself and taking copious quantities of laxatives. Sex would prove to be his real nourishment, anyway. Byron was the Wilt Chamberlain of his day, reportedly bedding 250 women in Venice in one year alone. His long list of lovers included Lady Caroline Lamb (who famously described him as "mad, bad, and dangerous to know"), her cousin Anne Isabella Milbanke (who became Lady Byron in 1815), and, reportedly, his own half sister, Augusta Leigh. Nor did he restrict himself to one gender. Byron had numerous homosexual affairs, often with underage boys. Other than the exotic animals he kept for companionship, there didn't seem to be too many creatures he wasn't interested in having sex with.

As a consequence, Byron became Europe's most celebrated rake. His poetic achievements never garnered as much attention as did the wild rumors that sprang up about him. Oddly enough, a lot of the gossip involved Byron drinking wine out of someone's skull. (Sometimes it was a dead monk's, sometimes an old mistress's. . . . The legends tended to outrace reality.) Fed up with the philandering, Lady Byron gave her husband his walking papers in 1816—just one year into their marriage. He then left

England for the Continent and never returned. It was the only way to avoid public censure by British society.

Byron spent that summer in Switzerland with his personal physician, John Polidori. They struck up a friendship with poet Percy Bysshe Shelley and his fiancée, Mary Godwin. During a stretch of rainy weather, the group entertained themselves by writing monster stories. Mary produced an early version of what would become her novel *Frankenstein*, while Polidori used Byron as the inspiration for "The Vampyre." The story of a suave British nobleman who sucks the blood out of unsuspecting victims, it would prove to be major influence on Bram Stoker's *Dracula*.

From Switzerland, Byron traveled to Italy, where he had an affair with the very married Countess Teresa Guiccioli. He remained there until 1823, when he left for Greece and a rendezvous with destiny, helping the Greek independence movement repel the Ottoman Turks. Despite a complete lack of military experience, Byron helped drill troops and provided needed cash to the rebel forces. To this day, he is still considered a Greek national hero.

Before he could see any action, Byron was felled by an attack of malarial fever and died on Easter Sunday 1824. Soon after his death, which was mourned throughout England, a group of his friends gathered in London to read over his memoirs. The manuscript was filled with vivid descriptions of Byron's sexual escapades, which, the group felt, might just destroy his hard-won "heroic" reputation. Determined that the memoirs never see the light of day, they proceeded to set them on fire.

!

YOU'VE GOT ME BY THE SHORT HAIRS

In the days before photography, Byron had an unusual way of memorializing his former lovers. He placed snippets of his old girlfriends' pubic hair in envelopes, marking each with the name of the woman immortalized within. Well into the 1980s, the envelopes and their curly contents remained on file at Byron's publishing house in London. After that the trail goes cold.

SHE'S MY NIECE *AND* MY DAUGHTER!

Byron's many paramours may have included his own half sister, Augusta Leigh. She was married at the time, but hey, if you're going to commit incest, why not go all the way and commit adultery as well? Many scholars now contend that Augusta's daughter Medora was in fact the product of Byron's loins, making him, well, an even more complicated figure than we thought.

ANIMAL LOVER

Along with married women and young boys, Byron loved animals. At times his menagerie included horses, geese, monkeys, a badger, a fox, a parrot, an eagle, a crow, a heron, a falcon, a crocodile, five peacocks, two guinea hens, and an Egyptian crane. While a student at Cambridge, Byron kept a pet bear as a cheeky protest against university rules prohibiting dogs in the dormitories. In one of his letters, he even went so far as to suggest that his ursine companion "sit for a fellowship."

Byron also kept more conventional pets. He traveled with five cats, including one named Beppo (also the title of one of his poems). Perhaps the best known of Byron's animal pals is his Newfoundland, Boatswain, who died of rabies in 1808, at age five. In "Epitaph to a Dog," Byron immortalized Boatswain in verse and erected a monument to him in the family burial vault that is larger than Byron's own.

Lady Byron did not share her husband's love of fauna. After they split, she wrote pointedly that "the reason why some tyrannical characters have been fond of animals and humane to them is because they have no exercise of reason and could not condemn the wickedness of their master."

LET IT BLEED

Byron's death at age thirty-six was unnecessary—the byproduct of one of the most misguided medical techniques of the nineteenth century. He contracted a fever during a rain-soaked horseback ride through the Greek countryside and was quite literally bled to death by his doctors. They affixed twelve leeches to Byron's temples in an attempt to "draw out" the cause of his high temperature. They also fed him castor oil to induce diarrhea, another common practice deemed insane by today's medical authorities. All told, the leech

brigade sapped more than four pounds of blood from a man already weakened by fever. No wonder Byron grew delirious, calling out in English and Italian. He was probably asking for his lawyer. Less than twenty-four hours later, he was dead.

> LORD BYRON WAS THE WILT CHAMBERLAIN OF HIS DAY, REPORTEDLY BEDDING 250 WOMEN (AND AN OCCASIONAL YOUNG MAN) IN VENICE IN ONE YEAR ALONE.

ONE LAST LOOK

Byron had hoped to be interred in Poets' Corner at Westminster Abbey, but the dean felt he was too notorious to be included alongside such paragons of virtue as Geoffrey Chaucer and Edmund Spenser. Instead, Byron was laid to rest in his family vault at Hucknall Torckard. That rest was disturbed in June 1938 when, in a ghoulish examination conducted for reasons that remain unclear, forty people crowded into his freshly opened tomb hoping to glimpse his body. When the lid was finally lifted off the dead poet's casket, only three stout souls remained. One of the gawkers described the poet's corpse as being "in an excellent state of preservation." Minus his heart and brains (removed during autopsy) and a detached right foot, Byron looked pretty good for a guy who had been decomposing more than 114 years. One witness remarked that his "sexual organ showed quite abnormal development." Well hung even in death, Byron appeared to have the last laugh on his exhumers. The next day they sealed up his vault and left him in peace.

HONORÉ DE BALZAC

MAY 20, 1799–AUGUST 18, 1850

NATIONALITY:
FRENCH

ASTROLOGICAL SIGN:
TAURUS

MAJOR WORKS:
LE PÈRE GORIOT (1834–35),
LA PEAU DE CHAGRIN (1831),
LA COUSINE BETTE (1846)

CONTEMPORARIES & RIVALS:
GUSTAVE FLAUBERT, VICTOR HUGO

LITERARY STYLE:
PANORAMIC, WITHERINGLY SATIRICAL

WORDS OF WISDOM

"IF WE ALL SAID TO PEOPLE'S FACES WHAT WE SAY BEHIND ONE ANOTHER'S BACKS, SOCIETY WOULD BE IMPOSSIBLE."

I am not deep," Honoré de Balzac once remarked, "but very wide." It is unclear whether he was wryly observing his physical appearance or the intellectual breadth of his work (or both). Certainly Balzac was among the fattest of the world's great novelists. A five-foot-three-inch mound of adipose flesh mounted atop two spindly legs, he was notorious for his gargantuan appetites, eccentric dress, and coarse behavior. While dining at a restaurant in Paris, he reportedly devoured a dozen mutton cutlets, a duck with turnips, a Normandy sole, two partridges, and more than one hundred oysters. He finished things off with a dessert of twelve pears plus a variety of sweets, fruit, and liqueurs. His table manners were revolting. He ate directly off his knife and sprayed bits of food around the room as he chewed. Is it any wonder most people considered him a crass, distasteful boor? Born Honoré Balssa, he changed his surname and added an aristocratic-sounding "de" to convince people he was a nobleman.

Whatever people thought of his personal habits, none would begrudge Balzac for being one of the world's greatest novelists. His signature multivolume work, *The Human Comedy*, was the product of a lifetime spent closely observing the many layers of post-Napoleonic French society. It was not, however, the product of his life's ambition. Initially, Balzac fancied himself a tragedian. But his play about the life of Oliver Cromwell went over about as well as Cromwell had fared with the English people. One college professor who read it advised Balzac's mother that her son should pursue any career *but* literature.

Undeterred, Balzac pressed on. He tried his hand at popular fiction, cranking out five novels in 1822. The books weren't great, and neither were the pseudonyms he wrote them under. One, "Lord R'Hoone," was just a lazy anagram of his first name. Still, there's something to be said for persistence. Balzac was soon writing as many as fifteen hours each day while dressed in a monk's robe and amped up on copious cups of coffee. (About the only stimulant Balzac didn't consume was tobacco, which he considered enfeebling.) He garnered material for his novels by attending parties, where a single overheard conversation was often enough to fill out the plot of yet another installment of *The Human Comedy*.

During a twenty-year period, Balzac churned out ninety-seven works totaling more than eleven thousand pages. Some of them were racy, bordering on pornographic. Others were just plain weird. Take the novel *Seraphita,* which concerns a hermaphroditic angel who tutors a young couple in mysticism amid the fjords of Norway. Balzac's personal life was somewhat less strange, though just as racy. He was intimate with hundreds of women, which, considering his beggarly appearance and indifference to hygiene, was quite an accomplishment. And he spent whatever money he earned. Convinced he should live like an aristocrat, Balzac never did square that illusion with his moderate income. As a result, he was constantly in debt. Late in life, he became involved with a Polish noblewoman who had oodles of cash—just the sort of sugar mama he needed. But as smitten as she was with his genius, even she realized his spendthrift ways posed a mortal danger to her solvency. She married him only a few months before his death, when ill health had made him an object of pity.

Returning home to Paris after the wedding, Balzac discovered that his longtime servant had gone mad in his absence. "What an omen!" he wailed. "I shall never leave this house alive." He was right. A few months later, his heart finally gave out from years of overconsumption and hard living. To the end, he was immersed in the world of his fiction. His last words—"Send for Bianchon . . . he'll save me"—were a shout-out to his physician alter ego from *The Human Comedy*.

THE COFFEE DEGENERATION

What was fueling Balzac's prolific literary output? Why, the same thing that helps millions of Americans get through those interminable nine-o'clock meetings: good old-fashioned high-octane java. The strung-out Frenchman drank up to fifty cups of thick, black Turkish coffee per day. In a pre-Starbucks age, this level of intake required real ingenuity. When he couldn't get his fix in brewed form, he simply pulverized a handful of beans and popped them into his gullet, Limbaugh-style.

"Coffee is a great power in my life," Balzac admitted. "I have observed its effects on an epic scale." And he suffered from them, too. The high quantities of industrial-strength joe gave him stomach cramps, contributed to his high blood pressure, and left him with an enlarged heart. Caffeine poisoning—not to mention his generally gluttonous lifestyle—contributed to his early demise at age fifty-one.

BLIND TASTING

Coffee wasn't Balzac's only beverage. He was also a connoisseur of fine teas. One of his favorites came to him by way of a Russian government official, who had received it from the czar via the emperor of China. The exotic and expensive brew, harvested by the "imperial plucking" method and carried by caravaneers into Russia, was the stuff of legend. It was said that anyone who drank it would go blind. Not surprisingly, Balzac saved it for only his closest friends. His longtime pal Laurent-Jan sipped the concoction on numerous occasions, each time declaring, "Once again I risk losing an eye—but hell, it is worth it!"

A CASE OF MISTAKEN IDENTITY

There's a fine line between genius and madness, as one of Balzac's dinner companions could attest. The great Prussian naturalist and explorer Friedrich von Humboldt once asked a psychiatrist friend to introduce him to a genuine madman. The doctor arranged a lunch with Humboldt, Balzac, and one of his patients. As usual, Balzac—who was meeting Humboldt for the first time— showed up disheveled and ungroomed and proceeded to babble on throughout the meal. As the conversation wound down, Humboldt leaned over to his friend and thanked him for bringing along such an engaging basket case. The psychiatrist did a double take. "But it's the other who's the lunatic," he informed Humboldt. "The man you're looking at is Monsieur Honoré de Balzac!"

SLINGING HASH

Accompanied by the poet Charles Baudelaire, Balzac tried hashish under the supervision of an alienist. The setting was a magnificent seventeenth-century mansion overlooking the Seine. But the outcome did not match the serene environment. Balzac was underwhelmed by the effects of the drug, which failed to elicit the "celestial voices" in his head that he had been expecting. He left feeling slightly disappointed that the hash had not driven him completely mad.

THE STARVING ARTIST

Though he styled himself a nobleman, Balzac was no stranger to poverty. During his lean years, he lived in a hovel without heat or furniture. Undaunted, the great writer supplied his own interior décor using the power of his imagination. He simply wrote on the bare walls what he wished to see there. On one he scribbled "Rosewood paneling with commode." On another: "Gobelin tapestry with Venetian mirror." And over the empty fireplace: "Picture by Raphael."

Balzac's squalid Paris garret was on the top floor of a building in one of the most dangerous parts of the city. For a man of his appetites, such conditions must have been especially arduous. He was so poor that most dinners consisted of a stale roll dipped in a glass of water. A Paris bookseller once rescinded his offer on Balzac's next novel after seeing his appalling apartment. Another time, a burglar tried to rob him by picking the lock on his desk. Aroused from his slumber, Balzac just laughed. "What risks you take to try to find money in a desk by night," he said, "where the legal owner can never find any by day!"

> HONORÉ DE BALZAC WAS NOTORIOUS FOR HIS GARGANTUAN APPETITES AND COARSE BEHAVIOR. HE ATE DIRECTLY OFF HIS KNIFE AND SPRAYED BITS OF FOOD AROUND THE ROOM AS HE CHEWED.

PRECIOUS SUBSTANCE

Talk about retaining fluids. Balzac revealed to friends that, while having sex, he preferred not to ejaculate out of fear it would sap his creative energy. "Lovey-dovey and amorous play, up to ejaculation, would be all right," a confidant reported, "but only up to ejaculation. Sperm to him meant emission of purest cerebral substance, and therefore a filtering, a loss through the member, of a potential act of artistic creation." Or, as Balzac himself once put it after climaxing during intercourse with one of his many lovers: "This morning I have lost a novel!"

EDGAR ALLAN POE

JANUARY 19, 1809–OCTOBER 7, 1849

NATIONALITY:
AMERICAN

ASTROLOGICAL SIGN:
CAPRICORN

MAJOR WORKS:
"THE FALL OF THE HOUSE OF USHER" (1839),
"THE TELL-TALE HEART" (1843), "THE RAVEN" (1845)

CONTEMPORARIES & RIVALS:
NATHANIEL HAWTHORNE, JAMES RUSSELL LOWELL,
HENRY WADSWORTH LONGFELLOW

LITERARY STYLE:
VERBOSE AND BYZANTINE

WORDS OF WISDOM ➤ *"IN MY MIND, ALL TIME IS A MIDNIGHT DREARY."*

*T*oday you can find Edgar Allan Poe's face reproduced on everything from bookstore walls to bottles of beer. But that wasn't always the case. America's most famous literary export died penniless and largely unloved in his own country. It was up to the French (who insist on referring to him as "Edgar Poe" for reasons unknown) to resuscitate his reputation and exalt him to the iconic status he enjoys today. Thank you, François. We can talk about Jerry Lewis later.

Edgar Allan Poe was the father of macabre fiction, a writer whose eerie stories and atmospheric poems paved the way for H. P. Lovecraft and Stephen King. He was also afraid of the dark. "I believe that demons take advantage of the night to mislead the unwary," he once confessed to a friend. "Although, you know," he quickly added, "I don't believe in them." Maybe Poe just sensed he was living under a dark cloud. You couldn't blame him. An orphan at age three, he was raised by a wealthy couple named John and Frances Allan in Richmond, Virginia. Raised, not adopted, because snooty John Allan refused to allow the son of theatrical performers to taint his pristine family tree. Nevertheless, Poe took his stepfather's surname as his middle name. He also inherited some of John's priggish manner.

Besides affection, the other thing John Allan failed to give his stepson in any great quantity was money. Indeed, destitution was a hallmark of Poe's short life. At the University of Virginia, he ran up gambling debts to meet his needs, which by then included copious amounts of alcohol. The pattern repeated itself when Poe entered the U.S. Military Academy at West Point in 1830. A disgrace to the uniform, he spent most of his time drinking and dreaming up ways to get booted out. In January 1831 he finally succeeded. He disobeyed direct orders and failed to show up for drills often enough that he was court-martialed for "Gross Neglect of Duty." He retains the dubious dual distinction of being the only major American writer to attend West Point, and the only one to get kicked out.

Poe fit the mold of the classic, falling-down drunk. A college classmate wrote that his "passion for strong drink was as marked and as peculiar as that for cards . . . without a sip or a smack of the mouth he would seize a full glass and send it home at a single gulp." That one glass was usually enough to put him into an alcoholic stupor. Part of the problem was no doubt due to his slight build and sickly disposition. At West Point, Poe appeared so frail and old that the other cadets joked that his stepfather had taken his place. John Allan eventually got so fed up with Poe's dissolute ways that he disowned him, promising to have his stepson arrested if he ever appeared on Allan's property.

Bereft of both money and family, Poe moved in with an aunt, Maria Clemm, at her home in Baltimore. He also began cranking out short stories for magazines. In 1836, at age twenty-seven, he married his thirteen-year-old cousin Virginia, Clemm's daughter, after a bizarre three-year courtship during which he was repeatedly warned of the impropriety of marrying someone so young. Together they moved around a lot—to New York, to Philadelphia, back to New York again. Poe was always one step ahead of his creditors and one stiff drink away from a three-day bender. Then, just when his writing career began to pick up, his wife contracted tuberculosis and died.

Poe's life was indeed a nightmare, and it had a fittingly oneiric conclusion. Stopping off in Baltimore on a trip to New York in late September 1849, he disappeared for five days. He was picked up off the street in front of an Irish tavern, semiconscious and drunk as a skunk, dressed in ragged clothes that clearly belonged to someone else. Admitted to Washington College Hospital, the delirious versifier spent the next two days calling out for a mysterious man named Reynolds and begging the attending physician to blow his brains out. At last, crying out from his sickbed, "Lord, help my poor soul!" he keeled over and died.

No one's sure what happened during those five lost days. Evidence suggests that Poe may have been shanghaied by a gang of electoral goons, plied with drink, and forced to stuff ballot boxes in the Baltimore mayoral election. The ensuing alcoholic binge may have exacerbated an existing health condition, such as syphilis, diabetes, or perhaps rabies. Whatever the cause, his death was an unpleasant one—as was the reputation concocted for him by his earliest biographer, an embittered editor named Rufus Griswold, whose work Poe had once slogged in print. Griswold's 1850 "memoir" maliciously depicts Poe as a drug-addicted degenerate who had incestuous sex with his own aunt. It was all false, cheap, posthumous score settling, but it was decades before the literary establishment (with a little help from the French) accepted Poe into the pantheon of great American authors.

THE SUM OF ALL FEARS

It's no wonder Poe was afraid of the dark. He was educated in a ceme-tery—literally. When Poe attended boarding school in England, the classroom abutted a graveyard. Too cheap to buy textbooks, the head-master conducted math lessons outside among the slumbering dead. Each child was instructed to choose a headstone and then find the deceased's age by subtracting the year of birth from the year of death. Gym class took place in the same cheery environment. On the first day of school, each student was presented with a small wooden shovel. If a parish member died during the semester, the children were sent out to dig the grave, thereby engaging in some invigorating aerobic exercise.

QUOTH THE RAVEN, "YOU GOT HOSED"

Poe was very proud of "The Raven," calling it "the greatest poem that was ever written." (Modesty was not his strong suit.) Yet he earned nearly nothing from the work, thanks in large part to his ignorance of copyright law. Eager to get his creation in print, he published it in a newspaper, *The New York Evening Mirror*, unaware that doing so released him from all copyright protection. Any-one could then reprint the poem—and many people did, making a killing. When Poe finally got around to publishing his own edition, the poem was already so widely circulated that no one bought it.

DICKENS LOSES HIS GRIP

Poe's famous raven was in fact inspired by the avian pet of British author Charles Dickens. Grip, Dickens's babbling bird, appears as a character in his serialized mystery novel *Barnaby Rudge*, which Poe reviewed in 1841. Poe com-plimented Dickens on the use of the talking raven, deeming that it should have played a larger role in the plot.

When Dickens and Poe met for the first and only time, in 1842, the beloved bird had recently died. (It had apparently drunk from an open paint bottle Dickens left lying around the stable.) Dickens related the sad story to Poe, who returned home that night and inserted an ominous talking raven into an exist-ing poem called "To Lenore," which he had put aside. "Lenore" rhymed perfectly with "Nevermore," which became the sinister black bird's now-famous mantra.

WHEN POETS ATTACK

There's nothing as entertaining as a catfight between poets. Poe's arch nemesis was Henry Wadsworth Longfellow, the eminent author of "Song of Hiawatha" and other poems. For reasons still unclear nearly two centuries later, Poe went from fawning admiration to outright hostility toward the man, his poetry, and his character. In 1840 he wrote a scathing review of Longfellow's latest poem, accusing him of plagiarizing it from Alfred Lord Tennyson. When that provoked no response, Poe claimed that Longfellow had ripped off one of *his* poems as well. The so-called "Longfellow War" was on. Unfortunately for Poe, it was nothing but a waste of ammunition. He never produced a shred of evidence that Longfellow was a plagiarist, and the New England poet serenely refused to respond to the younger man's ad hominem attacks. After Poe's death, Longfellow had nothing but nice things to say about him, adding: "The harshness of his criticisms I have never attributed to anything but the irritation of a sensitive nature, chafed by some indefinite sense of wrong." Oh, smack!

AS A CHILD, POE WAS LITERALLY EDUCATED IN A CEMETERY. HE LEARNED MATH BY ADDING AND SUBTRACTING THE DATES ON GRAVESTONES.

UP, UP, AND AWAY

Poe was not above a little journalistic hoaxing, especially when he was hard up for cash. In April 1844, a destitute Poe sold a story to the *New York Sun* about the world's first transatlantic balloon crossing. "The great problem is at length solved," he wrote triumphantly. "The Air, as well as Earth and the Ocean, has been subdued by science, and will become a common and convenient highway for mankind." Poe's incredibly well thought out, five-thousand-word article went on to describe in exquisite detail the dirigible in question, its operator (a real-life balloonist named Monck Mason), and the voyage itself. The only problem: It was all a lie. The next day, the *Sun* printed a retraction: "The mails from the south ... not having brought confirmation of the balloon from England ... we are inclined to believe that the intelligence is erroneous."

STONED AGAIN

The black cloud of bad luck that seemed to follow Poe throughout his life lingered awhile even after his death. The headstone ordered to mark his grave was run over by a runaway train. As a result, until his body was exhumed and reburied in 1875, he rested beneath a generic lot marker that read "No. 80."

CHEERS, MATE!

Anyone who tries to market Poe-branded kitchen appliances has to reckon with a shadowy figure known as the Poe Toaster. Every year since 1949, this mysterious black-cloaked stranger has appeared at Poe's gravesite on the night of the author's birthday. The graveyard groupie may sound like a character from one of Poe's macabre tales, but as the cemetery groundskeepers (and the numerous scholars who debate his identity) will tell you, he is all too real. The ritual is always the same: He drinks a toast to the deceased and then leaves behind a half-empty bottle of cognac and three red roses as tokens of admiration. Why three roses? They may represent Poe, his mother-in-law, and his wife, all of whom are interred in the same plot. Why cognac? Nobody knows. Why any of it? No one has ever tried to intercept the toaster to ask—out of respect for Poe and the solemnity of this annual ceremony.

EVERYONE'S A CRITIC

Poe seems to divide the literary community. There are those, like the French, who revere him as a god. And then there are those who can't stand him or any of his works. Notable Poe detractors include T. S. Eliot, who described him as having "the intellect of a highly gifted person before puberty"; Mark Twain, who once remarked, "To me, his prose is unreadable—like Jane Austen's" (a rare two-for-one literary smackdown!); and W. H. Auden, who took the most personal potshot, dismissing Poe as "an unmanly sort of man whose love life seems to have been largely confined to crying in laps and playing mouse."

POE RELATION

Actor Edgar Allan Poe IV, a direct descendant of the master of the macabre, has gotten a lot of career mileage out of the association with his great-great-uncle. Poe the fourth played Poe the first in the feature film *Monkeybone* and on a 1999 episode of *Sabrina the Teenage Witch*. When not aping his legendary relative, he has specialized in portraying crazed lowlifes and carnival barkers in such movies as *Sex Puppets* and *Oliver Twisted*.

ARE YOU READY FOR SOME FOOTBALL?

In 1996 professional football returned to Baltimore after a thirteen-year absence. A contest was conducted to select a name for the new franchise; in a tribute to the city's most famous resident, Ravens won out over Marauders and Americans. After two years without a mascot, in August 1998 the team unveiled not one but three. In an elaborate and bizarre on-field ceremony before a preseason game against the Philadelphia Eagles, each of the ravens was "hatched" from an enormous egg. They are, in order of emergence: Edgar, a "tall, strong, competitive Raven with long, flowing feathers, and sharp, pointy eyes"; Allan, a "short, skinny, and agile" bird; and Poe, the "chubby, lazy, but undeniably lovable" runt of the litter. So far, none of the trio seems to have developed the raging alcohol problem that was Poe's defining characteristic.

CHARLES DICKENS

FEBRUARY 7, 1812–JUNE 9, 1870

NATIONALITY:
ENGLISH

ASTROLOGICAL SIGN:
AQUARIUS

MAJOR WORKS:
THE PICKWICK PAPERS (1836–37),
BLEAK HOUSE (1852–53), *DAVID COPPERFIELD* (1849–50),
GREAT EXPECTATIONS (1860–61)

CONTEMPORARIES & RIVALS:
EDGAR ALLAN POE, WILLIAM MAKEPEACE THACKERAY

LITERARY STYLE:
FLORID, LARGER-THAN-LIFE, EPISODIC

WORDS OF WISDOM

"ANNUAL INCOME: TWENTY POUNDS. ANNUAL EXPENDITURE: NINETEEN SIX. RESULT: HAPPINESS."

A young boy endures a miserable, joyless childhood working in a dreary factory that reeks of the accumulated futility of all those who have gone before him. It sounds like the premise of one of Charles Dickens's novels—and it is—but it could also be the first line of his own biography. Up to a time, Dickens's life was as Dickensian as Oliver Twist's. And then—well, then he got famous and didn't have to worry about working in factories anymore.

Dickens's futility mill of choice was Warren's boot-blacking factory, where he was sent to work after his father, John, was thrown into debtor's prison in 1824. Young Charles's task was to glue labels on bottles of shoe polish, which doesn't sound so bad until you contemplate doing it for ten to twelve hours a day for six shillings a week. Then it becomes a living hell that makes you want to write about the plight of poor kids in factories for the rest of your life, which is exactly what Dickens did.

He became famous with incredible ease. *The Pickwick Papers*, published when Dickens was only twenty-four years old, became one of the bestselling books in the history of English literature, catapulting its young author to worldwide celebrity almost overnight. Gone were the days of shoe black and debtor's prisons. Dickens now lived in a world where people lined up to purchase the latest installments of his long, serialized novels. In New York, six thousand crowded onto a dock to await the arrival of the final chapters of *The Old Curiosity Shop* in 1841. "Does Little Nell die?" they cried out to sailors on the approaching steamer, eager to know the fate of the novel's plucky young heroine. (Yes, she does, prompting Oscar Wilde to quip that, "One would have to have a heart of stone to read the death of Little Nell . . . without laughing.")

Dickens was the Stephen King of his day—unloved by critics (and foppish wits like Wilde) but revered by legions of passionate fans. "We do not believe in the permanence of his reputation," the *Saturday Review* declared in 1858. "Our children will wonder what their ancestors could have meant by putting Dickens at the head of the novelists of his day." Tell that to Tolstoy, Dostoyevsky, Henry James, and the many others who considered Dickens the finest English writer since Shakespeare. Or tell it to his business partners, who benefited enormously from his uncanny marketing savvy. The idea of serializing the novels was his alone, as were various schemes for publishing and republishing the works in several different "special editions," all of which made Dickens a wealthy man. Even the immense length of his novels redounded to his financial benefit. Dickens published his books in serial form and was paid by the installment. The more installments, the more gold crowns were deposited in the wily author's pocket.

Although his novels and stories remained consistently, almost supernaturally excellent over the course of more than thirty years, Dickens did have some ups and downs. In 1836 he married Catherine Hogarth, a respectable newspaper editor's daughter, but was unusually close to her two younger sisters. When Mary Hogarth died in 1837 at the age of seventeen, Dickens reacted as if his own wife had perished. He cut off a lock of Mary's hair and kept it in a special case. He slipped a ring off her finger and wore it for the rest of his life. He kept all the dead girl's clothes and was still taking them out for review more than two years later. Dickens even professed a desire to be buried in the same grave as his sister-in-law; he would be haunted by visions of her ghost for years. No one knows what, if anything, had happened between them, but Catherine and her ten children could not have been happy.

More trouble lay ahead. Dickens separated from his wife in 1858. He had recently hooked up with Ellen Ternan, an eighteen-year-old actress twenty-seven years his junior. He played sugar daddy and may have fathered a child by her, and she traveled with him under false names to avoid a scandal. When returning from France in 1865, their train plunged over a bridge between Dover and London. Mortified at being spied amid the wreckage with his inamorata, Dickens fled the scene with the manuscript of *Dombey and Son* stashed under one arm. He never fully recovered from nagging injuries suffered during the crash, and physical strain from his breakneck public reading tours began to take a toll as well. He suffered a stroke and died June 9, 1870, exactly five years after the train accident. He was buried—against his wishes—in the Poets' Corner of Westminster Abbey.

OCD(ICKENS)

Bob Cratchit may have had to work in dismal, cramped conditions, but not so his creator. Dickens was a compulsive rearranger who refused to write in any room if the tables and chairs weren't ordered just so. He had an uncanny ability to remember the precise location of every piece of furniture in any given room and he would spend hours reorganizing to suit his whims. When he was a guest at a private home or swanky hotel, his first task was to rearrange everything in his room to match his own interior plan.

Not surprisingly, Dickens was also something of a neat freak. He brushed his thinning hair hundreds of times a day, even whipping out a comb in the middle of a dinner party if he sensed a single strand out of place. When friends left the room, he invariably tidied up after them and would boil with anger if others showed the slightest sloppiness. On a visit to the United States Capitol in 1842, he was appalled at the slovenly behavior of the nation's elected representatives, particularly their inability to hit spittoons with expectorated streams of chewing tobacco. "I strongly recommend all strangers not to look at the floor," Dickens groused, "and that if they happen to drop anything . . . not to pick it up with an ungloved hand on any account."

MAGNETIC FIELDS

Even weirder than Dickens's neatness tics were his superstitions. He touched everything three times for luck, considered Friday his "lucky day," and always left London on the day the latest installment of one of his novels was published. Most curious of all were his sleeping habits—he insisted on sleeping with his head facing the North Pole. "He maintained that he could not sleep with it in any other position," a friend revealed. Asked to explain his preference, Dickens responded with some mumbo-jumbo about "earth currents and positive and negative electricity." Alignment with the planet's magnetic fields, he believed, helped foster creativity.

MESMERIZE ME

When he wasn't entrancing readers with his eight-hundred-page novels, Dickens was hypnotizing people with Mesmerism. Developed by a German crackpot named Franz Anton Mesmer, Mesmerism was the "science" of harnessing the healing rays of "animal magnetism" to cure the sick. It was all the rage in continental Europe in the second half of the nineteenth century. By Dickens's day, it had found its way across the Channel to England, where he first learned its tenets from the respected British physician John Elliotson, an early adopter of the stethoscope who was later drummed out of the medical profession for his hypnotic heresy. Dickens was so, well, mesmerized by this pseudoscience that he started practicing it himself. He mesmerized people for fun at parties or to help friends overcome minor ailments. He was even known to work miracles. In 1844 he took on the case of one Madame de la Rue, who was afflicted with acute anxiety attacks that made her face twitch. After just a few weeks of treatment, Dickens had her relaxed, sleeping soundly, and functioning normally. He continued their sessions for some time afterward, trying to get at the root of her anxiety through dream interpretation (another hobby of his). And when his friend John Leech suffered a concussion in 1849, Dickens harnessed the power of Mesmerism to heal him in just a few days.

Just about the only affliction Mesmerism seemed powerless to cure was the one that plagued Dickens the most: asthma. So he found relief the old-fashioned way: He took opium.

HANS OFF

Hans Christian Andersen got an up-close look at the Scrooge-like side of Dickens during an ill-fated visit to the novelist's home in 1857. The two had met a decade earlier, when an excited Dickens burst into the Danish fairy-tale writer's London book signing, screaming: "I must see Andersen!" They became fast friends. When Andersen prepared to return to Denmark, Dickens presented him with an autographed edition of his complete works as a parting gift. It seemed like a match made in heaven

For ten years, Andersen cherished the prospect of returning to England to stay with his dear friend. When he did, however, he found a very different person. Dickens had become a cold, bitter man on the brink of separation from his wife and about to set up house with his mistress, Ellen Ternan. A visit from an eccentric Dane who could barely speak English was the last thing he needed; but when Andersen invited himself for a two-week stay, Dickens couldn't refuse. The imposition put the already dyspeptic novelist in an even fouler mood. "Hans Christian Andersen may perhaps be with us," he wrote to a visiting friend, "but you won't mind him—especially as he knows no language but his own Danish, and is suspected of not even knowing that."

Andersen knew he was in for trouble the moment he arrived. Dickens was nowhere to be found, having high-tailed it to London to attend to personal business. He left his guest in the care of his obnoxious, disrespectful children. They made fun of the Dane behind his back, refused to attend to his needs, and spoke ill of his novels to his face. Even five-year-old Edward got in on the act, threatening to throw the beloved children's author out the window. Andersen was reduced to flinging himself face forward on the lawn, sobbing uncontrollably.

They may have worn him down, but Andersen wouldn't leave. Five weeks later, he was still hanging around. "We are suffering a good deal from Andersen," wrote Dickens, who had returned and quickly longed to be rid of his old "friend." When the unwelcome guest finally left, the Dickens family unloaded with both barrels. "He was a bony bore, and he stayed on and on," daughter Kate observed. Charles himself left a nasty note in the room where Andersen had stayed. "Hans Andersen slept in this room for five weeks," it read, "which seemed to the family *ages*." He was never invited back again.

DEADHEAD

"I am dragged by invisible force into the morgue," Dickens once admitted. The Paris Morgue, to be precise, where public display of unidentified dead bodies took place throughout the nineteenth century. Dickens had a strange fascination with the place. He would hang out there for days, obsessing over the corpses of drowned vagrants and other unclaimed wretches. He called the feeling that came over him at these times "the attraction of repulsion." It also compelled him to visit the scenes of famous murders and to dwell on the details of sensational crimes with a morbid curiosity worthy of his contemporary, Edgar Allan Poe.

PIMP MY BOOKSHELF

If you visit Dickens's home at Gad's Hill Place in Kent, prepare to be punk'd. The mischievous author had a secret door installed in his study. Designed to resemble a bookcase, it comes complete with phony shelves filled with the spines of fictitious books whose titles were dreamed up by Dickens himself— probably on an afternoon when he'd had a little too much sherry. Be sure to check out the three-volume *Five Minutes in China*, the nine-volume *Cat's Lives*, as well as such punny favorites as *Noah's Arkitecture* and *The Gunpowder Magazine*. Dickens's twisted side shines through in *The Wisdom of Our Ancestors*, a multivolume set that covers disease and torture implements, as well as its companion volume, *The Virtues of Our Ancestors*, the spine of which is so narrow that the title is printed sideways.

> DICKENS HAD A CURIOUS OBSESSION WITH THE PARIS MORGUE, WHERE HE WOULD SPEND DAYS STUDYING THE CORPSES OF DROWNED VAGRANTS AND OTHER UNCLAIMED WRETCHES.

WHERE THE NELL AM I?

Where is the world's only known statue of Dickens located? The answer, oddly enough, is Philadelphia. Dickens so detested monuments that, in his will, he forbade the erection of a statue. Some of his admirers made one anyway. When his family rejected it, they found a home for it in the City of Brotherly Love's Clark Park. The life-size bronze sculpture depicts the author cavorting with Little Nell, the beloved heroine of his novel *The Old Curiosity Shop*.

THE DICKENS–BONADUCE NEXUS

Dickens is the great-great-great-grandfather of actor Brian Forster, who played Chris Partridge on the television series *The Partridge Family* from 1971 to 1974.

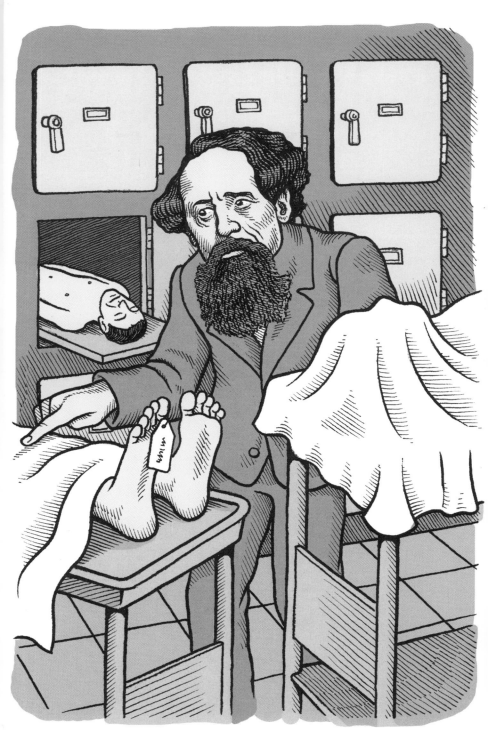

THE BRONTË SISTERS

CHARLOTTE BRONTË

APRIL 21, 1816–MARCH 31, 1855

NATIONALITY:
ENGLISH

ASTROLOGICAL SIGN:
TAURUS

MAJOR WORKS:
JANE EYRE (1847), *VILLETTE* (1853)

CONTEMPORARIES & RIVALS:
ANNE BRONTË, EMILY BRONTË

LITERARY STYLE:
MEASURED PROSE THAT MASKS A WORLD OF
EMOTIONAL PAIN

WORDS OF WISDOM

*"I WOULD RATHER UNDERGO THE
GREATEST BODILY PAINS THAN HAVE
MY HEART CONSTANTLY LACERATED
BY SEARING REGRETS."*

EMILY BRONTË

JULY 30, 1818–DECEMBER 19, 1848

NATIONALITY: ENGLISH

ASTROLOGICAL SIGN: LEO

MAJOR WORKS: *WUTHERING HEIGHTS* (1847)

CONTEMPORARIES & RIVALS:
ANNE BRONTË, CHARLOTTE BRONTË

LITERARY STYLE: OVERWROUGHT, GOTHIC

"HONEST PEOPLE DON'T HIDE THEIR DEEDS."

ANNE BRONTË

JANUARY 17, 1820–MAY 28, 1849

NATIONALITY: ENGLISH

ASTROLOGICAL SIGN: CAPRICORN

MAJOR WORKS: *AGNES GREY* (1847),
THE TENANT OF WILDFELL HALL (1848)

CONTEMPORARIES & RIVALS:
EMILY BRONTË, CHARLOTTE BRONTË

LITERARY STYLE: RESTRAINED AND NEOCLASSICAL

"HE THAT DARES NOT GRASP THE THORN SHOULD NEVER CRAVE THE ROSE."

From earliest childhood, the Brontë sisters were serious about their literary ambitions. Where most children call their nursery "our room," they called theirs "our study." And study they did: the great works of English literature, their own behavior, even the wicked weather on the surrounding moors. Everything they examined eventually entered the poems and novels that would one day make them famous.

Their house was almost unbearably bleak and awful. Surrounded on three sides by graveyards, it was described by one visitor as "a dreary, dreary place literally paved with rain-blackened tombstones." Charlotte, Emily, and Anne loved the place. That should have been the first clue that these were not normal English schoolgirls.

Their father, a poor Irish farmer turned Evangelical preacher named Patrick Brunty, had changed the family name in emulation of the British naval hero Lord Nelson, also known as the Duke of Brontë. The umlaut, he believed, would lend an air of distinction. To be frank, old man Brontë was a bit of a kook. He grew even more eccentric after the death of his wife in 1821. The six Brontë children were largely left to their own devices as Dad secluded himself in his study to read and work on his weekly sermons.

The one attempt at formal schooling ended in tragedy. The two oldest girls, Maria and Elizabeth, died of tuberculosis after being exposed to the appallingly unsanitary conditions at the nearby boarding school. The devastated Mr. Brontë immediately summoned Charlotte and Emily to come home. There they remained for the next six years, educating and entertaining themselves with improvised games and stories.

In their most intricate and imaginative collaboration, the three sisters and their brother Branwell split into groups and created two elaborate fantasy kingdoms. Emily and Anne called theirs Gondal; Charlotte and Branwell countered with one named Angria. For the next decade, they chronicled adventures led by the inhabitants of their imaginary kingdoms, recording them in books fashioned from scraps of paper and cardboard sugar boxes. The game passed the time and provided a creative outlet, for the girls faced stultifying career prospects unless some wealthy swains arrived to offer a hand in marriage.

Unfortunately, no such swains were forthcoming, so the girls took turns teaching, tutoring, and minding other people's children. Charlotte spent time in Brussels, where she fell in love with a married man, and Emily started secretly writing poetry. The three sisters considered opening their own school out of the family home, but they failed to entice pupils to gloomy Haworth on the moors.

Ever the ringleader, Charlotte was struck by the idea that each of them should write a novel and try to publish it. Charlotte wrote two. Her first, *The Professor*, was roundly rejected. But her second attempt, *Jane Eyre*, joined Emily's *Wuthering Heights* and Anne's *Agnes Grey* in finding its way into print. Informed by their publisher that it wasn't proper to publish a book under a woman's name, the sisters adopted the pseudonyms Currer, Ellis, and Acton Bell. *Jane Eyre* in particular was an immediate critical and commercial success.

Sadly, what could have been a new beginning turned out to be the beginning of the end. Branwell drank himself to death in 1848, just months after his sisters' novels were published. Emily thought the best way to pay tribute to him was to attend his funeral in bare feet . . . during a hellacious rainstorm. She contracted tuberculosis. In typically eccentric Brontë fashion, Emily refused all medical treatment, food, and even sympathy. She wasted away and died less than three months later. In fact, she had lost so much weight that her coffin measured only sixteen inches wide—the narrowest the local undertaker had ever built. Finally, in a cruel coda, Anne caught Emily's TB. She tried to hide her illness, waiting just long enough to make its effects irreversible. A few months later, she followed her sister to the grave.

Charlotte was now completely alone. She passed the time editing her sisters' works and occasionally bad-mouthing them in print. (She called Anne's second novel, *The Tenant of Wildfell Hall*, a "mistake" and excluded it from the sisters' official canon.) She also wrote a few more novels and began making the rounds of the literary scene. She befriended novelists Elizabeth Gaskell and William Makepeace Thackeray, among others. But she rarely left home and remained the caretaker of her aging, invalid father. In 1854 she married, against her father's wishes, but the union was short-lived. She became pregnant and died before bringing the baby to term. Possible causes include typhus, TB (the family curse), and hyperemesis gravidarum (a rare pregnancy disorder characterized by severe and persistent vomiting). According to local legend, a mysterious figure in black watched the funeral proceedings from the moors. At the time, many believed it to be Emily. If so, it would provide a fittingly Gothic finale for the Brontë family saga.

!

LOOKS AREN'T EVERYTHING

Of the three novel-writing Brontë sisters, Emily was by far the most attractive. At five-foot-seven, she was strikingly tall for a woman of her time. Graced with a lovely figure and beautiful face, she exuded an air of mystery that men found intriguing. Her sister Anne was also quite the looker. Charlotte, on the other hand ... well, not so blessed. Small and birdlike at four-feet-ten-inches tall, she wore glasses to correct her severe myopia and considered herself quite plain. Other assessments were harsher. "I met Miss Brontë tonight, and I would have to say she would have to be twice as good-looking as she actually is to be considered homely," remarked one young man who ran into her at a party. To her credit, Charlotte channeled any anxiety about her appearance into her writing. She modeled her greatest literary creation, the ungainly governess Jane Eyre, on herself.

THE BRONTË SISTERS (FROM LEFT TO RIGHT: EMILY, CHARLOTTE, ANNE) LIVED IN A HOUSE SURROUNDED ON THREE SIDES BY GRAVEYARDS.

A WINDOW ON HER WORLD

Emily was the most eccentric of the three sisters, famous for standing at her window for hours at a time, gazing in silent contemplation. What was she thinking about? Window treatments, apparently. Charlotte once caught her staring at what she assumed were the moors, only to discover that the blinds were closed. The moony teenager had been standing for six hours gazing into the white window blinds.

THE REJECTION COLLECTION

It took Charlotte Brontë a while to learn the publishing game. Her first novel, *The Professor*, was turned down by several editors. Each time the manuscript was returned to her, she sent it to the next publisher without removing the rejection letter. Soon it was circulating with a collection of rejection slips piled on top—not exactly a ringing endorsement for her writing ability. No wonder *The Professor* was published only posthumously.

BRANWELL, THE FORGOTTEN BRONTË

Once there were six Brontë siblings. Two died in childhood. Three went on to become literary legends. And then there was Branwell. The fourth child—and the only boy—he may have been the most talented. A triple threat, Branwell excelled as a poet, a painter, and a tutor—although his penchant for hopping into the sack with the mothers of his pupils landed him in trouble at least once. His poems attracted the attention of Samuel Taylor Coleridge, and his portraits of his sisters are considered to be their definitive likenesses. Clearly, Branwell was on a similar path to immortality.

Unfortunately, his other weaknesses included alcohol and laudanum, a powerful opiate that was prescribed for almost everything in the nineteenth century. Fired from a series of jobs and beset by delirium tremens, in his late twenties Branwell grew increasingly dissolute and irrational. He contracted tuberculosis, the disease of choice among Brontës (and nineteenth-century writers in general), and died at age thirty-one. Rumor has it he died standing up, leaning against a mantelpiece, just to prove it could be done.

HERE'S TO YOU, MRS. ROBINSON

Anne Brontë was regarded as the best governess of the three. (Dreamy Emily was ill suited for the job, and stern Charlotte once likened caring for children to slavery.) Her specialty was getting incorrigible kids to behave—a talent that won her praise from beleaguered parents. One couple, the Rev. Edmund and Lydia Robinson, was so grateful that they asked her to recommend a tutor for their son. Anne made the mistake of proposing her dissolute, drug-addicted brother Branwell. He soon embarked on a two-and-a-half-year adulterous affair with Mrs. Robinson, who was seventeen years his senior. Upon discovering the infidelity, her incensed husband fired both Branwell and Anne, castigating her for having "brought this viper into the bosom of our family."

JANE ERR

Charlotte Brontë wrote *Jane Eyre* under a pseudonym, but she never really struggled to conceal her true identity. When sending her manuscript to be published, she included a note advising editors "in future to address Mr. Currer Bell, under cover to Miss Brontë, Haworth, Bradford, Yorkshire, as there is a risk of letters otherwise directed not reaching me at present." She also failed to include any postage, promising instead to send the stamps later. Not surprisingly, the novel was rejected by five publishing houses before it eventually won favor with Smith, Elder and Co. of London. The initial reviews were unenthusiastic. They dismissed "Currer Bell" as an "unsexed" female who desired "to trample upon customs established by our forefathers." William Makepeace Thackeray was a rare early supporter. Charlotte's sweeping saga touched him so deeply he reportedly broke down in tears in front of his butler.

HENRY DAVID THOREAU

JULY 12, 1817–MAY 6, 1862

NATIONALITY:
AMERICAN

ASTROLOGICAL SIGN:
CANCER

MAJOR WORKS:
A WEEK ON THE CONCORD AND MERRIMACK RIVERS (1849), "CIVIL DISOBEDIENCE" (1849), *WALDEN* (1854)

CONTEMPORARIES & RIVALS:
RALPH WALDO EMERSON, NATHANIEL HAWTHORNE

LITERARY STYLE:
PLAINSPOKEN, PELLUCID, RAPT WITH NATURAL WONDER

WORDS OF WISDOM

"I AM A MYSTIC, A TRANSCENDENTALIST, AND A NATURAL PHILOSOPHER TO BOOT."

ong before Jewish dissidents in the Soviet Union popularized the term, Henry David Thoreau was the world's first refusenik. He was always refusing one thing or another. To wit:

He refused to pay the $5 fee to receive his Master of Arts diploma from Harvard. "It isn't worth five dollars," he groused. "Let every sheep keep its own skin."

He refused to administer corporal punishment to children in his care at Concord Academy. The school board fired him for insubordination, costing him one of the few promising career opportunities he ever had.

He famously refused to pay his $1 poll tax in 1847 in protest of America's involvement in the Mexican War. That offense landed him in jail, where (according to legend) he brushed off his patron Ralph Waldo Emerson, who had come to bail him out. "Henry, why are you here?" Emerson reportedly asked. "Waldo, why are you *not* here?" was Thoreau's riposte. The next morning, Thoreau wasn't there anymore either. His aunt paid the tax for him, and he left his cell just in time for that afternoon's huckleberry party.

Thoreau even refused his given name. Born David Henry Thoreau, he insisted that everyone call him Henry David. Yes, he was as dedicated a contrarian as America's notoriously contrarian literary tradition has ever produced. Bartleby the Scrivener had nothing on David Henry—oops, excuse me—Henry David Thoreau.

One thing that Thoreau was *not* was inconsistent. He stuck to his plan for living, peculiar as it was, even in the eccentric milieu of nineteenth-century Concord, Massachusetts. Among his personal passions were fending for himself, communing with nature, traveling along rivers by boat, and writing long, digressive accounts of his experiences. Friends found him odd but somehow endearing. Ralph Waldo Emerson practically bankrolled his entire adult life. Thoreau served as bodyguard to Emerson's wife and children, handyman, and Concord court jester, leading children on expeditions into the woods, where he taught them about local flora, fauna, and birdsong. When he was really desperate for cash, he simply went back to work in his father's thriving pencil factory.

Thoreau's books sold dismally during his lifetime, but local legend grew after his death from tuberculosis at age forty-four. With the possible exception of Herman Melville's *Moby-Dick*, Thoreau's *Walden* is the most revered book no one has ever actually read. On the flip side, his great essay "Civil Disobedience" *was* read, and by some pretty important people. Gandhi, Leo Tolstoy, and Martin Luther King Jr. all cited it as inspiration.

Thoreau's personal life had several ups and downs. He never married, though he tried hard to land a wife. His beloved brother John died of tetanus in 1841. In April 1844, Thoreau and a friend accidentally destroyed more than three hundred acres of the Concord woods when their campfire blazed out of control. Emerson's terrible financial advice sent Thoreau into a spiral of debt that took him years to get out of, seriously straining their friendship. Yet, Thoreau lived the life he wanted. He was content with *not* becoming the "head of American engineers" that Emerson wanted him to be, preferring instead to reign as the "captain of a huckleberry party." It's that stubborn determination to be himself for which he continues to be admired to this day.

BUTTER BATTLE

Civil disobedience seemed to run in Thoreau's family. His grandfather Asa Dunbar was the ringleader of Harvard College's "Great Butter Rebellion" of 1766. Peeved about the quality of food served in the university dining halls, Dunbar did what any self-respecting undergraduate would do: He organized a student revolt. "Behold, our butter stinketh!" he railed. "We cannot eat thereof. Give us therefore butter that stinketh not!" Alas, Harvard faculty did not follow Dunbar's inexorable logic. Citing him with "the sin of insubordination," they suspended half the college as punishment. The Butter Rebellion, great though it may have been, failed utterly. However, it did pave the way for future Harvard food protests, including the Bread and Butter Rebellion of 1805 and the Cabbage Rebellion of 1807.

UGLY HENRY

By all indications, Thoreau was quite the charmer. But his appeal had nothing to do with good looks or personal hygiene. The Concord lothario cut a decidedly ungainly figure. His neighbor Nathaniel Hawthorne described him as being "as ugly as sin, long-nosed, queer-mouthed, and with uncouth and rustic, though courteous, manners, corresponding very well with such an exterior." Indeed, Thoreau rarely bathed or bothered to tamp down his unkempt hair or replace his shabby clothes. He was also notorious for his appalling table manners. Oliver Wendell Holmes often complained about Thoreau's tendency to eat with his fingers. Nevertheless, people seemed willing to overlook these deficiencies. "His ugliness is of an honest and agreeable fashion, and becomes him much better than beauty," Hawthorne concluded. Louisa May Alcott, who had a crush on Thoreau, wrote: "Beneath the defects the Master's eye saw the grand lines that were to serve as the model for the perfect man."

A 'SHROOM OF ONE'S OWN

Just because Thoreau was a free thinker by the standards of his day doesn't mean he wasn't a bit of a prude. One day in the fall of 1856, while walking in the woods, he was mortified to discover a large mushroom in the shape of a human penis. "It may be divided into three parts: pileus, stem, and base—or scrotum—for it is a perfect phallus," he wrote in his journal. "In all respects a most disgusting object, yet very suggestive.... It was as offensive to the eye as to the scent, the cap rapidly melting and defiling what it touched with a fetid, olivaceous, semiliquid matter. In an hour or two the plant scented the whole house wherever placed, so that it could not be endured. I was afraid to sleep in my chamber where it had lain until the room had been well ventilated. It smelled like a dead rat.... Pray, what was Nature thinking of when she made this? She almost puts herself on a level with those who draw in privies."

ROCK BOTTOM REMAINDER

When it came to book sales, well, let's just say Thoreau was no J. K. Rowling. Now considered a minor classic, his 1849 breakthrough *A Week on the Concord and Merrimack Rivers* sold so poorly that children would travel to his house to get a look at the "strange man . . . [who] had written a book no copy of which had ever been sold." That was an exaggeration, but only slightly. In fact, Thoreau's publisher wrote to him asking what to do with all the unsold copies piling up in his office.

Thoreau took 706 remainders, which he stacked in his attic and tried to sell to anyone who dropped by. "I now have a library of nearly nine hundred volumes," he confessed at one point, "over seven hundred of which I wrote myself."

RAISIN HELL

If you like raisin bread, you can thank Thoreau. He invented it during a bread-making phase at Walden Pond. The ladies of Concord were said to be amazed at his culinary innovation.

> THOREAU RARELY BATHED, NEVER BOTHERED TO TAMP DOWN HIS UNKEMPT HAIR, AND DRESSED IN RAGS. THAT DIDN'T STOP LOUISA MAY ALCOTT FROM FALLING IN LOVE WITH HIM.

PENCIL PUSHER

Studding bread dough with dried grapes was child's play compared with Thoreau's innovations in the realm of pencil making. Pencillery—if such a word exists—was in Thoreau's blood. Charles Dunbar, his uncle, had founded the family business in 1821 after stumbling upon a plumbago, or graphite, deposit in Bristol, New Hampshire. Thoreau's father, John, soon joined the firm and so revolutionized the manufacture of pencils that the Massachusetts Agricultural Society awarded him a special citation. At an early age, Henry David Thoreau pledged that he, too, would make his mark on the world of pencils. He finally got his chance in 1838. Devoting himself to pencils full-time, he soon developed an improved lead formula whose quality equaled that made in Germany. A new grinding mill for graphite was another of young Thoreau's revolutionary inventions. If only he had bothered to patent these ideas, he might have become a wealthy man.

Resting on his laurels, Thoreau vowed to never again make another pencil. "Why should I?" he told friends. "I would not do again what I have done once." But, like a seductive siren, the pencil trade lured him back; beset with debts, he returned with renewed vigor in 1843. He became thoroughly absorbed in his work, even admitting to Ralph Waldo Emerson that he dreamed about pencil machines all night long. The hard work paid off, for Thoreau developed what company advertisements pitched as "a new and superior drawing pencil, expressly for Artists and Connoisseurs"; it was harder, blacker, and more durable than any on the market. Before long, art teachers in Boston were insisting that students use nothing but Thoreau pencils. Only increased competition, prompted in part by Thoreau's own manufacturing innovations, kept the family from dominating the American pencil industry.

HENRY DAVID THE RED?

In 1954, at the height of the "Red Scare," the gentle individualist from Concord became an unlikely target of anticommunist hysteria. The U.S. Information Service ordered that all copies of *Walden* be removed from its libraries in American embassies worldwide. The book, it claimed, was "downright socialistic."

STING ALONG WITH ME

Thoreau considered himself a naturalist above all else, so he would probably be tickled to know there's an insect named after him. Entomologist A. A. Girault named a genus of wasp *Thoreauia*, in his honor.

WALT WHITMAN

MAY 31, 1819–MARCH 26, 1892

NATIONALITY:
AMERICAN

ASTROLOGICAL SIGN:
GEMINI

MAJOR WORKS:
LEAVES OF GRASS (1855)

CONTEMPORARIES & RIVALS:
JOHN GREENLEAF WHITTIER,
GERARD MANLEY HOPKINS

LITERARY STYLE:
EXUBERANT, UNMETERED

*"WHATEVER SATISFIES
THE SOUL IS TRUTH."*

WORDS OF WISDOM

Today, Walt Whitman is a beloved, avuncular figure—the "Good Gray Poet," with his flowing salt-and-pepper beard. But in his day he was quite the iconoclast. One critic called him "the dirtiest beast of his age." The Boston *Intelligencer*, in a review of his magnum opus *Leaves of Grass*, savaged him in highly personal terms: "The beastliness of the author is set forth in his own description of himself, and we can conceive of no better reward than the lash for such a violation of decency. The author should be kicked from all decent society as below the level of the brute. He must be some escaped lunatic raving in pitiable delirium."

The issue, of course, was sex. Whitman celebrated sex in his poetry with a frankness never before seen in America. His advocacy of male "brotherhood," lusty depictions of the human body, and repeated references to the virtues of touching oneself made him the object of censors' wrath almost from the moment he first sounded his "barbaric yawp" in 1855.

Whitman was also an unabashed American populist. His patriotic boosterism, in such poems as "I Hear America Singing," paved the way for a thousand sappy car commercials, not to mention Ronald Reagan's "Morning in America" reelection campaign. Any time you hear Woody Guthrie or Bob Dylan cataloging the virtues and sins of the U.S. of A., they're following Whitman's example.

Whitman liked to say that he and his work were one, that *Leaves of Grass* was the story of his life. That was true to a point, but he had a life away from poetry as well. He was one of nine children, and two of his siblings suffered from severe mental illness. Whitman was as healthy as a horse, in mind and body, and felt pent up only when he had to work indoors, in cramped newspaper offices, or as a schoolteacher on Long Island. He finally found an outlet for his creative energy in 1849, when he started on the first edition of *Leaves of Grass*, the evolving poetry collection he would revise and reissue throughout his lifetime.

Six years later, the collection's publication was showered with praise by the leading lights of the American literary community even as it provoked condemnation in the establishment press. "I greet you at the beginning of a great career," Ralph Waldo Emerson wrote to Whitman in a letter the less-than-humble poet included in a subsequent edition of the book. Whitman now had followers, but he also became a target. In 1865 Secretary of the Interior James Harlan fired him from his job at the Bureau of Indian Affairs as part of a campaign to improve the department's "moral character." He had found a copy of the latest edition of *Leaves of Grass* while snooping around Whitman's desk. That incident would prompt H. L. Mencken to remark many years later that "one day in 1865 brought together the greatest poet America had produced and the world's damnedest ass."

Whitman spent most of the Civil War years as a volunteer nurse in Washington, tending to sick and injured soldiers. He also found time to commit his brother Jesse to a lunatic asylum. In 1863 another troubled sibling, Andrew, died of tuberculosis at age thirty-six. He left behind two children and a pregnant, alcoholic wife, who later became a prostitute. It's no wonder Whitman preferred the company of the maimed.

After the war, he continued to revise and reissue *Leaves of Grass*. He attended baseball games, wrote essays on democracy, and nurtured what was apparently his only long-term relationship, a liaison with Irish-American streetcar conductor Peter Doyle. Whitman suffered a stroke in 1873 and was paralyzed on his left side. He moved into his brother's house in Camden, New Jersey, and would never live anywhere else. He spent much of his time in the bathtub, splashing around and singing "The Star-Spangled Banner," "When Johnny Comes Marching Home," and various Italian arias. His final years also saw a parade of visiting dignitaries—including Oscar Wilde—who dropped by to shoot the breeze and drink in the old man's wisdom. Enfeebled by a second stroke in 1888, Whitman died four years later at what was then considered the ripe old age of seventy-two.

THE GOOD GAY POET

Whitman's sexual orientation wasn't much of a secret, even in his lifetime. Everyone got the picture once they met him. If they didn't, a glance at "Song of Myself"—with its frankly erotic descriptions of the male body—would have quickly convinced them. This was a guy who liked guys—mostly of the rough-and-ready, unlettered, working-class variety. Whitman's notebooks are filled with descriptions of bus drivers, ferry-boat workers, and other "rude, illiterate" men he met—or picked up, to be precise—on the streets of Manhattan. In the afterglow, Whitman recorded their names, attributes, and addresses in his little black book:

> George Fitch—Yankee boy—Driver . . . Good looking, tall, curly haired, black-eyed fellow
>
> Dan'l Spencer . . . somewhat feminine . . . slept with me Sept 3d
>
> Wm Culver, boy in bath, aged 18

Later in life, Whitman cut down on the tomcatting and settled into a long-term relationship with Peter Doyle, a streetcar conductor he met in 1865 in Washington, D.C. Doyle was certainly Whitman's type: "A great big hearty full-blooded everyday divinely generous working man" was how the poet described him. "We were familiar at once," Doyle said of the night they met. "I put my hand on his knee. We understood. He did not get out at the end of the trip—in fact went all the way back with me. . . . From that time on we were the biggest sort of friends." They would remain friends and, by all indications, lovers until Whitman's death in 1892.

Still, homosexual relations, however discreet, were considered scandalous enough that Whitman went to some lengths to conceal them. He made a point of changing the pronouns in some of his more erotic poems from "he" to "she," suppressing passages, and even deleting entire selections from later editions of Leaves of Grass. When writing about Pete Doyle in his notebooks, he identified him as "16.4" (for his initials "P," the sixteenth, and "D," the fourth letters of the alphabet). In other places he referred to Doyle as "her." When asked by an interviewer whether his ideal of male friendship involved homosexual union, a panicked Whitman claimed to have fathered six illegitimate children by a female lover. Needless to say, the whereabouts of this purported paramour were never discovered.

ABE THE BABE

Whitman had a serious crush on Abraham Lincoln, whom he eulogized in his 1865 poem "O Captain! My Captain!" While working as a nurse in Washington, D.C., during the Civil War, Whitman often saw the president with his cavalry guard on the streets. His written description of their encounters leaves little doubt that he considered the lanky railsplitter quite the dish:

> I see very plainly Abraham Lincoln's dark brown face, with the deep-cut lines, the eyes, always to me with a deep latent sadness in the expression. . . . Probably the reader has seen physiognomies (often old farmers, sea-captains, and such) that, behind their homeliness, or even ugliness, held superior points so subtle, yet so palpable, making the real life of their faces almost as impossible to depict as a wild perfume or fruit-taste, or a passionate tone of the living voice—and such was Lincoln's face, the peculiar color, the lines of it, the eyes, mouth, expression. Of technical beauty it had nothing—but to the eye of a great artist it furnished a rare study, a feast and fascination.

I TOUCH MYSELF

Many a doctoral dissertation has been written on Whitman's supposed love of masturbation. Indeed it's hard to read his poems, with their constant references to touching (not to mention such lines as "Straining the udder of my heart for its withheld drip"), without coming to the conclusion that America's greatest poet was also its most dedicated practitioner of self-love. Of course, in Whitman's day, it was usually referred to as "self-abuse." Masturbation, or its clinical designation "onanism," was considered a gateway to homosexuality. It was dubbed "the worst form of venereal indulgence" by no less an eminence than Sylvester Graham, the nineteenth-century dietary reformer and father of the graham cracker.

WILDE MAN

If ever two great writers were destined to meet, they were Walt Whitman and Oscar Wilde. The gay icons met for the first time in January 1882, when Wilde visited Whitman at his home in Camden, New Jersey. The Irish writer told the American poet how much he loved *Leaves of Grass*, which his mother used to read to him as a child. Whitman responded by kissing Wilde square on the lips. They drank some elder-

berry wine and hot toddies and talked about the state of poetry. Wilde later sent the older man a portrait of himself as a keepsake. Assessing their meeting after the fact, both men were ebullient. Whitman described Wilde as "a fine, large, handsome youngster," while Wilde boasted to friends that "the kiss of Walt Whitman is still on my lips."

> WHEN NOT WRITING POETRY OR RHAPSODIZING ABOUT HIS LOVE FOR ABRAHAM LINCOLN, WALT WHITMAN WOULD IDLE AWAY THE HOURS IN HIS BATHTUB, SPLASHING AROUND AND SINGING "THE STAR-SPANGLED BANNER."

SWELLED HEAD

Whitman lived in the golden age of phrenology, the study of the physical characteristics of a skull to determine a brain's mental characteristics. Though dismissed today as quacks, nineteenth-century phrenologists attracted many celebrity adherents, including Whitman. The poet frequented phrenological parlors and subscribed to phrenological journals throughout the 1840s. In 1849 he even had his head "read" by a phrenological practitioner. Whitman's noggin was found to be of above-average size, "marvelously developed," and indicative of high levels of friendliness, sympathy, and self-esteem. He scored low marks for "indolence, a tendency to the pleasure of voluptuousness . . . a certain reckless swing of animal will . . . [and] an overabundance of sheer humanity." No wonder he went on to become one of the leading proponents of this pseudoscience. It described him perfectly.

MIND BOGGLING

The nineteenth century was the heyday of butterfingered lab assistants. Hoping to advance science, Whitman donated his brain to the American Anthropometric Society. But a careless technician dropped the Good Gray Poet's gray matter and then failed to scrape up the splattered remains. The mess was tossed in the trash. When word got out, a run on the brain bank ensued. The society's inventory of notable noodles plummeted from two hundred to eighteen.

LEO TOLSTOY

SEPTEMBER 9, 1828–NOVEMBER 20, 1910

NATIONALITY:
RUSSIAN

ASTROLOGICAL SIGN:
VIRGO

MAJOR WORKS:
WAR AND PEACE (1865),
ANNA KARENINA (1875)

CONTEMPORARIES & RIVALS:
IVAN TURGENEV

LITERARY STYLE:
OMNISCIENT, DIALECTICAL,
AND RICH WITH CHARACTER DETAIL

WORDS OF WISDOM

"THE ONE THING THAT IS NECESSARY, IN LIFE AS IN ART, IS TO TELL THE TRUTH."

Until experiencing a midlife spiritual conversion, Leo Tolstoy lived the life of an ordinary Russian nobleman, albeit one who also produced two of the most enduring classics in all world literature. In his diary, he recounted some day-to-day activities:

> I put men to death in war, I fought duels to slay others, I lost at cards, wasted my substance wrung from the sweat of peasants, punished the latter cruelly, rioted with loose women, and deceived men. Lying, robbery, adultery of all kinds, drunkenness, violence, murder. . . . There was not one crime which I did not commit.

It certainly sounds like a full, rich, rewarding existence, but for Tolstoy it was a crushing weight on his conscience. He sought something more than just torturing serfs to death and forcing sex on their widows. But it took him almost half his life to find it.

Born into a wealthy family (his fourth cousin was Alexander Pushkin, the great Russian poet), Tolstoy was an indifferent student whom his professors deemed "both unable and unwilling to learn." He spent most of his time gambling and contracting venereal diseases, although early on he was struck with the urge to write. While still in his twenties, he published several major works and cataloged his faults in the voluminous journal that he considered something of a confessional autobiography-in-progress.

His notebooks reveal a man obsessed with death. A veteran of the bloody Siege of Sevastopol, during the Crimean War, Tolstoy offered detailed accounts of battlefield atrocities and executions. He was so freaked out by the Grim Reaper that he would sometimes break into a sweat, convinced that Mr. Death lurked behind him, ready to tap on his shoulder. The demise of his brother Nicholas in 1860 served as another reminder of his own mortality. Although only in his mid-thirties, Tolstoy became convinced he was already too old and ugly to settle down and enjoy a normal family life. He was shocked when comely Sofia Andreyevna ("Sonya") Behrs, a doctor's daughter, agreed to marry him in 1862.

There followed a period of relative calm and stability, during which Tolstoy sired thirteen children and wrote his two masterworks, *War and Peace* and *Anna Karenina*. Although these novels brought him fame and additional wealth, they also deepened his belief that his life was not a virtuous one. He descended into a spiritual malaise, which health problems only compounded. Tolstoy was said to have "sinews of steel, and the nerves of a fainting female." He suffered from rheumatism, enteritis, toothaches, fainting spells, malaria, phlebitis, and typhoid fever. He also experienced several small strokes.

Clearly, this was a man primed for a midlife crisis. And his version resulted in a radical spiritual transformation. Tolstoy renounced sex, booze, tobacco, and meat and dedicated himself to a life of "Christian anarchism." He was committed to living out Jesus' teachings but without acknowledging the authority of the Russian Orthodox Church; not surprisingly, he won few friends at church HQ. They excommunicated him in 1901. He did win admirers among his serfs, however, whom he liberated and to whom he started donating his vast fortune. Such newfound altruism did not sit well with the missus.

Indeed, for all his problems, Tolstoy believed he knew the true cause of his earthly distress. "My illness is Sonya," he once declared, referring to his wife. Although she bore and raised a small nation of children, and copied *War and Peace* by hand *seven* times, she proved to be a constant irritant to the increasingly preoccupied holy man. A devotee of the Moscow party scene, Sonya was put off by her husband's intense Christian spiritualism, which she called a "disease." The constant parade of pilgrims to their country estate only made matters worse. She was also understandably perturbed by Tolstoy's decision to renounce all property rights, including proceeds from his books and inheritance. When he started giving away his money by the sackful, she hit the ceiling.

The last straw came when a scheming hanger-on named Chertkov convinced the doddering Tolstoy to bequeath to him all his riches. Fed up, Sonya began exerting more control. She followed him around, spying on him with a pair of opera glasses. When he suggested they end the marriage, she threatened suicide. Finally, Tolstoy discovered she was snooping through his diary—he'd had enough. He snuck out in the middle of the night, leaving a note thanking her for forty-eight years of marriage. "I am doing what people of my age very often do," the eighty-two-year-old legend wrote. "Giving up the world, in order to spend my last days alone and in silence."

Unfortunately for Tolstoy, those last days were spent in a freezing train station, where he collapsed with fever and chills. Delirious, his long white beard frozen into the ice, he died on the floor of the stationmaster's office on November 20, 1910.

SON OF KHAN

The man who once warned the world about the danger of "Genghis Khan with a telephone" knew whereof he spoke. Tolstoy was a direct descendant of the Mongol warrior.

BOOBY PRIZE

Tolstoy never won a Nobel Prize in Literature. Although considered the front-runner when the first such honor was awarded in 1901, he was passed over in favor of the obscure (and oddly named) French poet Sully Prudhomme. No official reason was given, but perhaps Tolstoy's politics didn't sit well with the culturally conservative Nobel committee. One of the judges cited his "narrow-minded hostility to all forms of civilization," whatever that means. At least Tolstoy was in good company. Henrik Ibsen and Émile Zola were also bypassed for similar reasons.

FULL DISCLOSURE

On their wedding night, thirty-four-year-old Tolstoy forced his eighteen-year-old bride to read his diary accounts detailing his sexual escapades with other women, including female serfs. Apparently, that was his idea of openness and honesty, but it was "T.M.I." as far as Sonya was concerned. The next day, she wrote in *her* diary of the disgust she felt at being subjected to such "filth."

JUST SAY NYET

There was nothing half-hearted about Tolstoy's religious conversion. Believing that eliminating meat was the key to mastering one's passions, he became a strict vegetarian, subsisting on a meager diet of oatmeal porridge, bread, and vegetable soup. He also gave up alcohol and tobacco and tried to convince the peasants on his estate to follow suit. In his essay "Why Do Men Stupefy Themselves?" Tolstoy decried both substances as drugs that people use to anesthetize their uneasy consciences. "The confusion and above all the imbecility of our lives," he railed, "arise chiefly from the constant state of intoxication in which most people live."

TALK ABOUT ROMANTIC: ON HIS WEDDING NIGHT, LEO TOLSTOY SHARED HIS EXTENSIVE SEXUAL HISTORY WITH HIS 18-YEAR-OLD BRIDE, SONYA, BY ENCOURAGING HER TO READ HIS PRIVATE JOURNALS.

BABEL ON

Along with abstinence, vegetarianism, and Christian anarchism, Tolstoy was a big proponent of Esperanto, the artificial international language designed to foster worldwide peace through ease of communication. He claims to have mastered it in three or four hours. Like everything Tolstoy adopted, it became something of a holy cause. "For he who knows what Esperanto stands for, it is immoral not to promote it," he wrote.

SHOWS BEFORE BROS

For such a spiritual guy, Tolstoy could be downright cold. He left his own brother Dmitry to rot on his deathbed, even refusing to look at him because he had forsaken God for a life of debauchery. "I honestly believe that what bothered me most about his death," Tolstoy later wrote, "was that it prevented me from attending a performance at court to which I had been invited." Ouch.

PISTOLS AT DAWN!

Another "friend" who bore the brunt of Tolstoy's cold-shoulder treatment was the Russian writer Ivan Turgenev. The two were close chums for a long time, but they grew apart, mostly due to Tolstoy's increasingly contrarian demeanor. When Turgenev complained about his bronchitis, a callous Tolstoy brushed him off, calling it an "imaginary disease." "We are poles apart," the author of *Fathers and Sons* later observed. "If I like the soup, I am certain Tolstoy will hate it—and vice versa."

The final blow-up occurred during a dinner party at a friend's estate. The conversation was going fine until Tolstoy started criticizing Turgenev for the way he was raising his daughter (she had been born out of wedlock to one of Turgenev's servants). "If she were your legitimate daughter, you would educate her differently," Tolstoy declared. An enraged Turgenev rose from his chair. "If you keep on talking like that," he screamed, "I'll slap your face!"

The dinner party ended but the feud simmered on. In an ensuing exchange of angry notes, Tolstoy challenged Turgenev to a duel. He even sent for his pistols. Although the two literary giants didn't go head to head, they did resolve never to speak to each other again. "We ought to live as though we existed upon different planets," Turgenev concluded. And they did, despite the proximity of their homes, only reconciling when Tolstoy found religion and started making amends with those he had wronged (a long list, apparently). Turgenev accepted his apology, but the two remained distant.

A BOOK ABOUT NOTHING?

Sorry, *Seinfeld* fans. Tolstoy's original title for *War and Peace* was not *War: What Is It Good For?* (as Elaine Benes informs Russian novelist Yuri Testikov in a classic episode of the nineties sitcom). The actual working title was the Shakespearean *All's Well That Ends Well*.

GROUP SCENE

Tolstoy was one of the first authors to attract a cult following. Some might even say he attracted a cult. Near the end of his life, about one hundred groupies camped out around his country estate, hoping for a tug on the great man's cloak.

THE LAST WORD

Tolstoy remained a committed iconoclast until the end. As he lay dying, his friends urged him to reconcile with the Russian Orthodox Church. Tolstoy refused. "Even in the valley of the shadow of death," he insisted, "two and two do not make six." That declaration is often mistakenly attributed as his final utterance. Tolstoy's actual last words were more cryptic, though less profound: "But the peasants. . . . How do the peasants die?"

EMILY DICKINSON

DECEMBER 10, 1830–MAY 15, 1886

NATIONALITY:
AMERICAN

ASTROLOGICAL SIGN:
SAGITTARIUS

MAJOR WORKS:
"WILD NIGHTS! WILD NIGHTS!" (1924),
"BECAUSE I COULD NOT STOP FOR DEATH" (1924)

CONTEMPORARIES & RIVALS:
WILLIAM CULLEN BRYANT, JOHN GREENLEAF WHITTIER,
WALT WHITMAN

LITERARY STYLE:
CLIPPED, GNOMIC VERSES SET TO THE METER
OF OLD HYMNS

WORDS OF WISDOM

"IF I READ A BOOK AND IT MAKES MY WHOLE BODY SO COLD NO FIRE CAN EVER WARM ME, I KNOW THAT IS POETRY."

J. D. Salinger, Harper Lee, and Thomas Pynchon, take heed. In the pantheon of literary recluses, you all vie for second place. Top spot goes to the demure poet from Amherst, Massachusetts, who perfected the author-as-hermit archetype long before you three limelight avoiders e'er were born.

How reclusive was Emily Dickinson? She was so reclusive that she often "visited" people by speaking to them from behind the door of an adjoining room. She was so reclusive that when she saw strangers approaching her house, she would run away crying, "Donkeys, Davy!" (a line from *David Copperfield*, one of her favorite novels). She was so reclusive that friends who had traveled great distances to see her often arrived to find her incommunicado. "Emily, you damn rascal!" pal Samuel Bowles upbraided her on one such occasion. "No more of this nonsense. I've traveled all the way from Springfield to see you. Come down at once!" A chastened Emily soon emerged from her locked room and engaged Bowles in conversation as though nothing had happened.

Why did Dickinson so delight in avoiding society? When people asked her, she was typically coy, miming the act of locking herself in her room and calling it the ultimate gesture of freedom. Some ascribed her retreat from the world to the psychological effects of a broken love affair. Others cited grief over the death of her dog Carlo, who invariably accompanied her on walks around town. Maybe she was just trying to avoid attending religious services. "Some keep the Sabbath by going to church," she once observed. "I keep it staying at home." Whatever the reason, by 1869 she was openly declaring, "I do not cross my Father's ground to any House or town." She would live by that precept for the rest of her life.

To be fair, Dickinson's seclusion wasn't as absolute as, say, the Unabomber's. She did keep in contact with friends and family through cards and letters. She played the happy homemaker—baking bread, tending to the conservatory and garden, and caring for her bedridden mother. She also made a point of trying to interact with the neighborhood children, whipping up treats that she lowered in a basket from her second-floor bedroom window. Oftentimes she would emerge from the house to join them in their games. But if ever she heard an adult approaching, she'd scamper off and disappear into her world of darkness and solitude.

And it was a dark world, both physically and spiritually. Scholars now believe that Dickinson suffered from rheumatic iritis, a painful eye inflammation that caused her to avoid all light. Refusing to sign an oath declaring her allegiance to Jesus Christ, Dickinson left Mount Holyoke Female Seminary, finding no solace in either academics or religion. As a result, she turned to poetry. She wrote nearly two thousand untitled, concise, cryptic poems using her own idiosyncratic syntax and punctuation. Only a handful were published during her lifetime. And the few who read them were not impressed. Critics derided "the incoherence and formlessness of her versicles," labeling Dickinsion "an eccentric, dreamy, half-educated recluse in an out-of-the-way New England village . . . [who] cannot with impunity set at defiance the laws of gravitation and grammar." A reviewer for *The Atlantic* fumed, "These poems are obviously the work of an oversensitive, coy, ill-disciplined, well-bred, hysterical spinster."

No wonder she left orders to have all her poems burned after her death. Her sister Lavinia tried to comply, but after torching hundreds of manuscripts and letters, she opened up one of Emily's desk drawers and found a sewing box containing more than a thousand handwritten poems—some scrawled on the backs of recipe cards or old scraps of paper. None were titled or ordered; some were incomplete. But with help from neighborhood busybody Mabel Loomis, Lavinia prepared them for publication. The first small volume of Dickinson's verse was published in 1890. It sold six printings in just five months. More than twenty years after the Belle of Amherst had signaled her retreat from the world, her innermost feelings about life, death, God, and the power of imagination were exposed to the world. It would be another half century before she was accepted into the pantheon of America's greatest poets.

WHITE WONDER

Daguerreotypes of Emily Dickinson depict her as a wan, thin, harmless-looking woman. But she had a way of making people nervous. "I never was with anyone who drained my nerve power so much," said Thomas Wentworth Higginson, her literary mentor, upon meeting her for the first time. "Without touching her, she drew from me. I am glad not to live near her." Perhaps her most off-putting affectation was her legendary all-white wardrobe, which may have been a subtle commentary on the Puritan notion of sin or simply a way to avoid leaving the house to visit expensive dressmakers. Whatever the reason, Dickinson stuck with the alabaster attire to the bitter end. She was buried in a white flannel burial robe, lying inside a white coffin.

JUST SIT RIGHT BACK AND YOU'LL HEAR A TALE . . .

Popular legend has it that you can sing almost any Emily Dickinson poem to the tune of "The Yellow Rose of Texas," "Amazing Grace," or the theme from *Gilligan's Island*. Was the clairvoyant poet sending us secret messages across the space/time continuum? Hardly. She simply wrote most of her poems in iambic tetrameter, the same rhythm used in such songs.

THE "L" WORD

When Dickinson's neighbors labeled her "gifted but queer," they might have been on to something. Speculation has been growing that America's beloved spinster poet may have been a closet lesbian. As Exhibit A in their case for Emily's Sapphic secret life, "queer studies" scholars point to Dickinson's complicated relationship with Susan Gilbert, a schoolteacher who married the poet's brother Austin in 1856. Dickinson and Gilbert did seem unusually close. They exchanged numerous letters, many of which read like mash notes. Emily wrote to her future sister-in-law in April 1852:

> Sweet Hour, blessed Hour, to carry me to you, and to bring you back to me, long enough to snatch one kiss, and whisper. . . . I have thought of it all day, Susie, and I fear of but little else, and when I was gone to meeting it filled my mind so full, I could not find a chink to put the worthy pastor; when he said 'Our Heavenly Father,' I said 'Oh Darling Sue.' . . . I think of ten weeks—Dear

One, and I think of love, and you, and my heart grows full and warm, and my breath stands still. The sun doesn't shine at all, but I can feel a sunshine stealing into my soul and making it all summer, and every thorn, a rose. And I pray that such summer's sun shine on my Absent One, and cause her bird to sing!

What did Susan Gilbert think of such blandishments? We'll never know. The Dickinson family had all her letters to Emily burned after Emily's death. Fearing they'd reveal the truth about the relationship, perhaps?

WRITE WHAT YOU DON'T KNOW

The commonly proffered writer's maxim "Write what you know" seemed not to apply to Dickinson. She wrote several poems about the seashore, for example, although she'd never been.

EMILY DICKINSON WAS SO RECLUSIVE, SHE FORCED DOCTORS TO "EXAMINE" HER FROM BEHIND A CLOSED DOOR.

MASTER AND SERVANT

More than a century after Dickinson's death, scholars are still trying to figure out the identity of the mysterious "Master" cited in a series of passionate love letters she wrote in her early thirties. Identifying the recipient of these hot-and-heavy missives—who appears to be an older male lover—has long been considered crucial to understanding the psychosexual underpinnings of her poetry. Candidates for her "Dear Master" include the Rev. Charles Wadsworth, a Philadelphia clergyman; Samuel Bowles, a Springfield newspaper editor; and Professor William Smith Clark, the founder and president of Massachusetts Agricultural College.

RECLUSE ENDANGERMENT

Dickinson never renounced her eremitic lifestyle—even while dying. Diagnosed with a terminal case of Bright's Disease, she allowed her doctor to examine her only through a partially closed door.

LONG-DISTANCE CALL

Dickinson must have known the end was coming. Shortly before she died, she dashed off a quick note to her cousins Louise and Frances Norcross. "Little Cousins," the note read, "Called back. Emily." The two-word farewell would become her epitaph.

SILENT BUT DEADLY

One day, taciturn U.S. president Calvin Coolidge visited the Amherst, Massachusetts, home of his fellow New Englander and came away unimpressed—that is, if his typically terse parting comment truly sums up his impression. After being given a guided tour of the premises and allowed to examine several rare and valuable Dickinson manuscripts, "Silent Cal" had but one observation: "Wrote with a pen, eh?" he said. "I dictate."

LEWIS CARROLL

JANUARY 27, 1832–JANUARY 14, 1898

NATIONALITY:
ENGLISH

ASTROLOGICAL SIGN:
AQUARIUS

MAJOR WORKS:
ALICE'S ADVENTURES IN WONDERLAND (1865),
THROUGH THE LOOKING-GLASS (1872)

CONTEMPORARIES & RIVALS:
EDWARD LEAR, DANTE GABRIEL ROSSETTI,
ALFRED LORD TENNYSON

LITERARY STYLE:
EXUBERANT AND RICH WITH WORDPLAY

"EVERYTHING'S GOT A MORAL, IF ONLY YOU CAN FIND IT."

WORDS OF WISDOM

Lewis Carroll may have inspired more psychedelic rock music than any other writer in history. Just think "White Rabbit" by Jefferson Airplane, "I Am the Walrus" by the Beatles, the entirety of Donovan's *Hurdy Gurdy Man* album. (Hey, no one said it was good psychedelic rock music.) All this from a man who probably never took drugs, may have never had a real adult relationship, and spent most of his life as a mathematics lecturer at a small English church.

Oh, and he also created one of the most beloved children's book heroines of all time.

Long before he met Alice, Charles Lutwidge Dodgson was a shy, stammering vicar's son from Daresbury, Cheshire. The third of eleven children, he began writing early in life. Even after earning a degree in mathematics from Christ Church College, Oxford, he continued to write comic verse, some of which was published in the *Comic Times*. Determined to keep his writing and mathematics careers separate, he invented the pen name "Lewis Carroll" by inverting his first two names, translating them into Latin, and then translating back to English. This kind of whimsical, smart-guy wordplay became a hallmark of his writing style.

Tall, slender, and handsome, Carroll lived the life of a cloistered academic. His principal outlets were writing and photography. After he was named a church deacon in 1861, it was assumed he would become an Anglican priest, but something stopped him from taking the leap to ministry. In his diaries, he spoke of a pervasive sense of sin and guilt, though it's unclear whether these feelings kept him from taking his vows. Certainly he remained devout. He once broke down in tears on a visit to the Cologne cathedral and was known to walk out of theatrical performances if anything sacred was defamed on stage.

In 1862 Carroll took a boat ride with friends, including Alice Liddell, a ten-year-old girl with whom he had developed an unusually close friendship. He passed the time by telling a story featuring Alice as the central character, which the little girl urged him to write down. Originally called *Alice's Adventures Underground*, he retitled it *Alice's Adventures in Wonderland*. Published in 1865, the book was an immediate and phenomenal success, spawning a sequel, *Through the Looking-Glass*, in 1872. Filled with such bizarre characters as the Mad Hatter and passages of nonsense verse, like "Jabberwocky" and "The Walrus and the Carpenter," the Alice tales were enjoyed by scores of readers of all ages. Shy, bookish Charles Dodgson was now world-renowned children's author Lewis Carroll (although he still found time to pen the occasional arid math treatise, notably the riveting *The Dynamics of a Particle* in 1865).

Carroll continued to write, take photographs, invent things, and muse on matters mathematical for the last two decades of his life. His photographic portraits are now seen as ahead of their time, although his prepubescent female subjects have raised questions for biographers. Carroll was unquestionably an eccentric. He lived an unconventional lifestyle, never marrying and, by all accounts, forming no long-term relationships with adult women. When he died of bronchitis in 1898, he left behind a never-ending pasta bowl of colorful characters, weird situations, and trippy bits of wordplay that writers, musicians, and children the world over still draw inspiration from today.

--- INSPECTOR GADGET ---

Carroll created more than just an endearing children's story. He was also a gadget freak who loved inventing in his spare time. Among his innovations: an electric pen; a new kind of postal money order; a tricycle; a method for justifying right margins on a typewriter; an early type of double-sided mounting square; and a mnemonic system for remembering names and dates, known as *Memoria Technica*.

Carroll also came up with the idea of printing a book's title on the spine of its dust jacket so that it could be found easily on a bookshelf. Words he coined that are still in use today include the portmanteaus *chortle* (a combination of *chuckle* and *snort*) and *galumph* (*gallop* plus *triumph*). An inveterate puzzle solver, Carroll devised many card and logic games, improved backgammon, and created an early form of Scrabble.

MEDICAL MARVEL

Rumors that Carroll used psychoactive drugs have been greatly exaggerated, but who could blame him, given his medical history? You'd want to dull the pain, too, if you suffered from ague, cystitis, lumbago, boils, eczema, synovitis, arthritis, pleurisy, diarrhea, laryngitis, bronchitis, erythema, vesical catarrh, rheumatism, neuralgia, insomnia, and toothaches—as Carroll did at various times. He also experienced chronic agonizing migraines accompanied by bizarre hallucinations, including "moving fortifications." Throw in a lifelong stammer, possible ADHD, and partial deafness, and it's a wonder Carroll wasn't a hardcore opium smoker. Then again, maybe he was.

LEWIS CARROLL'S FAVORITE MODE OF TRANSPORTATION WAS THE TRICYCLE. HE EVEN INVENTED ONE OF HIS OWN.

OH, MY ACHING HEAD!

Were Alice's adventures the by-product of a bad headache? Researchers for the British medical journal *The Lancet* reached that conclusion in 1999, when they analyzed the migraine hallucinations Carroll recorded in his dairies. Recurring images from the years leading up to the publication of *Alice's Adventures in Wonderland* in 1865 supported the thesis "that at least some of Alice's adventures were based on Carroll's personal migraine aura perceptions."

YOU CAN'T SPELL "CHARLES DODGSON" WITHOUT "OCD"

Along with other health problems, Carroll may have suffered from obsessive-compulsive disorder. He certainly was extremely anal retentive. Before leaving on any journey, no matter how short, he mapped out the route and estimated the time to complete each stage. Absolutely nothing was left to chance. He then calculated exactly how much money was needed and placed just the right amount of coins in each pocket to pay fares, tip porters, and buy

food or drink. When brewing tea, he insisted that it steep for precisely ten minutes, not a second more or less.

Like a nineteenth-century Felix Unger, Carroll often imposed his compulsive orderliness on others. When hosting a dinner party, he drew up a seating chart and then recorded in his diary each diner's menu choices so that "people would not have the same dishes too frequently." On a visit to a library, he left a note in the suggestion box outlining a more efficient system for organizing the books. He once rebuked his own niece for leaving an open book facedown on a chair. He even corrected other writers when he found small mathematical errors in their works. Yet, like most eccentrics, Carroll somehow managed to make these annoying traits seem endearing. No one seems to have been overly bothered by them. Then again, he never had to live with Oscar Madison.

GO ASK ALICE

The "P" word continues to haunt Lewis Carroll more than a century after his death. Was he a pedophile? The debate rages. Clearly, he had a special affinity for young girls. He took hundreds of photographs of them, occasionally in the nude (the girls, not Carroll). None depict explicitly sexual situations, although at least one girl's mother was creeped out enough to deny his request to photograph her without a chaperone. Carroll had an especially close relationship with Alice Liddell, the real-life model for *Alice's Adventures in Wonderland*, which ended abruptly in 1863. No one is sure why. The pages in Carroll's diary from this period were torn out by his family—possibly to protect his reputation. Carroll's interest in photography also ceased rather suddenly, in 1880, and he speaks in his diaries of a lifelong sense of sin and guilt. About what, he does not say. Was he doing more than snapping photos? Some recent biographers say that Carroll was nothing more than a Willy Wonka–type figure—an innocent man-child who was fascinated with children but did nothing to abuse or exploit them. Certainly no evidence exists that Carroll ever touched anyone inappropriately. Only the White Rabbit knows for sure.

CHUCK THE RIPPER?

Was Alice's eccentric creator really a woman-hating serial killer? In his 1996 book *Jack the Ripper, Light-Hearted Friend*, author Richard Wallace makes the case that Lewis Carroll was Victorian London's notorious murderer of prostitutes. For proof, Wallace relies on passages from Carroll's writing, which he claims contain anagrams revealing detailed descriptions of the Ripper's crimes. For example, the letters in the opening lines to Carroll's "Jabberwocky," which are

> 'Twas brillig, and the slithy toves
> Did gyre and gimble in the wabe
> All mimsy were the borogoves,
> And the mome raths outgrabe.

can be rearranged to read:

> Bet I beat my glands til,
> With hand-sword I slay the evil gender.
> A slimey theme; borrow gloves,
> And masturbate the hog more!

It's a bit unclear what hog masturbation has to do with Jack the Ripper. Nor does Wallace admit that Carroll was nowhere near London at the time of the murders. In fact, errors abound in many of the anagrams Wallace claims to have "deciphered." And then there's the fact that anagrams can be devised to make any written passage say almost anything, as one of Carroll's biographers proved when she rearranged the letters in a sentence from *Winnie the Pooh* to reveal that Christopher Robin was the real "Saucy Jack." Other than that, though, his theory is airtight.

LOUISA MAY ALCOTT

NOVEMBER 29, 1832–MARCH 6, 1888

NATIONALITY:
AMERICAN

ASTROLOGICAL SIGN:
SAGITTARIUS

MAJOR WORKS:
LITTLE WOMEN (1868)

CONTEMPORARIES & RIVALS:
MARK TWAIN, HENRY DAVID THOREAU

LITERARY STYLE:
GENTEEL, CHARMING, A TAD PREACHY

WORDS OF WISDOM

"MONEY IS THE ROOT OF ALL EVIL, AND YET IT IS SUCH A USEFUL ROOT THAT WE CANNOT GET ON WITHOUT IT ANY MORE THAN WE CAN WITHOUT POTATOES."

Like Jo March, the heroine of her great novel *Little Women*, Louisa May Alcott was temperamental and headstrong. Such qualities really bugged her father, the great Transcendentalist guru Bronson Alcott. "She is still the undisciplined subject of her own instincts," he complained. At the time, Louisa was a one-year-old infant. Clearly, growing up in this family was going to be tough.

Louisa remained the black sheep her entire life. She was also the breadwinner—a volatile and often toxic combination. By any standard, Bronson Alcott was a useful idiot for anyone looking to promulgate a crackpot remedy or start up a utopian vegetarian community. He was also a bit of a hypocrite. He loudly and repeatedly denounced private property but accepted handouts of cash and rent-free lodging from his wealthy friends. As a consequence, the family was always one generous gesture away from the poorhouse. That's where Louisa came in. She worked a series of tedious jobs to provide for her three sisters and two eccentric parents. She sewed, she taught school, she minded other people's children. But inside she burned to live—and to write about—a different kind of life.

On a trip to Boston, Alcott tried to sell some of her early jottings. "Stick with your teaching," the eminent publisher James Fields told her when she presented him with her manuscript. "You can't write." Undaunted, she continued to perfect her craft. As it turned out, her writing became the family's main source of income. She made a killing penning sensational Gothic thrillers under the pen names A. M. Barnard, Aunt Weedy, Flora Fairfield, Oranthy Bluggage, and Minerva Moody. In fact, the name Louisa May Alcott might have been lost to history had her publisher not asked her in 1868 to write a story for girls. There was just one problem: she hated kids. "I don't really enjoy this sort of thing," she wrote in her journal, "Never liked girls or knew many, except my sisters, but our queer plays and experiences may prove interesting, though I doubt it." She would later dismiss her juvenile fiction as mere "moral pap for children."

Alcott dashed off *Little Women* in just three months. It became an instant success and made her a literary celebrity. Still she remained a spinster, eerily dependent on her now-no-longer-penurious family. She was also sort of a busybody. Alcott led the campaign to ban Mark Twain's *Adventures of Huckleberry Finn* in Massachusetts. It was this type of demagoguery that prompted literary historian Odell Shepherd to remark that she "preserved to the age of fifty-six that contempt for ideas which is normal among boys and girls of fifteen."

Alcott's social activism had a positive aspect as well. She was an early proponent of the abolitionist cause as well as an advocate of women's suffrage. During the Civil War, she traveled to Washington, D.C., to work as a nurse in the Union Hospital. She was overwhelmed by the sights, sounds, and smells of wounded soldiers returning from the Battle of Fredericksburg. (Not to mention that they were the first naked men she had ever seen.)

She contracted pneumonia as well. Or maybe it was typhoid. Doctors couldn't say for sure. Whichever malady afflicted her, the treatment was the same, according to insane nineteenth-century medical practices. Alcott was pumped full of calomel, a mercury compound believed to cleanse the body of toxins. It gave her mercury poisoning. Her tongue swelled, her gums became inflamed, her hair fell out. The condition was incurable and irreversible, and she battled its debilitating effects for the last twenty-five years of her life. As it turned out, she survived her eccentric, domineering father by just two days. Right until the end, she was taking care of business. While arranging Bronson Alcott's funeral, she confided in her trusty journal, "Shall I ever find time to die?" On March 6, 1888, she finally did.

More than a century later, Louisa May Alcott's life and work continue to attract scholarly interest. However, getting people to see her as more than just a talented children's author has proved difficult. In the late 1980s, two professors researching a book on Alcott found the hand-written manuscript of her unpublished first novel in the Harvard University library. The manuscript, worth an estimated $1 million, had been sitting on the shelf, virtually unread and gathering dust, for almost 150 years.

----------------------- *OY, NEIGH!* --------------------

Alcott was a rambunctious child—so much so that she became convinced she'd been a horse in a previous life. Her father, who did not believe in such karmic twaddle, was not amused.

FRUITCAKES

When Alcott was eleven years old, her father moved the family to the utopian Fruitlands community in Harvard, Massachusetts. The experiment in "plain living and high thinking" was an unmitigated disaster, which Alcott memorably satirized in her 1873 memoir *Transcendental Wild Oats*. Forbidden to eat meat or exploit animals in any way, the Alcotts subsisted on unleavened bread, porridge, and water for nearly half a year. Proscribed from using horse manure or planting anything deep in the soil for fear of disturbing earthworms, the residents discovered that—surprise, surprise—all attempts at farming proved futile. They quickly grew cold (wool was also verboten), malnourished, and sick. Worst of all, the "utopian" settlement attracted all manner of crackpots and lunatics, some of whom had to be forcibly expelled by an ad hoc Council of Elders. The group lasted less than six months before most of the members—including the Alcotts—simply gave up and left.

CRACKERS ABOUT GRAHAM

Papa Bronson wasn't the only Alcott with nutty ideas. His wife, Abba, was a follower of Dr. Sylvester Graham, inventor of the graham cracker, who sold her on his theory that men's brains and lungs were weakened by the loss of semen during sexual intercourse. Maybe Abba was just looking for an excuse to avoid doing the wild thing after four difficult and painful pregnancies.

--- MY HEROES ---

Talk about a transcendental twofer. As a girl, Alcott had the hots for both Henry David Thoreau and Ralph Waldo Emerson, also residents of Concord, Massachusetts. Her first love was Thoreau, the dreamy outdoorsman who taught her all about the birds and the bees—literally. Thoreau was an avid

naturalist who could wax poetic about birdsong and insects. He was also known to toodle his flute for her, but strictly in the musical sense. With the older, crustier Emerson she developed more of a student-teacher-type crush. The so-called Yankee Plato presented her with a copy of *Goethe's Correspondence with a Child*, in which a nubile young woman falls madly in love with a randy, aging poet. Was he sending her a message? Apparently Alcott thought so. She spent hours composing passionate love letters to Emerson but never sent them. On moonlit nights, she would sit in the walnut tree outside his window, singing in German. Sometimes she left flowers on his doorstep. But Emerson, a married man, never seemed to notice or reciprocate. She was, after all, just six years older than his eldest daughter.

> OPIUM PLAYED AN OUTSIZED ROLE IN LOUISA MAY ALCOTT'S FICTION—PERHAPS BECAUSE SHE WAS ADDICTED TO IT IN REAL LIFE.

AI, POPPY!

Opium played an outsized role in Alcott's fiction, perhaps because she was addicted to it in real life. She first picked up the habit when her doctor prescribed laudanum, a drinkable opiate remedy popular throughout the nineteenth century. She used it to help her sleep during her long battle with the effects of mercury poisoning. Before long, Alcott was a full-fledged opium fiend. Many of the characters in her pseudonymous thrillers are opium eaters, as is the gambling and drug-addicted heroine of her autobiographical 1872 novel *Work: A Story of Experience*.

SMUT PEDDLER

Wholesome children's stories may have paid the bills, but deep down Alcott preferred to write steamy potboilers. Whenever she really wanted to cut loose, she adopted the pseudonym A. M. Barnard and crafted yarns of Gothic suspense and intrigue, known as "blood and thunder tales" in the parlance of the day. These books, which boasted such lurid titles as *A Whisper in the Dark* and *Pauline's Passion and Punishment*, were serialized in sensational periodicals, including *Frank Leslie's Chimney Corner*. Their female protagonists did things that were decidedly "unladylike" by Victorian standards, like taking opium and smoking hashish. One novel begins with the heroine proclaiming, "I'd gladly sell my soul to Satan for a year of freedom!" Hardly a declaration one can imagine being uttered by *Little Women*'s Jo March, that's for sure.

HASHING IT OUT

Louisa May Alcott came by her opium addiction honestly—she took up the drug for medicinal reasons. Her fictional characters, on the other hand, had no such excuse. In her 1869 short story "Perilous Play," a group of jaded young socialites pig out on hashish bonbons. And in her 1877 novel *A Modern Mephistopheles*, the villainous Jasper Helwyze seduces an innocent young wife with his patented "sleep compeller," an opiate confection that he dispenses from a tortoiseshell and silver candy case. Before long, the blissed-out woman is "slipping fast into the unconscious stage of the hasheesh dream, whose coming none can foretell but those accustomed to its use." Like Louisa May herself, for instance.

MARK TWAIN

NOVEMBER 30, 1835–APRIL 21, 1910

NATIONALITY:
AMERICAN

ASTROLOGICAL SIGN:
SAGITTARIUS

MAJOR WORKS:
THE ADVENTURES OF TOM SAWYER (1876),
LIFE ON THE MISSISSIPPI (1883),
THE ADVENTURES OF HUCKLEBERRY FINN (1884)

CONTEMPORARIES & RIVALS:
**AMBROSE BIERCE, WILLIAM DEAN HOWELLS,
OSCAR WILDE**

LITERARY STYLE:
AMERICAN REGIONAL VERNACULAR

*"THE ROAD TO HELL IS
PAVED WITH ADVERBS."*

WORDS OF WISDOM

is name may have been phony, but few authors have been more doggedly honest and authentic than the one formerly known as Samuel Langhorne Clemens.

"Mark Twain" was just one of Clemens's many pseudonyms. He also wrote under the pen names Thomas Jefferson Snodgrass, Rambler, Josh, Sergeant Fathom, and W. Epaminondas Adrastus Blab. His best-known moniker is a nautical term meaning "two fathoms deep," which young Sam picked up during his time working steamboats on the Mississippi River. Although the rechristened Mark Twain never legally changed his handle, he did trademark the pseudonym and incorporate himself as a business under that name. It was one of many, many ways this humorist, satirist, and teller of tall tales was years ahead of his time.

Most of us associate Twain with Missouri, his home state, but in fact he hated the place. "If you are born in my state, you pronounce it *Missourah*," Twain once remarked. "If you are not born in my state, you pronounce it *Missouree*. But if you are born in my state, and you have to live your entire life in my state, you pronounce it *misery*." Fed up with his life of misery, Twain left home at age eighteen and never went back.

He took a job on a riverboat, hoping to work his way up to captain, then the third highest-paying job in the country. He convinced his younger brother Henry to join him. In May 1858, Twain had a disturbing dream in which he saw Henry lying dead in a metal casket. A month later his nightmare came true, for Henry was killed in a steamboat explosion. The incident—and the foreboding dream—would haunt Twain the rest of his life.

During the Civil War, Twain served briefly in a Confederate militia, but it would be hard to find a man less fit to be a soldier. After a few weeks spent marching in place, he lit out for the American West, eventually winding up in San Francisco, where he found work as a journalist. He got his first taste of literary success in 1865 with the publication of his short story "The Celebrated Jumping Frog of Calaveras County." Two books of travel writing, *The Innocents Abroad* and *Roughing It*, cemented his growing reputation as one of the keenest observers of the American character.

To cash in on his newfound success, Twain headed out onto the lecture circuit. Some now go so far as to call him history's first stand-up comic. His ribald anecdotes and barbed observations about Gilded Age life may be a long way from Larry the Cable Guy, but it's fair to say that Twain invented the role of "humorist" now claimed by everyone from Dave Barry to Bill Maher. That alone would have ensured the sardonic Missourian's place in American cultural history. But then he had to go and write what many critics consider *the* most important novel in American literary history to boot.

The Adventures of Huckleberry Finn generated controversy from the moment it was published in 1885. Louisa May Alcott put it down in disgust, writing to Twain that "if you can't write a better book for our young people than *Huckleberry Finn*, I suggest you don't write anything at all." Then she went out and got it banned in her home state of Massachusetts. It was the first of many instances in which Huck Finn's story was suppressed, either for its (undeniable) vulgarity or its (arguably) racist portrayal of African Americans. Alcott's particular campaign had a predictable effect: Sales shot up 300 percent. Twain was now a bona fide literary celebrity.

Over the last two decades of his life, Twain extended his fame worldwide. He made a boatload of money on the after-dinner speaking circuit but squandered his wealth through a series of bad investments. (The Twain Bed Clamp, a wildly impractical device designed to keep babies from getting caught up in their bed covers, may be one of the worst inventions ever foisted on the public.) He filed for bankruptcy in 1895, recovered, but was dealt an even harsher blow by the death of his beloved wife, Livy, in 1904.

Twain spent his final years cranking out his last few bitter blasts at humanity, with special vitriol directed at organized religion. When he died in 1910, he left instructions for the posthumous publication of some of his more, shall we say, "adult-oriented" writings. One last kiss-off to his would-be censors? Or maybe it was just Twain's way of proving what he himself had once observed: "I think we never become really and genuinely our entire honest selves until we are dead. People ought to start dead, and then they would be honest so much earlier."

— CIGAR AFICIONADO —

It would be an understatement to say that Twain loved cigars. From the age of eight, he smoked between twenty and forty stogies a day until the day he died. He sometimes tried to quit, or reduce his intake, but invariably he failed. "To cease smoking is the easiest thing," he once observed. "I ought to know. I've done it a thousand times." He often fell asleep with a lit cigar clamped in his mouth.

You might expect a man of Twain's wealth and prominence to at least seek out some high-quality smokes. You'd be wrong. Twain smoked the cheapest, foulest cigars he could lay his hands on. Fellow puffers would make a point of bringing their own when they visited Twain's house, lest he offer them one of his. A reporter for the *New York World* remarked upon the "long, black, deadly-looking cigars" that Twain indulged in during an interview in 1902. "Their mere appearance compels comment," wrote the newspaperman. "You express surprise that the first one was not guilty of murder."

> MARK TWAIN ONCE DELIVERED AN ENTIRE SPEECH ON BREAKING WIND TO AN AUDIENCE THAT INCLUDED QUEEN ELIZABETH I.

THE TWAIN VEIN

Long before Lenny Bruce and Redd Foxx, Twain mastered the art of "working blue." He often gave after-dinner speeches to private audiences, during which he vented his unconventional opinions on sex, flatulence, and other taboo topics. In one such address, "Some Remarks on the Science of Onanism," he riffed on the subject of masturbation, advising, "If you *must* gamble away your lives sexually, don't play a Lone Hand too much." On another occasion, he devoted an entire speech to the idea of breaking wind in front of Queen Elizabeth I.

Perhaps Twain's most notorious oration was his 1902 "Address to the Mammoth Cod Club of Boston," a masterpiece of bawdy satire fashioned as a thoughtful defense of undersized male genitalia. "I fail to see any special merit in penises of more than usual size," Twain said to the club members, whose "mammoth cods" he also derided in verse. He went on to confess that he had once tried to enhance the size of his own member with an injection of silver nitrate, but that "as soon as I could get it out of its sling," he felt ashamed and regretted the decision.

GENERAL PATENT

Twain loved gadgets—making them, buying them, and investing in them. He was close friends with Nikola Tesla, the Serbian American engineer and inventor who was derided in his time as a "mad scientist." The pair spent a lot of time together in Tesla's lab, shooting the breeze and tinkering with various scientific innovations.

Twain patented three inventions: a self-adjusting vest strap, a self-adhesive scrapbook, and a historical memory-building game that, according to one critic, "looked like a cross between an income tax form and a table of logarithms." Of the three, only the scrapbook made any money.

Twain had no one but himself to blame for his lack of success. He missed out on some potentially lucrative ground-floor opportunities. Though he was one of the first to have a telephone installed in his house, he passed on investing in Alexander Graham Bell's invention because he believed that static on the line would doom its chances for widespread acceptance.

Twain was also an early adopter of the typewriter. After purchasing one of the earliest "typemachines" in 1874, he made literary history as the first person to turn in a typewritten manuscript (for *Life on the Mississippi* in 1883). This time, he did put his money where his mouth was— virtually all his money, in fact. But he backed the wrong horse. The typesetting device in which he sunk his fortune was a colossal failure. (You could even say the investment scheme had sucked him dry; one of his fellow investors was *Dracula* author Bram Stoker.) Not long after, Twain went bankrupt. He ended up trading in his old Remington typewriter because he needed the cash. To add insult to injury, the Remington Typewriter Company hyped their association with the famous author in its advertisements—without paying him, of course.

--- WHEN GREAT AUTHORS COLLIDE ---

When he moved to Hartford, Connecticut, in 1874, Twain found he had a literary giant for a neighbor: Harriet Beecher Stowe, author of *Uncle Tom's Cabin* and the woman Abraham Lincoln credited with sparking America's Civil War. Twain was not yet at the height of his celebrity, whereas Stowe was one of the most famous women in America. Nevertheless, Twain owned the more tricked-out house, by far. His enormous Gothic manse boasted nineteen rooms and seven bathrooms—each equipped with that wonder of modern wonders, the flush toilet. Twain lived there until 1891, when his declining financial fortunes forced him to move to Europe.

CAT FANCIER

Twain adored cats. In fact, in his later years he would rent kittens from his neighbors to keep him company during his summer-long sojourns in New Hampshire. "If man could be crossed with the cat," Twain once observed, "it would improve the man, but it would deteriorate the cat."

OH, BABY

As much as he loved kittens, Twain detested human infants—or so he claimed. One time a friend was showing off the newest addition to her family. "Don't you adore babies, Mr. Clemens?" she asked. "No, I hate them," he replied, and proceeded to tell her a story about the time his sister's son climbed on his bed and kissed him while he was recovering from an illness. "I made up my mind, if I lived I would put up a monument to Herod," Twain said.

THE MARK TWAIN DIET

Twain was a strong believer in the healing power of fasting. When he had a cold or fever, he often went without eating for two days or more, claiming remarkable recuperative results. "A little starvation can really do more for the average sick man than can the best medicines and the best doctors," he observed.

------------ SHOOTING STAR ------------

Twain wasn't so hot at placing his financial bets, but when it came to foretelling his own death, he was a regular Nostradamus. Born in November 1835, when Halley's Comet was visible, Twain correctly predicted he would die when it returned. "I came in with Halley's Comet," he declared in 1909. "It is coming again next year, and I expect to go out with it. It will be the greatest disappointment of my life if I don't go out with Halley's Comet. The Almighty has said, no doubt: 'Now here are these two unaccountable freaks; they came in together, they must go out together.'" Sure enough, the comet came back the following April, and Twain died the next day.

WHAT A LOAD OF SCRAP

Not all of Twain's inventions proved disastrous. In fact, one of his more successful brainstorms became an inspiration for homemakers and memorabilia collectors everywhere. In 1873 Twain patented the world's first self-pasting scrapbook. Scrapbooking helped Twain commemorate his travels around the globe. It also earned him a fair bit of cash. Twain's scrapbook, which came in a variety of leather-band cloth bindings, sold more than 25,000 copies.

MARGARITAVILLE ON THE MISSISSIPPI

When he's not looking for his lost shaker of salt, singer/songwriter Jimmy Buffett likes to curl up with a little Samuel Clemens. The Mississippi-born musician often includes quotations and paraphrases from Twain in his lyrics. He's written three songs inspired by the author's 1897 travelogue *Following the Equator*. Buffett even named a horse in his 2004 novel "Mr. Twain."

OSCAR WILDE

OCTOBER 16, 1854–NOVEMBER 30, 1900

NATIONALITY:
IRISH

ASTROLOGICAL SIGN:
LIBRA

MAJOR WORKS:
THE PICTURE OF DORIAN GRAY (1891),
THE IMPORTANCE OF BEING EARNEST (1895)

CONTEMPORARIES & RIVALS:
GEORGE BERNARD SHAW,
THE MARQUESS OF QUEENSBURY

LITERARY STYLE:
BITINGLY SATIRICAL AND BRIMMING WITH BARBED WIT

"IT IS ONLY BY NOT PAYING ONE'S BILLS THAT ONE CAN HOPE TO LIVE IN THE MEMORY OF THE COMMERCIAL CLASSES."

WORDS OF WISDOM

Cultivated leisure is the aim of man," Oscar Wilde once said. And he set out to prove it by barely working a day in his life. Except for a brief two-year stint as editor of the magazine *The Woman's World*, the legendary playwright and wit never held a real job, giving him ample time to compose the acid bon mots for which he became famous.

Not surprisingly, many of these witticisms centered on the theme of laziness. "I was working on the proof of one of my poems all the morning, and took out a comma," he declared on one occasion. "In the afternoon I put it back again." He once reproved a beggar who informed him he had no work to do and no bread to eat. "Work!" Wilde exclaimed. "Why should you want to work? And bread! Why should you eat bread?" (To be fair, Wilde did slip the poor man some spare change at the end of his tirade.)

No one seemed bothered by Wilde's indolence, as long as he remained one of the world's most engaging dinner companions. He came by his eccentricity honestly, as the son of a slightly dotty Irish nationalist poet and her skilled ear-and-eye surgeon husband, William (so skilled, in fact, that a type of surgical incision named after him is still performed today). Yet outside the operating room, the Wilde name was dogged by controversy. One of Dad's patients filed suit, accusing him of raping her while she was under anesthesia. He lost the case—a bad omen for young Oscar's future prospects in the courtroom.

At school, Wilde was always a bit, well, different. He eschewed all "manly" sports and instead developed a flair for interior decorating, tricking out his college quarters in peacock feathers, lilies (his favorite flower), and blue china. He may have been one of the first noteworthy victims of what today we would call gay bashing. Legend has it that his fellow students wrecked his dorm room and dunked him in the river Cherwell for "odd" behavior that may have included homosexual activity. Nevertheless, it's unclear how, at that time, he perceived his sexual identity. In 1884 he married Constance Lloyd but spent an inordinate amount of time before the big day working on the design for her wedding dress—a harbinger of how unconventional their marriage would be. Shortly after meeting his longtime lover Robert "Robbie" Ross in 1886, Wilde informed Constance he could no longer have sex with her for fear of giving her syphilis.

Certainly, by the time he started producing the plays that established his reputation in the 1890s, Wilde was as out as out could be, by the standards of the day. For fun, he favored hooking up with working-class "rent boys," in encounters he likened to "feasting with panthers." But he also formed a number of longer-term relationships; the most fateful was with Lord Alfred Douglas, son of the Marquess of Queensbury, of boxing rules fame. A virulent homophobe (before such a word existed), Queensbury blew a gasket upon learning of Wilde's affair with his then twenty-two-year-old son. He threatened to pelt Wilde with rotten turnips at the opening-night performance of *The Importance of Being Earnest* and left a rude calling card identifying the playwright as a "sodmomite."

Egged on by Lord Alfred, Wilde filed suit against Queensbury for libel. He lost, and things only got worse from there. Queensbury countersued, accusing Wilde of gross indecency. A private investigator uncovered evidence of Wilde's homosexual behavior, and the author's writings and personal letters were used as evidence against him. He was found guilty and sentenced to two years of hard labor in Reading Jail. (Standing in the rain awaiting transport to the hoosegow, he quipped, "If this is the way Queen Victoria treats her prisoners, she doesn't deserve to have any.") The scandal put an end to Wilde's writing career and made him persona non grata in the highfalutin social circles through which he had once flitted so effortlessly.

The prison experience left Wilde a broken man, spiritually and physically. Penniless, he immigrated to France, adopted the alias Sebastian Melmoth, and lived off the generosity of friends. Ironically, his devotion to leisure may have played a role in his demise. Rousted from his prison bed at Reading and forced to attend chapel service, after he had begged to be allowed to sleep in, Wilde fell down and cracked his skull. Upon his release, he underwent surgery to relieve the ensuing chronic pain. The doctor performed a mastoidectomy of a type pioneered by Wilde's father, using the famed "Wilde incision." Something went awry, however, and Wilde contracted a fatal case of cerebral meningitis. After uttering one last witticism about his hotel room's hideous wallpaper—"One or the other of us has got to go"—he died in his Paris lodgings on November 30, 1900.

GONNA DRESS YOU UP IN MY LOVE

What do Oscar Wilde and Ernest Hemingway have in common? Not much, beyond the shared history of transvestitism, of course. Both men spent much of their childhood wearing girl's clothes at the behest of their mothers. Wilde's mum, Lady Jane Wilde, was an eccentric poet who liked to outfit herself in outlandish costumes, each one topped with a bejeweled, feathered headdress. Apparently starved for a dress-up companion, she felt she had missed out by not giving birth to a girl. To compensate, she simply pretended little Oscar *was* a girl, hiding him behind a series of frilly Victorian frocks. But before you jump to conclusions, there's no link between such behavior and homosexuality—although it would explain much about Hemingway's macho posturing. Did someone say *over*compensating?

BRIDE OF DRACULA

Wilde faced some stiff competition for the hand of Florence Balcombe, his first fiancée and the beautiful daughter of a lieutenant colonel. Bram Stoker, the author of *Dracula*, was a regular houseguest of Wilde's parents and a fixture of Lady Wilde's literary salon. In 1878 he beat out Wilde for Florence's hand. Apparently she decided that a loveless marriage with an avowed gay man was less appealing than spending the rest of her life sleeping next to the world's foremost vampire expert.

THE TOOTH WILL OUT

Wilde may have been a legendary wit, but he wasn't the world's handsomest man. Most heinous among his features were his fetid, blackened teeth, a by-product of the mercury treatment he had been given to alleviate the symptoms of syphilis contracted in late adolescence. Throughout his adult life, when engaged in intimate conversation, Wilde always spoke with one hand covering his mouth, lest his rotten choppers disgust his conversation partner.

WILDE WEST

Oscar Wilde and "cowboy" might not seem to go together—unless you're auditioning performers for a new-jack version of the Village People. But the flamboyant Irishman got along famously during his yearlong speaking tour of the American West in 1881–82. Clad in a velvet coat and lace cuffs, he appeared before large and appreciative audiences in such cities as Leadville, Colorado, where he declared the local miners "polished and refined compared to the people I met in larger cities back East." He also quipped that a saloon sign he passed that read "Please do not shoot the pianist. He is doing his best." represented "the only rational method of art criticism I have ever come across."

GOIN' SOUTH

While touring the United States, Wilde wanted to meet one man above all others. No, not Walt Whitman, although the two did meet and share a kiss (see page 65). It was Jefferson Davis, former president of the Confederacy. Wilde finally got his chance on June 27, 1882, when he blew through Beauvoir, Mississippi, on his way to Montgomery, Alabama, to deliver a lecture on "Decorative Art" at the local opera house. The seemingly mismatched pair found much in common. Wilde remarked on the similarities between the American South and his native Ireland: Both had fought to attain self-rule and both had lost. He went on to declare that "the principles for which Jefferson Davis and the South went to war cannot suffer defeat."

As for the lecture, it proved to be something of a letdown. "An immense assemblage of the morbidly curious will greet him," declared the *Selma Times* in an article previewing the event. The *Montgomery Advertiser* was also eager to hear what the famous wit had to offer. "No lady has heard of Mr. Wilde that is not anxious to see and hear him; and, 'tis said, he 'adores the fair sex.'" But the Irishman's observations on aesthetics, delivered in such a strange and exotic accent, were wasted on the Southern audience. "The lecture was one of the peculiar nature that should be heard to be appreciated," the *Advertiser* summed up afterward, "and a synopsis or even a brief sketch will not be attempted."

DORIAN GOES GRAY

Many scholars consider *The Picture of Dorian Gray*, Wilde's novel about a debauched dandy who uses supernatural means to defy the aging process, to be semiautobiographical. Wilde certainly went to great lengths to disguise his graying hair. In fact, the dyes he used to color his flowing locks triggered a severe skin condition that caused his face, arms, chest, and back to itch like crazy during the last decade of his life.

ENGLAND IS BEHIND ME

During the early stages of his indecency trial, Wilde was still confident he would prevail. One day in Piccadilly Circus he ran into an old friend who seemed skittish about broaching the subject. Wilde bucked him up. "You've heard of my case?" he asked. "Don't distress yourself. All is well. The working classes are with me ... to a boy."

SURELY, OSCAR WILDE WAS NO ORDINARY FIANCÉ. IN THE WEEKS LEADING UP TO HIS WEDDING, HE OBSESSED OVER EVERY LAST DETAIL OF HIS BRIDE'S DRESS.

A REHABILITATED MAN

After his release from prison, Wilde tried one last time to prove his "decency" to the British public. He and his friend Ernest Dowson, a poet, visited a brothel in France. Pooling their resources, they had enough cash for one of them to sample the services. Dowson encouraged Wilde to give it a try, insisting his reputation could be salvaged if he acquired a more "wholesome"—that is, heterosexual—taste. Word got out about the visit, and soon a crowd gathered around the house of ill repute. When Wilde emerged, he reported to Dowson: "The first these ten years, and it will be the last. It was like cold mutton." He then addressed the crowd: "But tell it in England, for it will entirely restore my character!"

MEMBERS ONLY

Public outrage over Wilde's alleged "perversity" continued long after his death. In 1912 a memorial depicting him as a flying sphinx was erected on the site of his grave in Paris's famous Père Lachaise cemetery. But the sculpture's enormous phallus apparently scandalized an anonymous graveyard visitor, who took a hammer to it and knocked it off. (Cemetery caretakers later retrieved the broken ding-a-ling and used it as a paperweight.) The sphinx remained sexless until 2000, when multimedia artist Leon Johnson commissioned a sterling silver prosthetic penis and affixed it to Wilde's shattered crotch during a forty-minute ceremony entitled, fittingly, *Re-membering Wilde*.

IN DEPP

Early in his career, actor Johnny Depp spent a night sleeping in the Paris hotel room where Wilde had died. "I didn't see Oscar," reported the Hollywood heartthrob, although he admitted he "was a little paranoid that I might be buggered by his ghost at 4 A.M." To which the ghost of Wilde would have no doubt replied: "A pity, because you're just my type."

ARTHUR CONAN DOYLE

MAY 22, 1859–JULY 7, 1930

NATIONALITY:
SCOTTISH

ASTROLOGICAL SIGN:
GEMINI

MAJOR WORKS:
A STUDY IN SCARLET (1887), *THE SIGN OF FOUR* (1890),
THE HOUND OF THE BASKERVILLES (1902),
THE LOST WORLD (1912)

CONTEMPORARIES & RIVALS:
H. G. WELLS, RUDYARD KIPLING

LITERARY STYLE:
STATELY VICTORIAN PROSE

"IF IN ONE HUNDRED YEARS I AM ONLY KNOWN AS THE MAN WHO INVENTED SHERLOCK HOLMES, THEN I WILL HAVE CONSIDERED MY LIFE A FAILURE."

WORDS OF WISDOM

Arthur Conan Doyle was a failure as a physician and a complete disaster as an ophthalmologist. The historical novels he hoped would be his literary legacy went largely unread, even during his own lifetime. And he never could convince people that fairies were real or that Houdini had psychic powers. But he succeeded at the one thing that changed the publishing world forever: making oodles of money by creating the most popular detective franchise in history. Anytime you go to your grave with "Sir" before your name, you did something right.

A Scotsman by birth, Conan Doyle lived the life of the consummate English gentleman. He was named after King Arthur, whom his mother revered, and was raised on the novels of Charles Dickens and Sir Walter Scott. He studied medicine at the University of Edinburgh, spent time as a ship's doctor, and eventually settled in Portsmouth, England, the birthplace of his idol, Dickens. Conan Doyle had trouble scrounging up patients, however, relying instead on traffic accidents to keep his medical practice afloat. He married Louisa Hawkins, the sister of one of his patients, in 1885.

Conan Doyle began writing mystery stories soon thereafter, although Sherlock Holmes was hardly an overnight success. The first Holmes adventure, *A Study in Scarlet*, appeared in the 1887 edition of *Beaton's Christmas Annual*. Three years later, Conan Doyle left England for Vienna to study ophthalmology. His hopes of earning a good living as an eye doctor foundered for lack of patients, however, and the now two-time loser returned to writing to make ends meet. He hoped to win fame as an author of historical fiction. But his 1889 epic *Micah Clarke*, and others that followed, met with critical and public disdain. Then, in 1891, a new magazine called *The Strand* started publishing the Holmes adventures in serial form. The brilliant, high-strung consulting detective character, whom Conan Doyle had based loosely on his old university professor named Joseph Bell, struck a chord with Victorian readers. Conan Doyle's career took off. He wrote twenty-four Holmes stories before tiring of the character and killing him off in 1893's "The Final Problem."

Holmes was now a bona fide hit, and fans protested his "murder" in front of the author's house. Some sported black armbands to mourn the master detective's demise. Conan Doyle was forced to bring Holmes back in 1902—to the considerable benefit of his bank account. By now he had given up his medical practice and fallen in love with another woman, Jean

Leckie, although the relationship remained platonic out of respect for his wife, who was ill with tuberculosis. They married following Louisa's death in 1906.

Once an international celebrity, Conan Doyle increasingly devoted himself to pet causes. He became involved in two celebrated criminal cases, helping draw attention to the plight of a pair of men he felt had been falsely accused. He also penned a strident defense of British policy in the Boer War, an act of rhetorical jingoism that earned him a knighthood in 1902. He twice ran unsuccessfully for Parliament. Later, he focused almost exclusively on his belief in spiritualism, communicating with the dead, and the existence of fairies. It was a bizarre turnabout for a writer long associated with rational deduction. These stances made him a laughingstock in the literary world, although they endeared him to his second wife, who reportedly took an airplane ride shortly after his death in 1930 to see if she could contact him by séance from the cabin. The transmission, she believed, would be clearer if she were closer to heaven.

A MAN FOR ALL SEASONS

An avid sportsman, Conan Doyle excelled at cricket, golf, and skiing. He considered boxing the most sublime individual sport and was known to spar late at night while dressed in formal evening attire. During a visit to New York City in 1914, he took in a baseball game between the Philadelphia Athletics and the New York Yankees. He once played on a celebrity cricket team with fellow writers J. M. Barrie (creator of Peter Pan) and A. E. W. Mason, author of *The Four Feathers*. Fans of English football (what Americans call soccer) can thank him for helping found the Portsmouth Football Club in 1884. Doyle also served as the team's first goalkeeper, using the name A. C. Smith—a sign of the low esteem in which the game was held by the gentlemen of that time.

"NO SH*T, SHERRINGFORD"

Literary history—not to mention vernacular English—would have been quite different had Conan Doyle stuck with Sherringford Hope as the original name for the world's most famous detective. ("Hope" was the name of a whaling ship that he was especially fond of.) Calling the name dreadful, his wife, Louisa, convinced him to come up with something else. So he combined "Sherlock," after his favorite musician, violinist Alfred Sherlock, and "Holmes," for the famed jurist Oliver Wendell Holmes, who had recently written a book on criminal psychology. It should not go unremarked that Sherlock Holmes and the main character on the TV sitcom *Green Acres* were named after the same person.

AN ARDENT SPIRITUALIST, ARTHUR CONAN DOYLE BELIEVED THAT TINY WINGED FAIRIES WERE REAL AND COULD BE FOUND IF YOU ONLY LOOKED HARD ENOUGH.

HOW HOLMES BECAME A HOTTIE

If Conan Doyle had had his way, Holmes would have been saddled with more than just an awkward-sounding name; he'd also look nothing like the character we know today. When *A Study in Scarlet* was published in 1887, Conan Doyle insisted that his alcoholic father—at the time confined in a mental institution—be commissioned to do the illustrations. The drawings that Charles Doyle produced were amateurish and slipshod. They depicted Holmes as a short, fat, bearded man who resembled the French painter Henri de Toulouse-Lautrec. Many have attributed the book's poor sales to this ungainly rendering. When editors at *The Strand* began serializing Holmes stories a few years later, they made a point of hiring Sidney Paget, a top-notch illustrator, to makeover the great detective. Paget immediately rejected the elder Doyle's conception of Holmes as an ugly fop. "Absolutely not," he said. "We need to make him sexually attractive to women, an 1890s dandy. I am going to draw a Sherlock Holmes that all the women will yearn for and all the men will want to emulate in his flawless tailoring." The depiction that emerged—lean, angular, handsome, immaculately dressed—went a long way toward making Sherlock Holmes the international icon he is today.

TAPPING THE TABLE

Conan Doyle was devastated by the death of both his son and his brother during World War I. So devastated, in fact, that he turned his back on a life of rational thought and embraced the concept of Spiritualism, or talking to the dead. Today these conversations take place on daytime TV under the guidance of blow-dried "ghost whisperers" such as John Edward and James Van Praagh. But in Conan Doyle's era, séances took place around a wooden table, which would levitate or be tapped upon when a communication from the spirit world was transmitted. The John Edward of Conan Doyle's day was Margaret Fox, an upstate New York matron who, with her two sisters, buffaloed wealthy, gullible patrons for years, finally confessing it was all just an act. Conan Doyle was one of the few who refused to accept her admission, and for many years he wrote and lectured on the subject of spiritualism, often to public derision. Once while giving an address on the subject at New York's Carnegie Hall, he was interrupted by a high-pitched whistle. Thinking it was a message from the Great Beyond, he became very excited. Then an old man in the crowd admitted it was only his hearing aid on the fritz again. The audience burst into laughter, and newspapers used the anecdote as further evidence that Sherlock Holmes's creator was off his rocker.

— NO HOLMES FOR YOU! —

Conan Doyle's belief in the occult had at least a minor impact on his royalty statements. For many years, *The Adventures of Sherlock Holmes* was officially banned in the Soviet Union.

FAIRYLAND

Perhaps Conan Doyle's most infamous trip around the deep end of the spirit world came in 1921, when he published *The Coming of the Fairies*, a ringing defense of two teenage cousins from Cottingley, England, who claimed to have befriended a group of tiny, winged fairies. Photographs of the girls cavorting with the supposed sprites were clearly doctored—and later exposed as fakes—but once again Conan Doyle proved to be a willing dupe. He continued to herald the fairies' advent in articles and speeches throughout the 1920s, long after everyone else had moved on.

WILD ABOUT HARRY

Conan Doyle developed an unlikely friendship with escape artist Harry Houdini, whom he believed possessed genuine psychic power. Both men were internationally famous, and both held an interest in the spirit world, but that's where their similarities ended. Houdini didn't believe in mediums, and he used his association with Conan Doyle as an opportunity to meet and expose them. For his part, Conan Doyle was convinced Houdini could actually *do* magic—not merely use tricks to convince an audience of the illusions. Their relationship began to deteriorate after Conan Doyle's wife conducted a séance during which she claimed to receive a message from Houdini's late mother in English, a language the old woman had never spoken. Soon after, Houdini began publicly ridiculing Conan Doyle's belief in spiritualism. The two men had a falling out, exchanged a few nasty letters, and then stopped speaking to each other altogether.

DEM BONES

Was Sherlock Holmes's creator the mastermind behind one of the greatest hoaxes in history?

That's what anthropologist John Winslow contended in a 1983 article for the journal *Science*. Winslow claimed that Conan Doyle was the hoaxer responsible for Piltdown Man, a set of fossilized bone fragments found in a gravel pit in 1912 and passed off as the remains of the legendary "missing link" between apes and humans. Turns out this "early man" was mostly an orangutan, though it took anthropologists more than forty years to suss out the fake.

So how did Conan Doyle become a suspect? He was a neighbor and acquaintance of Charles Dawson, the amateur archaeologist who found the remains. He was also friends with a phrenologist who specialized in oddly shaped skulls and could have helped procure the orangutan's jawbone, a key part of the hoax. Some have even argued that, in his writing, Conan Doyle left clues about Piltdown Man. Specifically, his 1912 novel *The Lost World* allegedly contains a puzzle spelling out the location of the fossils. As for motive, accusers point to Conan Doyle's obsession with spiritualism, suggesting that he sought to discredit the scientific establishment by hoodwinking them with a deliberate forgery.

Today, other than a few crackpot anthropologists, no one really subscribes to the Conan Doyle-as-Piltdown-hoaxer theory. However, few can deny it's a scheme worthy of Moriarty himself.

W. B. YEATS

JUNE 13, 1865–JANUARY 28, 1939

NATIONALITY:
IRISH

ASTROLOGICAL SIGN:
GEMINI

MAJOR WORKS:
RESPONSIBILITIES (1914), *THE WILD SWANS AT COOLE* (1917), *THE TOWER* (1928)

CONTEMPORARIES & RIVALS:
JOHN MILLINGTON SYNGE, SEAN O'CASEY, EZRA POUND

LITERARY STYLE:
VISIONARY, MYTHOLOGICAL, POLITICAL

WORDS OF WISDOM

"I AM STILL OF OPINION THAT ONLY TWO TOPICS CAN BE OF THE LEAST INTEREST TO A SERIOUS AND STUDIOUS MOOD—SEX AND THE DEAD."

William Butler Yeats straddled the line between visionary poet and frothing lunatic. His friend and fellow poet Katharine Tynan recalled him swinging his arms, gesticulating wildly, and mouthing bits of verse whenever he would walk to her house outside Dublin. The police eyed him warily, unsure whether to arrest him or let him rave on. "'Tis the poetry that's disturbin' his head," they concluded, and left him alone.

Yeats was even more whacked-out on public transportation. When riding the bus, he would periodically fall into a trance. Staring straight ahead, he emitted a low humming noise as he beat time with his hands. When other riders asked if he was all right, he ignored them. His daughter once boarded the bus and found him in this unapproachable fugue state; she wisely opted not to disturb him. But when the bus reached their stop, Yeats snapped out of it. "Oh, who is it you wish to see?" he asked her, like a receptionist greeting a patient at a psych clinic.

If the poetry that was "disturbin' his head" hadn't been some of the finest ever composed, he would probably be remembered as just another doddering Irish versifier. But Yeats blazed a path from the late Romantic era to the dawn of modernism, crafting cryptic, idiosyncratic poems that drew heavily on his belief in the occult and his cyclical view of world history. Without him, the English language would be missing such oft-quoted phrases as "terrible beauty" and "the center cannot hold," not to mention the word "gyre" (a type of spiraling vortex).

After a relatively uneventful youth, Yeats's life picked up steam in his early twenties, when he began dabbling in mysticism, engaged in Irish politics, and felt the sting of unrequited love. He proposed four times to Maud Gonne, the woman he considered his soul mate, during a ten-year period. She turned him down every time. Fed up, he tried offering his hand to Maud's daughter Iseult. (She was twenty-two at the time; he was fifty-two.) She, too, spurned him. Convinced by his astrological charts that he *must* get married in 1917, Yeats moved on to Georgie Hyde-Lees, a medieval scholar who shared his love of horoscopes and the occult. As an added bonus, Georgie styled herself a psychic, and she occasionally channeled the spirit of Yeats's mystical alter ego, Leo Africanus.

Writing, opining on Irish affairs, conducting the odd séance—that was how a mature Yeats spent most of his time. He was a member of two very different, very exclusive societies: the Irish Senate (where he helped design coins and judicial robes) and the Hermetic Order of the Golden Dawn, a "white magic" cult that was the Church of Scientology of its day, drawing celebrity adepts from across Ireland and throughout Great Britain. He also helped found the Abbey Theatre, which hosted some of the era's great playwrights, including Yeats himself. The man was multitalented.

Late in life, Yeats settled into his role as a living legend. His poetry became more personal. He wrote frankly about his impotence and his attempts to overcome it. Death and the dissipation of his creative energy became a preoccupation as well. He died in 1939, leaving behind some of the most eloquent "old man" poems ever composed. The closing lines of one became his epitaph: "Cast a cold eye / On life, on death. / Horseman, pass by."

!

HEADBANGER'S BALL

Yeats was always fascinated by the supernatural. In January 1888 he attended his first séance at the home of a Dublin medium. The experience proved to be a moving one, in every sense. As the table tapping got under way, Yeats's anxiety increased. He felt urged to pray but couldn't remember any prayers. Instead, he started banging his head on the table and reciting the opening lines from Milton's *Paradise Lost*: "Of man's first disobedience, and the fruit of that forbidden tree, whose mortal taste brought death into the world ... " That didn't help either. Terrified, Yeats suddenly felt his entire body thrown back against the wall, "moved like a suddenly unrolled watch-spring," to use his own description. That was it for Yeats and séances, at least for a while. The sudden violent impulse completely unnerved him, and he was never sure if it came from within or from somewhere "out there," in the spirit world.

MY FRIEND LEO

The spirit world's Abbott to Yeats's Costello was Leo Africanus, a sixteenth-century adventurer whom Yeats first "met" at a séance in Hampstead, England, in June 1914.

Leo introduced himself and, after professing to be affronted that the poet hadn't heard of him, struck up a conversation. Over the next few years, the two became close friends—as close as a flesh-and-blood human and a shade from the other side of the life/death divide can be. Yeats came to view Leo as his "daimon," or alter ego, a kind of spiritual opposite who embodied all the idealized characteristics he wished he had. Where Yeats was cautious, Leo was bold, and so on. Leo would often offer advice to the poet and support in the form of "automatic writing" that would pour forth from Yeats's own hand. Sometimes Yeats's wife, an avowed medium, would do the channeling. Over time, Leo's influence on Yeats began to wane, and their "correspondence" ended in 1917.

MR. CROWLEY

Yeats's occult dabbling put him in contact with some of the era's most eccentric supernaturalists. When he joined the Hermetic Order of the Golden Dawn in 1898, fellow members included horror writers Algernon Blackwood and Arthur Machen as well as the "Wickedest Man in the World," the celebrated hedonist and black magician Aleister Crowley.

Yeats and Crowley immediately disliked each other. Yeats considered Crowley immoral, if not outright insane, and Crowley believed that Yeats was secretly jealous of his literary and magical powers. Over the next few years, Yeats maneuvered to have Crowley expelled from the Golden Dawn on the grounds that "a mystical society should not have to serve as a reform school for juvenile delinquents." For his part, Crowley accused Yeats of using black magic to cast a spell against him—a hex the crafty Crowley had thwarted, of course. In the end, Yeats prevailed. Crowley was kicked out and went on to form his own magical order, but the Golden Dawn remained divided and never regained its former popularity.

The old magician would have the last word. In an essay entitled "My Crapulous Contemporaries," Crowley ridiculed Yeats directly, writing: "It is true that a sort of dreary music runs monotonously through your verses, only jarred by the occasional discords. It is as if an eternal funeral passed along, and the motor-hearse had something wrong with the ignition and the exhaust."

MUSSOLOONEY

Like his friend Ezra Pound, Yeats was a little too taken with the accomplishments of Benito Mussolini, Italy's Fascist dictator. Always suspicious of democracy, he once declared "despotic rule of the educated classes as the only end to our troubles." But it wasn't until the 1930s that he started putting his money where his mouth was. About that time, Yeats wrote three "marching songs" for the Irish Blueshirts, a homegrown Fascist movement modeled on the Nazi brownshirts. In late 1933 he wrote gushingly to his friend Olivia Shakespear: "The great secret is out—a convention of blueshirts—'National Guards'—have received their new leader with the Fascist salute and the new leader announces reform of Parliament as his business . . . Italy, Poland, Germany, then perhaps Ireland." By "reform of Parliament," Yeats meant the abolition of parliamentary government, which he favored, despite holding a seat in the Irish senate. (No one ever said he was consistent.)

W. B. YEATS WAS ACTIVELY INVOLVED WITH THE HERMETIC ORDER OF THE GOLDEN DAWN, A "WHITE MAGIC" CULT.

MONKEY MAN

In the days before Viagra, older men often resorted to quack remedies and experimental procedures to address their erectile dysfunction. Yeats was no exception. Determined to put a little more lead in his pencil, the aging poet traveled to Vienna to undergo the fabled "Steinach Operation," a revolutionary vasectomy touted by its namesake inventor as a surefire way to rejuvenate male sexual potency. (Sigmund Freud had been "Steinached" some years earlier, to no effect.)

The fifteen-minute operation, in which monkey glands were implanted into Yeats's scrotum, went off without a hitch. Yeats got his groove back. He later credited the surgery with reviving not only his creative powers but also his "sexual desire; and that in all likelihood will last me until I die." He soon began enjoying the fruits of his "strange second puberty" with a new mistress, twenty-seven-year-old actress and poet Margot Ruddock.

All the monkeying around did not come without a cost, however. Word soon spread, and the randy altercocker became an object of derision. Dubliners started calling him "the gland old man," and Irish writer Frank O'Connor likened the procedure to "putting a Cadillac engine into a Ford car."

THANK YOU, SUGAR DADDY!

Margot Ruddock must have really spun Yeats's top. The nubile actress wrote undistinguished and unmemorable poetry. Yet, when Yeats was commissioned to edit the *Oxford Book of Modern Verse* in 1936, he included a whopping *seven* of her poems—one more than the combined total allotted to Ezra Pound and W. H. Auden! Daddy must have gotten a few extra kisses the night that anthology hit the shelves.

H. G. WELLS

NATIONALITY:
ENGLISH

ASTROLOGICAL SIGN:
VIRGO

MAJOR WORKS:
THE TIME MACHINE (1895),
THE WAR OF THE WORLDS (1898),
THE INVISIBLE MAN (1897)

CONTEMPORARIES & RIVALS:
ARTHUR CONAN DOYLE, JOSEPH CONRAD,
HENRY JAMES

LITERARY STYLE:
STATELY, EDWARDIAN

"EVERY TIME I SEE AN ADULT ON A BICYCLE, I NO LONGER DESPAIR FOR THE FUTURE OF THE HUMAN RACE."

WORDS OF WISDOM

When Hitler's SS was drawing up its list of prominent British citizens to be executed immediately after the German occupation of England, H. G. Wells was near the top. His crime was being a socialist, although if Nazi authorities had taken a closer look, they would have discovered he was also a dyed-in-the-wool anti-Semite. The author who came to be known as "The Man Who Invented Tomorrow" was a study in contradictions, and his private life was almost as bizarre as his sci-fi flights of fancy.

The son of a professional cricketer, Wells grew up in dire straits after an injury prematurely ended his father's career. He failed as a draper's assistant, a pharmacist's assistant, and a teaching assistant before wisely concluding that the title "assistant" wasn't right for him. In 1891 he married his cousin Isabel Mary Wells, but that worked out about as well as his various jobs. He divorced her three years later to marry Amy Catherine Robbins, one of his students. She bore him two children and stuck by him despite a slew of extramarital affairs.

Beginning with *The Time Machine* in 1895, Wells cranked out dozens of stories and novels that helped define the conventions of the science-fiction genre. Among his innovations were the fictional depiction of time travel, nuclear war (he coined the term *atomic bomb*), and genetic manipulation. His lifelong fascination with eugenics represented the dark side of his futuristic vision, which was always tinged with more than a dollop of Jew hatred. Wells believed in the forcible relocation of racial and ethnic minorities, punishment of "deviants," and rule by a scientific and technocratic elite. He was also quite hostile to Roman Catholicism.

These prejudices rarely showed up overtly in his works, many of which stand up today as classics of the speculative genre. Although dismissed by some critics of his day—one famously called *The War of the Worlds* "an endless nightmare"—Wells won over readers in part through the uncanny accuracy of his predictions. He correctly foresaw the advent of air conditioning, commercial television, videotape recording, wheeled trucks, propeller airplanes, and aerial warfare. He also successfully predicted the start date of World War II and the coming sexual revolution—although this last may have been wishful thinking. He was known to be quite the ladies' man.

Naturally, not all his prognostications panned out. He did not foresee viable aircraft before 1950. He maintained that "my imagination refuses to see any sort of submarine doing anything but suffocating its crew and floundering at sea." And his cryptic dinner party prediction that the human race would destroy itself, die out as a species, and return to the primordial ooze within a thousand years has yet to play itself out. Still, Wells seemed to be preparing for his ultimate vindication when he chose his own epitaph, which reads, "God damn you all, I told you so."

THE SEX MACHINE

"I was never a great amorist," Wells once remarked. Tell that to the count-less women he bedded outside the constraints of marriage. (Or to the five children he reportedly sired out of wedlock.) Yes, this short, fat, balding intellectual with tiny hands and a high-pitched voice was quite the "playa," to use the parlance of a later time, or "the Don Juan of the Intelligentsia," as he liked to style himself. Even one of Wells's modern biographers described him as "something of a sex machine," an unlikely lothario with a "fatal attraction for the wrong women." His stable of famous lovers included celebrated French author Odette Keun, feminist writer Rebecca West, birth control advocate Margaret Sanger, venerable Boston Brahmin-turned-European-expatriate Countess Constance Coolidge, and Martha Gellhorn, a sassy socialite cum war correspondent who later married Ernest Hemingway.

So what was Wells's secret? For one thing, he had no conscience. "I have done what I pleased, so that every bit of sexual impulse in me has expressed itself," he wrote in his autobiography. A staunch advocate of "free love," Wells cheated on both wives, claiming at one point that he had the "right" to do so with impunity. (It's unclear whether he believed this "right" belonged to his wives as well.) Such brazen horndogging didn't seem to scare off too many paramours. Wells remained a veritable babe magnet well into his sev-enties. One lover attributed his erotic prowess to the fact that his body gave off an irresistible honeylike aroma.

STUCK IN AMBER

One of Wells's most sordid dalliances was with Amber Reeves, a free-thinking young woman from one of London's most prominent families. Her parents were friends of his and, like Wells, vociferous advocates of sexual liberation. After spending a weekend visiting with Wells and his wife, Amy, the voluptuous Amber began shagging the middle-aged author. Rumors started to circulate about the affair, which Wells made no effort to hide from Amy. The two were soon appearing together in public and made plans to elope to France. (What Wells planned to do with the wife he already had is unclear.) In his memoirs, Wells rhapsodized about the "sexual imaginativeness" of his younger partner, implying that her taste for kink put his wife to shame.

The bloom quickly came off the rose, however, when Amber became pregnant and friends warned Wells he could not survive the scandal of divorcing a second wife in such compromising circumstances. Amber was also showing signs of emotional volatility—no doubt exacerbated by Wells's demand that she wait on him hand and foot as if she were already his wife. Even great sex couldn't save this doomed relationship. A dispirited Wells convinced Amber to marry a young lawyer acquaintance of theirs, hoping that the scandal would die down and they could go on seeing each other. For a while, with the tacit acceptance of Wells's wife, they did. To add insult to injury, Wells wrote a thinly veiled account of the affair in the form of a novel, *Ann Veronica*, which saw print only after Wells's regular publisher rejected it on grounds of immorality. On December 31, 1909, Amber Reeves gave birth to Wells's daughter Anna-Jane. The girl did not learn the identity of her real father until 1928.

THE SPY WHO LOVED HIM

Was one of Wells's late-life paramours a Soviet spy? Some historians call Moura Budberg, the Ukrainian-born baroness whom Wells bedded in the early 1930s, the "Mata Hari of Russia," claiming she worked as a secret agent for the Bolsheviks while sleeping her way through various European capitals. Under the cover of their torrid affair, the twenty-seven-year-old Budberg shamelessly used the sixty-something Wells to gain access to his politically connected friends. She even set up a meeting between Wells and Soviet dictator Josef Stalin, after which Wells described "Uncle Joe" as the most "fair, candid, and honest" man he had ever met. Eventually, Wells woke up to the reality that he was being played, although his passion for the haughty noble left him powerless to end their affair. She eventually became pregnant by him and was compelled to have an abortion—an ironic twist given Wells's staunch belief in birth control.

WELLS MEETS WELLES

Their names will forever be linked—and not just because they sound the same. Orson Welles's 1938 radio dramatization of H. G. Wells's *War of the Worlds* sparked a nationwide panic and put the then-obscure theatrical director on the map. H. G. was reportedly less than pleased with both the adaptation and the ensuing controversy but had mellowed considerably by the time he met Orson two years later, on a visit to San Antonio, Texas. Wells was in town to address the U.S. Brewers Association. On his drive through town, he stopped to ask directions—of none other than Orson Welles. The two men spent the day together and later discussed the *War of the Worlds* broadcast in a joint interview on KTSA radio. The mismatched pair seemed to get along famously, and if Orson was offended by H. G.'s demeaning reference to him as "my little namesake," he didn't let on.

NOT SO BON VIVANT

Wells was known as a lively conversationalist, though you'd never know it from the anecdotes of some of his fellow partygoers. English novelist C. P. Snow recounted that the two were having a drink in a hotel bar when their conversation hit a dead spot. Suddenly, out of the silence, Wells posed the ultimate buzz-killing question: "Ever thought of suicide, Snow?" Snow reflected a moment and then answered, "Yes, H. G., I have." "So have I," replied Wells, "but not till I was past seventy." He was seventy years old at the time.

On another occasion, Wells nearly stopped time by announcing, apropos of nothing, "My father was a professional cricketer," as an icebreaker to *Jeeves and Wooster* author P. G. Wodehouse. "If there's a good answer to that, you tell me," Wodehouse later recalled. "I thought of saying 'Mine had a white moustache,' but finally settled for 'Oh, ah,' and we went on to speak of other things."

PASS THE HAT

When he wasn't taking their breath away with his chitchat, Wells was literally stealing people's clothing. One night, after yet another Cambridge party, Wells returned home with another man's hat. He liked it so much he decided to keep it, writing to its owner (whose address was written inside the brim): "I stole your hat. I like your hat. I shall keep your hat. Whenever I look inside it I shall think of you. . . . I take off your hat to you!"

WHEN HE WASN'T WRITING CLASSIC SCIENCE FICTION, H. G. WELLS PIONEERED THE FIRST MINIATURE WAR GAMES. IRONICALLY, HE CLAIMED TO BE A PACIFIST.

SHALL WE PLAY A GAME?

For a pacifist, Wells sure loved war—war gaming, that is. All his life, he enjoyed playing with toy soldiers. He even wrote two books on the subject, *Floor Games* (1911) and *Little Wars* (1913). Published on the eve of World War I, *Little Wars* is considered the definitive rulebook for the world's first recreational war game, the first game system that let players use commercially available toy soldiers as playing pieces. For these contributions, Wells is recognized today as the "the father of miniature war gaming."

So how did Wells square his pacifism with his passion for playing at war? He claimed that it made him *more* of a pacifist because when matched up against real generals, he found them to be incompetent buffoons. Wells clearly feared for the future of Britain should the country ever have to command armies in an actual battle. World War I, in which Britain lost more than 900,000 men, would prove him right soon enough.

STEAL THIS BOOK

In 1925 Wells became enmeshed in a plagiarism lawsuit. An obscure Canadian writer named Florence Deeks claimed that he had cribbed material from one of her unpublished manuscripts. The trouble started in 1920, when Deeks read a review of Wells's *Outline of History*. The two-volume tome bore an eerie resemblance to Deeks's own history of the world, *The Web of the World's Romance*, which had gathered dust for more than a year in the slush pile of Wells's North American publisher, MacMillan & Company—by an amazing coincidence, during the same period Wells was writing *his* book. A closer examination of the rejected manuscript revealed that it had been thumbed through extensively, and there were enough organizational similarities that Deeks considered suing right then and there. Still she was reluctant. The final straw came when other publishers started rejecting her manuscript because it was too similar to *his*. An outraged Deeks took Wells to court, accusing him of "literary piracy," but the Toronto spinster stood little chance of prevailing against the world-famous author. She lost, but her dogged pursuit of justice made her an inspiration to overlooked female writers everywhere.

ALL YOU NEED IS WELLS

Wells's belief in free love and women's liberation made him something of a patron saint of the flower-power generation. The Beatles even honored him with a place on their *Sgt. Pepper* album cover. He's in the second row from the top, third from the right, between Karl Marx and the Indian yogi Sri Paramahansa Yogananda.

KEEPING IT IN THE FAMILY

Wells's great-grandson is filmmaker Simon Wells, who directed the 2002 big-screen remake of *The Time Machine*, based on Great-Grandpa's novel.

GERTRUDE STEIN

FEBRUARY 3, 1874–JULY 27, 1946

NATIONALITY:
AMERICAN

ASTROLOGICAL SIGN:
AQUARIUS

MAJOR WORKS:
THREE LIVES (1909), *TENDER BUTTONS* (1914),
THE AUTOBIOGRAPHY OF ALICE B. TOKLAS (1933)

CONTEMPORARIES & RIVALS:
ERNEST HEMINGWAY, SHERWOOD ANDERSON,
VIRGINIA WOOLF

LITERARY STYLE:
PLAYFUL, EXPERIMENTAL, OCCASIONALLY INCOHERENT

"I'VE BEEN RICH AND I'VE BEEN POOR. IT'S BETTER TO BE RICH."

WORDS OF WISDOM

Gertrude Stein got a big kick out of herself. In fact, it's fair to say that no one enjoyed literary celebrity, or had a higher opinion of her own achievements, than this genial lesbian from Allegheny, Pennsylvania. "Besides Shakespeare and me," she once asked the sculptor Jacques Lipchitz during a discussion about great writers, "who do you think there is?"

Not everyone would agree with that lofty assessment. Many readers—and some critics—found her work impenetrable at best, puerile at worst. She cultivated an idiosyncratic, avant-garde writing style, marked by seemingly nonsensical repetitions and odd word choices, that could be off-putting to those weaned on more linear prose. *The New Yorker* spoke for many in the literary establishment when it declared of one of her novels: "Stein has succeeded in solving the most difficult problem in prose composition: to write something that will not arrest the attention in any way, manner, shape, or form."

Still, she had her staunch defenders. Whatever her merits as a writer, no one could deny her immense influence as a tastemaker and patron of the arts. Ernest Hemingway, Ezra Pound, and Pablo Picasso were just a few of the modern masters whom she took under her wing at her salon in Paris. If you were an expatriate artist in the 1920s and 1930s, and you *didn't* spend most of your downtime getting plastered and shooting the breeze at Stein's house, you weren't really living.

She moved to Paris in 1902, at the end of an uneventful young adulthood spent in America, studying psychology, embryology, and medicine. A few years later, she met the woman who became her longtime lover and amanuensis, Alice B. Toklas. Alice didn't mind living in Stein's zaftig shadow, seemingly content with her role as the great writer's muse, secretary, and bedtime playmate. Not to mention cook. Stein was a woman of immense appetites. Her principal passions were food, reading, and sex, in that order. "Books and food, food and books; both excellent things," she once observed. She luxuriated in the lardaceous American-style meals that Alice prepared for her, rhapsodizing about "the full satisfied sense of being stuffed up with eating." Is it any wonder one of Alice's pet names for her was "Mount Fattie"?

As Stein's notoriety grew, she and Alice became one of the unlikeliest celebrity power couples in world history. A pair of tiny Jewish lesbians who lived abroad in open defiance of bourgeois social mores don't seem like natural candidates to become the toast of Depression-era America—and yet they did. When the couple arrived in Manhattan for a six-month lecture tour in 1934, a revolving billboard reading "Gertrude Stein has arrived in New York" greeted them in Times Square. Like a cat preening on a windowsill, Stein basked in the glow of her fame. She took tea at the White House with Eleanor Roosevelt, partied with Charlie Chaplin in Hollywood, went on a tour of a spark-plug factory, and attended a production of her opera *Four Saints* in Chicago. At night, she and Alice took off to visit the slums to see how "the little people" were living.

Not that she cared. Although many people assume Stein was a political radical, she was actually something of a right-wing reactionary. "I cannot write too much upon how necessary it is to be completely conservative . . . in order to be free," she once wrote. She considered the unemployed to be lazy, opposed the New Deal, and—for a time at least—supported the collaborationist Vichy government in Nazi-occupied France. One of her closest friends was the notorious Nazi collaborator Bernard Fay, with whom she was known to discuss Adolf Hitler's "qualities of greatness." Stein even argued that Der Führer should be awarded the Nobel Peace Prize for ridding Germany of its troublesome Jews—an especially odd position given her own religious heritage.

Maybe she was just sucking up to the occupying authorities. Stein and Toklas lived in the French countryside throughout World War II, where they were left alone by the Nazis, presumably under orders from their friends in the Vichy government. When the war ended, they returned to Paris. But the golden age of expatriates was over, and Stein didn't have much time left. She died of cancer in 1946. According to Toklas, her final words were characteristically droll. "What is the answer?" she asked, before fading into unconsciousness. When Toklas didn't reply, Stein smiled knowingly and then added, "In that case, what is the question?"

LOVEBIRDS

Stein and Toklas were big on pet names and public displays of affection—often to the discomfort of those around them. Stein called Toklas gay, kitten, pussy, baby, queen, cherubim, cake, lobster, wifie, Daisy, and, most alarmingly, my little Jew. To Alice, Gertrude was king, husband, hubby, Mount Fattie, and fattuski. The two of them even left love notes for each other lying around the house, each one signed "DD" and "YD," for "Dear Dear" and "Your Dear."

AND DON'T FORGET TO DEDICATE THE BOOK TO ME!

Before agreeing to write Alice B. Toklas's "autobiography" for her, Stein encouraged her longtime lover to write it herself. Her suggested titles were typically Steinian exercises in self-aggrandizement: *My Life with the Great; Wives of Geniuses I Have Sat With*; and *My Twenty-Five Years with Gertrude Stein*.

TOUGH LOVE

Proving that criticism may have been her true calling, Stein once offered Pablo Picasso some constructive advice about his poetry. "I read his poems," she told friends afterward, "and then I seized him by the shoulders good and hard. 'Pablo,' I said, 'go home and paint.'"

AUTOMATIC WRITING

Stein's writing process was as formless as some of her prose. She refused to learn how to type, preferring to write her manuscripts in longhand. She worked at a furious pace—about two pages every five minutes—often while carrying on unrelated conversations. (While in college, she had developed a theory that people have an unconscious "second personality" that manifests itself in such situations.) As she filled pages, they floated to the floor where they were scooped up by a typist and transcribed for posterity. Stein rarely revised what she wrote and almost never worked for more than half an hour a day. Giving new meaning to the term "automatic transmission," she also occasionally wrote in one of her beloved Ford motorcars.

PAPA LOVES MAMA

Stein and Ernest Hemingway had a complicated relationship. Early in his career, she advised him to forsake journalism and concentrate full-time on fiction. She helped shape his first efforts by offering constructive criticism and introducing the element of repetition that would become a hallmark of his prose. She also encouraged him to travel to Spain and was the first to expose the young "Papa" to bullfighting. In gratitude, Hemingway asked Stein to serve as godmother to his firstborn son and used his growing influence to get some of her work published.

They remained close for many years. But their mother-and-son routine was Oedipally charged, to say the least. Hemingway always resented the presence of Alice B. Toklas and repeatedly urged Stein to "switch teams" and shack up with him instead. "I always wanted to fuck her and she knew it," he later confessed. "It was a good healthy feeling." Not to Stein, apparently. She successfully resisted all invitations to become Papa's hoochie mama.

MY FAIR FREDDY

Paul Bowles, author of *The Sheltering Sky*, was another of Stein's literary protégés. He joined her salon in 1931 and, at her urging, moved to Tangier in 1947. Stein took a liking to Bowles's middle name, Frederic, and referred to him only as "Freddy" for the time they knew each other.

ANIMAL FARM

Stein and Toklas were big-time animal lovers. Their personal menagerie included a cat named Hitler (so called because of his brush moustache) and dogs Polype, Byron, Babette, Pepe, and Basket. Polype was famous for eating his own excrement, Byron for his incestuous designs on members of his own litter, and Basket for his exquisite breathing, which Stein credited with teaching her the difference between sentences and paragraphs. Basket also received a daily sulfur-water bath. Paul Bowles was put in charge of drying him. Stein ordered him to don lederhosen and run the dog around the house while she egged him on from an upstairs window, shouting, "Faster, Freddy, faster!"

DON'T HAVE A COW

For reasons known only to her, Stein referred to orgasms as "cows." Coded references to "cows" can be found in a number of her poems and stories, including "As a Wife Has a Cow: A Love Story." For the record, she once called herself "the best cow giver in all the world." Go ask Alice.

IF I MAY QUOTE MYSELF . . .

Stein was quite fond of her most famous utterance: "A rose is a rose is a rose." She had the phrase painted on all her china and embroidered on all her bed linens.

AMONG THE MANY PETS KEPT BY GERTRUDE STEIN AND ALICE B. TOKLAS WAS A CAT NAMED HITLER.

--- POE RELATIONS ---

Edgar Allen Poe's great-nephew was the literary executor of Stein's estate.

TOMBSTONE BLUES

In keeping with Stein's literary stature, Alice B. Toklas made arrangements to have her lover buried in famed Père Lachaise Cemetery in Paris, alongside many other great authors. Unfortunately, she also got a few details wrong when it came time to inscribe the grave marker. Stein's hometown of Allegheny, Pennsylvania, is misspelled as "Allfghany" and the day of her death is erroneously listed as July 29, rather than July 27.

JACK LONDON

JANUARY 12, 1876–NOVEMBER 22, 1916

NATIONALITY:
AMERICAN

ASTROLOGICAL SIGN:
CAPRICORN

MAJOR WORKS:
THE CALL OF THE WILD (1903),
THE SEA WOLF (1904), *WHITE FANG* (1906)

CONTEMPORARIES & RIVALS:
FRANK NORRIS, SINCLAIR LEWIS, THEODORE DREISER

LITERARY STYLE:
SPARE, RUGGED, HARD-BITTEN, LIKE THE MAN HIMSELF

"I WRITE A BOOK FOR NO OTHER REASON THAN TO ADD THREE OR FOUR HUNDRED ACRES TO MY MAGNIFICENT ESTATE."

WORDS OF WISDOM

I was always willing to drink when anyone was around," Jack London once said. "I drank by myself when no one was around." In a literary universe teeming with galaxy-class drunks (Edgar Allan Poe, Jack Kerouac, and Dylan Thomas spring to mind), the author of such classic adventure tales as *White Fang* and *The Call of the Wild* may just have been the drunkest of all.

How drunk was he? His collection of "alcoholic memoirs," *John Barleycorn*, is on the recommended reading list of Alcoholics Anonymous. London boasted to friends that he started hitting the sauce at age five, when his alcoholic stepfather would send him to the local saloon to fetch his beer in a bucket. By fourteen, he was drinking hardened sailors under the table. At his peak, London consumed about a quart of whiskey a day, suffering the effects in the form of accidents and bouts of vagrancy. He once got so sloshed that he staggered off the Oakland wharf and into San Francisco Bay, where he floated along aimlessly until he was rescued by a Greek fisherman. While on a visit to Japan, London overindulged on sake. Cooped up in his sloop in Yokohama Harbor, he chugged rice wine night and day for a week, until local police ordered him to leave. Apparently convinced that if he was soused to the gills he must be able to breathe underwater, London dove into the harbor to evade the cops. Japanese authorities officially recorded him as drowned, but somehow London found his way back to the boat.

A true literary pioneer, London helped romanticize the image of the two-fisted, hard-drinking, devil-may-care American writer. Would there be an Ernest Hemingway or a Norman Mailer without his aggressively macho example? London lived the kind of hardscrabble life that writers from more refined backgrounds—like, say, Hemingway—envied and tried to emulate. He was born out of wedlock and raised in poverty along the Oakland waterfront, where he lived as a working-class outlaw, including a stint as an "oyster pirate" stealing the prized mollusks from commercial beds in San Francisco Bay. Beneath the roughneck facade, however, beat the heart of a thoughtful man of letters. London was almost entirely self-educated. A library rat, he amassed a personal book collection of some fifteen thousand volumes, which he referred to as "the tools of my trade." His trade paid off quite handsomely, and he became one of the twentieth-century's first celebrity authors. Fame, with its accompanying financial rewards, allowed London to pursue adventure, often on board his self-built sloop, the *Snark*.

After 1905, he was invariably accompanied on these excursions by his second wife, Charmian Kittredge, a brassy, uninhibited hellion whom he called "Mate Woman." In her, he'd met his match not only intellectually but sexually as well.

Although his adventurous lifestyle kept him physically fit, it also exposed London to a variety of illnesses and ailments that gradually wore him down and led to his untimely death. In his early twenties, he lost his four front teeth to a bout with scurvy. He contracted dysentery and pleurisy while working in Mexico and then malaria in the South Pacific. During a cruise to the island of Ontong Java, his hands swelled to twice their normal size and his skin started peeling off in clumps. He was diagnosed with pellagra, a vitamin-deficiency disease common among sailors. He was also plagued by kidney stones, rheumatism, shingles, infected ankle sores, tonsillitis, insomnia, weak joints, and uremia. This last would finally do him in at age forty, in 1916. Contrary to common misconception, London did not commit suicide but succumbed to either the cumulative effects of his poor diet and alcohol consumption or an accidental overdose of morphine to relieve the pain caused by the uremia. He is buried in what is now the Jack London State Historic Park in Sonoma County, California.

A STAR IS BORN

London may have been born in squalor, but a life of literary success was clearly written in the stars—as his dad could attest. London's birth father was almost certainly William Chaney, a mercurial ex-pirate who became a seminal figure in the history of astrology. After being turned on to the power of horoscopes by British astrological pioneer Dr. Luke Broughton, Chaney deemed the zodiacal portents "the most precious science ever made known to man" and devoted himself to popularizing them. He brought academic rigor to the study of the stars, lecturing and training acolytes and publishing an ephemeris, or chart used to calculate horoscopes. Apparently nothing in these charts told him he was Jack London's father, however. When London sought him out in 1897, Chaney denied paternity, claiming he was impotent during the period London was conceived. Most modern scholars now dispute this claim.

PLOT THIEF

London was the subject of numerous accusations of plagiarism. He was known to take plot elements from true stories published in newspapers (a common practice at the time) or simply to pay people for plots and story ideas, including a young Sinclair Lewis. Rumor has it that he also nicked ideas from Irish journalist Frank Harris as well as American novelist Frank Norris. Invariably London's defense was that he and the aggrieved author had merely relied on the same sources. It must have worked. London was never found guilty of plagiarism.

TO THE RAMPARTS!

London was the first American author to earn a million dollars from his writing. He was also a committed socialist—a contradiction that did not go unnoticed among his contemporaries. "It would serve this man London right to have the working class get control of things." Mark Twain once remarked. "He would have to call out the militia to collect his royalties."

Truth be told, London's radicalism was a bit of a pose. He was known for showing up at elegant dinner parties wearing a workingman's flannel shirt—but one so impeccably laundered and pressed that it ruined the intended effect. He signed his letters "Yours for the Revolution," though he did precious little to start one. London did run twice for mayor of Oakland under the Socialist party banner. The first time, in 1901, he got 245 votes. Four years later, he upped that paltry total to 981. After that he stopped running altogether.

YELLOW FEVER

For all his talk of class struggle and economic justice, London was a vicious racist who harbored a special contempt for Asian people. On a visit to Japan to cover the Russo-Japanese war for the Hearst newspapers in 1904, he remarked to a colleague that the Japanese "may be brave, but so are the South American peccary pigs in their herd charges." Koreans, he wrote, were "the perfect type of inefficiency—of utter worthlessness." The Chinese got off relatively easy. London praised them for their lack of cowardice and their industrious nature. But in a sickening 1904 essay entitled "The Yellow Peril," London warned of the consequences should the "brown" Japanese and the "yellow" Chinese one day join forces. "The menace to the Western world lies, not in the little brown man," he wrote, "but in the four hundred millions of yellow men should the little brown man undertake their management."

So how did London square such beliefs with his progressive political platform? He didn't. When one of his Socialist party comrades pointed out that Marx had called for a revolution to unite the workers of *all* nations and races, London practically flipped his wig. "I am first of all a white man and only then a socialist!" he thundered.

SATAN'S MINION

Every God-fearing schoolchild knows Jack London as the author of *The Call of the Wild*. But among Satanists, he is most famous for a book he didn't write. For decades, Anton LaVey's Church of Satan maintained—inexplicably—that London was "Ragnar Redbeard," the pseudonymous author of the 1896 screed *Might Is Right*. A weird mixture of Darwinian evolutionary theory and Friedrich Nietzsche's philosophy of the "Superman," *Might Is Right* espouses sentiments no one familiar with London's political views would ever think of attributing to him, such as, "The Strong must ever rule the Weak in grim primordial Law" and "On earth's broad racial threshing floor, the meek are beaten straw."

Not surprisingly, the book won favor with radical anarchists, Satanists, white supremacists, Stalinists, and others favoring a social order in which the powerful subjugate the weak by force. That was not exactly London's cup of tea, even if he didn't think kindly of Asians. While Ragnar Redbeard's true identity has never been established, most scholars now agree he was Arthur Desmond, a radical (and red-bearded) New Zealand writer and political activist.

DRINKING A QUART OF WHISKEY EVERY DAY CAUSED JACK LONDON TO EXPERIENCE COUNTLESS ACCIDENTS— LIKE THE TIME HE STAGGERED OFF THE OAKLAND WHARF AND LANDED IN THE SAN FRANCISCO BAY.

VIRGINIA WOOLF

JANUARY 25, 1882–MARCH 28, 1941

NATIONALITY:
ENGLISH

ASTROLOGICAL SIGN:
AQUARIUS

MAJOR WORKS:
MRS. DALLOWAY (1925), *TO THE LIGHTHOUSE* (1927),
A ROOM OF ONE'S OWN (1929)

CONTEMPORARIES & RIVALS:
JAMES JOYCE, E. M. FORSTER,
KATHERINE MANSFIELD

LITERARY STYLE:
AUDACIOUSLY EXPERIMENTAL, IMPRESSIONISTIC

WORDS OF WISDOM

"AM I A SNOB? FIRST THE QUESTION MUST BE ANSWERED: WHAT IS A SNOB?"

Few writers were as destined for literary immortality as Virginia Woolf. Her pedigree was impeccable. Her father was a distinguished biographer and editor who was once married to the eldest daughter of William Makepeace Thackeray. Her godfather was the American poet James Russell Lowell (a forebear of both Amy and Robert Lowell). For just the right note of added regality, her mother was descended from one of Marie Antoinette's ladies-in-waiting. Through her childhood home drifted such artistic and literary luminaries as Henry James, George Eliot, and photographer Julia Margaret Cameron, her mother's aunt.

It wasn't all teacakes and sherry, of course. As children, Virginia and her sister Vanessa were subject to repeated molestation by their half-brothers George and Gerald Duckworth. Their mother died suddenly of influenza in 1895, followed by half-sister Stella Duckworth in 1897. "The blow, the *second* blow of death, strick on me," Woolf wrote later, "tremulous, creased, sitting with my wings still stuck together in the broken chrysalis." Stella's death precipitated the first of more than a dozen nervous breakdowns she would suffer during her life.

Woolf was a manic-depressive, in an age when no one yet understood the condition. To those around her, she was simply prone to intermittent bouts of insanity. These tended to coincide with major life changes, such as the death of her father in 1904, or periods of creative difficulty. She tended to "go mad," as she put it, when nearing completion of a novel. In the manic phase of her illness, she was known to talk incessantly. She once babbled on for forty-eight hours straight. Such erratic behavior must have shocked those who knew her as shy and demure.

Another unspoken aspect of Woolf's interior life was her lesbianism. Although she forged a number of romantic attachments with men, it's clear that, from an early age, she preferred women. In her teens, she developed a mad crush on Violet Dickinson, a family friend seventeen years her senior. "I wish you were a kangaroo and had a pouch for small kangaroos to creep to," Woolf wrote Violet in one of her typically cryptic, sexually charged letters. In another she addressed her as a "blessed hell cat," declaring, "What a squalling and squeaking there must be inside you." Woolf may never have consummated her relationship with Violet, but she did later have a long-term same-sex relationship with Vita Sackville-West, the inspiration for her novel *Orlando*.

Woolf's most noteworthy heterosexual relationship, of course, was with her husband, Leonard Woolf, an author and intellectual gadabout. Together they helped found the influential Bloomsbury literary salon. They made an interesting pair: Virginia detested Jews (Leonard was one) and intercourse with men, in approximately equal measure. After a few years spent futilely trying to get Virginia to have sex with him, Leonard simply gave up entirely. Luckily they both believed in open marriage and shared a similarly gloomy view of humanity's future. They are one of literary history's most weirdly compatible odd couples.

Suicide was another of Leonard and Virginia's common interests. Convinced that the world was going to hell in a handbasket, and that Socialist Jews and feminist lesbians would likely bear the brunt of the coming apocalypse, the couple started storing extra gasoline in their garage in case, at a moment's notice, they needed to kill themselves by inhaling tailpipe fumes. They also stockpiled lethal doses of morphine. When World War II broke out and the Nazis began bombing London, Woolf descended into what would be her final tailspin. Their house was destroyed twice while she was struggling to complete her final novel, *Between the Acts*. She and Leonard relocated to their country estate outside London, where, during the winter of 1941, her mood darkened even further. Convinced she was about to "go mad" once more, she couldn't bear the prospect. On the morning of March 28, she wrote farewell letters to her husband and sister and walked out of the house, down to the nearby Ouse River. There, jamming a large stone into her pocket to weigh herself down, she walked into the water and drowned herself. Her body was found three weeks later.

PET NAMES

Woolf loved animals. As a young girl, she surrounded herself with an unusual menagerie that included a squirrel, a marmoset, and a pet mouse named Jacobi. As if there weren't enough wild creatures roaming around, she also liked to give animal nicknames to the people in her life. She chose the moniker "Dolphin" for her sister Vanessa, who in turn called her "Goat." Appropriately enough, Woolf's first published essay was an obituary for the family dog.

HANDS OFF MY BUST!

As a child, Woolf had a run-in with the famous French sculptor Auguste Rodin. On a visit to his studio with a group of friends, she was explicitly instructed not to examine any of the unfinished pieces Rodin was keeping under wraps. Eager as always to defy the limitations imposed upon her, Woolf immediately set about unwrapping one of the proscribed sculptures. Rodin proceeded to slap her in the face.

MERRY PRANKSTERS

Between nervous breakdowns, Woolf liked to yuk it up by putting on black-face and playing practical jokes on the British Navy. Well, okay, she did it only once—but it caused quite a stir.

In 1910 Woolf was one of six people—and the only female—behind the infamous "Dreadnought Hoax" that resulted in the public humiliation of the Royal Navy. The scheme involved convincing the commander of HMS *Dreadnought* that a delegation of "Abyssinian" (present-day Ethiopian) royals was coming to inspect his ship. Woolf and her fellow hoaxers then donned fake beards, turbans, rented theatrical robes, and black greasepaint and boarded the vessel without attracting suspicion. They passed out cards written in Swahili (which is not the language of Ethiopia) and shouted "bunga bunga" every now and then to show their excitement. Before leaving, the faux Africans even took the time to pin phony medals on the chests of some of the British officers. They then returned to land, where they revealed their ruse to the British press, causing much consternation in the nation's naval hierarchy. Some newspapers called for the prosecution of the pranksters, but the British public was more forgiving, even adopting the Abyssinians' "bunga bunga" rallying cry as a national catchphrase. Sufficiently bemused, Woolf quietly resumed her nascent literary career.

TAKING A STAND

Inspired by her sister Vanessa, who stood while painting, Woolf, until very late in her career, did all her writing in a standing position.

HARDY HAR HAR

In the summer of 1926, Woolf visited Thomas Hardy, one of her literary forebears, at his home near Dorchester. The meeting didn't go as smoothly as planned. The blasé Hardy seemed not at all interested in discussing literary matters. He dismissed her thoughtful queries about the nature of poetry, responding with platitudinous non-answers, and offered no insight into the tribulations of literary life. He did sign a book for her, misspelling her last name "Wolff." Woolf's reaction to the meeting? A few days later she had a nervous breakdown.

UNTIL VERY LATE IN HER LIFE, VIRGINIA WOOLF WROTE HER FICTION STANDING UP. SHE WAS INSPIRED BY HER SISTER VANESSA, A PAINTER.

VIRGINIA WOOF

In the mood for a little canine biography, Virginia Woolf–style? Check out *Flush*, the bizarre "dog's life" that Woolf wrote on a lark in 1933. The titular cocker spaniel belonged to poet Elizabeth Barrett Browning. Woolf read about Flush in Browning's letters to her husband, Robert, and "the figure of their dog made me laugh so I couldn't resist making him a Life." The book goes into extensive—some would say excruciating—detail about the devoted bow-wow's ancestry, incorporating material gleaned from Carthaginian legend, Basque lore, and the courts of the Tudors and Stuarts. Amazingly, the feisty spaniel's wagging tale struck a chord with the reading public. *Flush* became Woolf's bestselling book to date, selling nearly 19,000 copies within the first six months of publication. The *New York Times* called it

"a brilliant biographical tour de force." About the only person disappointed by this reception was the eternally saturnine Woolf herself. She fretted that the book would pigeonhole her as a "ladylike prattler." "I shall very much dislike the popular success of *Flush*," she said.

WHO'S AFRAID OF GETTING SUED?

Edward Albee, that's who. The playwright sought and received permission from Woolf's widower, Leonard, to use his late wife's name in the title of his 1962 play *Who's Afraid of Virginia Woolf?* The title derives from an actual snippet of graffiti Albee once saw scrawled on a barroom mirror. English playwright Alan Bennett responded comically with a 1978 play entitled *Me—I'm Afraid of Virginia Woolf.*

JAMES JOYCE

FEBRUARY 2, 1882–JANUARY 13, 1941

NATIONALITY:
IRISH

ASTROLOGICAL SIGN:
AQUARIUS

MAJOR WORKS:
DUBLINERS (1914), *A PORTRAIT OF THE ARTIST AS A YOUNG MAN* (1916), *ULYSSES* (1922), *FINNEGANS WAKE* (1939)

CONTEMPORARIES & RIVALS:
WILLIAM BUTLER YEATS, SAMUEL BECKETT, D. H. LAWRENCE

LITERARY STYLE:
STREAM OF CONSCIOUSNESS STUDDED LIBERALLY WITH ARCANE WORDPLAY

"THE ONLY DEMAND I MAKE OF MY READER IS THAT HE DEVOTE HIS WHOLE LIFE TO READING MY WORKS."

WORDS OF WISDOM

Lauded by one critic as that rarest of authors who "only wrote masterpieces," Joyce shared the world's high opinion of his work. Although he once told W. B. Yeats that "both you and I will soon be forgotten," in his less disingenuous moments Joyce considered himself God's gift to modern fiction. More than sixty years after his death, few would disagree with that assessment. (Fewer still have managed to read his last two masterpieces all the way through, but that's a whole other story.)

Joyce was born into a rather well-to-do Irish Catholic family whose circumstances were undermined by a drunken, spendthrift father. Asked after John Joyce's death what his father had been, James replied, "A bankrupt." Nevertheless, the old man's salary as a tax collector was more than enough to send little Jimmy to a fancy-pants boarding school and launch him well on the way to becoming a doctor. That's when the writing bug bit him, and all dreams of paying off his father's accumulated debts flew out the window. In 1904 Joyce met Nora Barnacle, the lusty chambermaid who became his lifelong consort. Told that his son had run off with a woman named Barnacle, John Joyce replied pithily: "She'll never leave him." (A barnacle, you see, is a creature that glues itself onto a ship's hull and, well, okay, James's jokes were funnier.)

The poster child for lapsed Catholics everywhere, Joyce eventually turned his back on every institution that had nurtured him—his family, his country, and his church. The phrase *Non serviam* ("I will not serve"), spoken by the protagonist of *A Portrait of the Artist as a Young Man*, could have been his personal motto as well. His short-story collection titled *Dubliners* was rejected by twenty-two publishers and burned by one, who declared it morally repugnant and "unpatriotic in its depiction of Dublin." *Ulysses* was banned in the United States until 1933. Due in part to not only his frustration with the ignorance of those around him but also his desire to live openly "in sin" with Nora without having to marry, Joyce spent most of his life in Europe, notably Paris, Zurich, and Trieste. There he wrote and lived largely undisturbed, but for the occasional outbreak of world war.

Health was his principal concern. Bad eyesight plagued him from early childhood. He wore thick Coke-bottle glasses and had eleven operations for myopia, glaucoma, and cataracts. At one point, the lens in his left eye was removed entirely. Another problem was toothaches. During his lean years as a young writer, Joyce subsisted on a diet of cocoa but couldn't afford the dental treatments that accompanied such a saccharine regimen. His teeth literally rotted out of his mouth, leading to an inflammation of the iris that exacerbated his failing eyesight. When he quipped that he had selected the right words for *Ulysses* but just needed to put them in the perfect order, he might not have been joking. During the last third of his life, he was almost totally blind.

On January 10, 1941, Joyce doubled over with stomach pain and was rushed to a Zurich hospital. Diagnosed with a perforated duodenal ulcer, he soon lapsed into a coma, waking only once to utter his final words: "Does nobody understand?" A Catholic priest offered to preside over his funeral, but Nora demurred, saying, "I couldn't do that to him." Joyce is buried beneath a simple marker in Zurich's Fluntern Cemetery.

BOOM AND BARK

All his life, Joyce was mortally afraid of two things: dogs and thunder. The former phobia was quite understandable. As a child, he had been bitten on the chin by a stray dog while throwing stones on the beach. As for the fear of boomers, Joyce could thank his childhood governess. A devout Catholic, she taught him that thunderstorms were a manifestation of God's wrath and insisted that he cross himself and say a prayer every time he saw a flash of lightning. Even as an adult, Joyce trembled every time he heard the rumble of thunder. When someone asked him why, he said simply, "You were not brought up in Catholic Ireland."

PORTRAIT OF THE ARTIST AS AN OLD PERV

To say that Joyce had an active sexual imagination would be a profound understatement.

"The two parts of your body which do dirty things are the loveliest to me," Joyce wrote in one of the numerous erotic letters he sent to his longtime lover, Nora Barnacle. "I wish you would smack me or flog me even," he gushed in another. "I would love to be whipped by you, Nora love!" And those are just a couple of the tamer passages. Joyce's love letters abound with explicit descriptions of sex acts he shared or wished to share with her. Among the graphic anatomical references, which Joyce used as a masturbatory aid, are repeated salacious encomia to Nora's "big full bubbies" and "arse full of farts." Indeed, Joyce seemed to have a special place in his, er, heart for the aroma of a woman's wind and the sight of her soiled underwear. Weird? Yes. Sexy? That's debatable. Was Nora on board with the panty sniffing? Her letters back to him have not survived, although some of his notes suggest that she was every bit as dirty-minded as he—perhaps even more so. "You seem to turn me into a beast," Joyce wrote in yet another lusty missive. "It was you yourself, you naughty shameless girl, who first led the way."

I LIKE BIG BUTTS AND I CANNOT LIE

Like Sir Mix-a-Lot, Joyce was attracted to one particular part of the female body above all others. When told a story about a cannibal king who selected his royal consorts based on the size of their posteriors, Joyce replied, "I sincerely hope that when Bolshevism finally sweeps the world, it will spare that enlightened potentate."

KVETCH SESSION

Sometimes a meeting between two literary legends doesn't quite live up to our lofty expectations. Case in point was Joyce's 1922 encounter with French writer Marcel Proust. At the time, the two men were the most acclaimed novelists in the world. When they turned up at the same Paris dinner party, the room fell silent. People assumed the literary geniuses would have a lot in common—and they were right. Like two alter cockers on a park bench, Joyce and Proust immediately started complaining to each other about their various ailments. "I've headaches every day. My eyes are terrible," Joyce groused. "My poor stomach. What am I going to do? It's killing me!" countered Proust. After a bit more awkward small talk about how much they enjoyed eating truffles, each admitted he had not read the other's work. With nothing left to chat about, the notoriously shy Proust made a beeline for the door. Joyce accompanied him home in his taxi, hoping to continue their conversation but, alas, it was not to be. The author of *Remembrance of Things Past* vanished into his Paris flat, without so much as offering his guest a madeleine for the ride home.

GENERATION GAP

Joyce's first encounter with another literary icon—William Butler Yeats—was nearly as disastrous. The revered Irish poet tried hard to get his younger counterpart to like him, but his efforts were a lost cause. Yeats even offered to read some of Joyce's terrible poetry, which Joyce reluctantly forked over with the snippy retort: "I do so since you ask me, but I attach no more importance to your opinion than to anybody one meets in the street." A general exchange on literature then ensued. When Yeats mentioned Honoré de Balzac, Joyce laughed at him. "Who reads Balzac today?" he cackled. Finally, the discussion turned to Yeats's own work, which he described as entering a more experimental phase. "Ah," Joyce replied, "that shows how rapidly you are deteriorating." When the conversation ended, Joyce was pointedly dismissive. "We have met too late," he told Yeats. "You are too old for me to have any effect on you." All through this barrage of insults, Yeats bit his tongue. Later he was more candid, writing of Joyce: "Such a colossal self-conceit with such a Lilliputian literary genius I never saw combined in one person."

TALK TO THE HAND

Some people did share Joyce's high opinion of himself. One day in Zurich, a young man approached him on the street. "May I kiss the hand that wrote *Ulysses?*" he asked. "No," replied Joyce. "It did lots of other things, too." As Nora could no doubt attest.

I FIND IT ETERNALLY LAME

Joyce hated monuments. One time as he was riding in a taxi past the Arc de Triomphe in Paris, a friend asked him how long the eternal flame inside would burn. "Until the Unknown Soldier gets up in disgust and blows it out," Joyce retorted.

QUARK MY WORDS

In the world of particle physics, a quark is one of the fundamental building blocks of matter. It is also the name of a French concept car, a character on *Star Trek: Deep Space Nine*, and the Szalinski family dog in the 1989 sci-fi comedy *Honey, I Shrunk the Kids*. All these usages owe a debt to James Joyce.

American physicist Murray Gell-Mann first dubbed the subatomic particles "quarks" after the derisive cheer three seabirds give to King Mark on page 383 of *Finnegans Wake*. (The full line is "Three quarks for Muster Mark!")

> JAMES JOYCE SENT MANY EROTIC LETTERS TO HIS LONGTIME LOVER, NORA BARNACLE, EXPRESSING HIS DESIRE TO BE SMACKED, FLOGGED, AND WHIPPED.

FINNEGAN'S DEAF

Speaking of *The Wake* (as it's known informally among Joyceophiles), Joyce's famously impenetrable final novel became a little more so thanks to Samuel Beckett's hearing problem. Joyce, who was nearly blind when he wrote the novel, had taken to dictating it to Beckett. During one such session, there was a knock at the door that Beckett—who was hard of hearing—didn't notice. "Come in!" said Joyce, and Beckett dutifully wrote that down in the manuscript. When Joyce had the passage read back to him later, he liked the way it sounded and decided to leave "Come in!" in the finished book.

FRANZ KAFKA

JULY 3, 1883–JUNE 3, 1924

NATIONALITY:
BOHEMIAN

ASTROLOGICAL SIGN:
CANCER

MAJOR WORKS:
THE METAMORPHOSIS (1915),
THE TRIAL (1925), *THE CASTLE* (1926)

CONTEMPORARIES & RIVALS:
MAX BROD, RAINER MARIA RILKE

LITERARY STYLE:
LUCID, CONCISE, MATTER-OF-FACT

WORDS OF WISDOM

"BEYOND A CERTAIN POINT THERE IS NO RETURN. THIS POINT HAS TO REACHED."

You know you're a great writer when your last name becomes an adjective. How could we describe something as "Kafkaesque" if not for Kafka? It's a question that probably never occurred to the nondescript haberdasher's son from Prague, who died without knowing how perfectly his nightmarish novels and stories captured an age, a society, and a universally recognized feeling of alienation and despair.

Kafka's domineering father helped foster that sentiment, belittling his son from early childhood as a physical weakling who would never match the old man's success as a purveyor of high-end walking sticks. Lord knows, little Franz tried. He excelled at school, made his bar mitzvah, and earned a law degree, but from a young age he found his only release came from reading and writing—pursuits that Hermann Kafka considered trivial and unworthy.

A flop as a lawyer, Kafka next tried his hand at insurance. He took a job as a claims manager at the Workers' Accident Insurance Institute of Bohemia, but the hours were brutal and the working conditions stultifying. He spent most of his time drawing severed, mangled, and truncated fingers to document defective apparatus and malfunctioning machines. As he wrote to his friend and fellow writer Max Brod: "You have no idea how busy I am. . . . People tumble off scaffolds and into machines as if they all were drunk, all planks tip over, all embankments collapse, all ladders slip, whatever gets put up comes down, whatever gets put down trips somebody up. And all those young girls in china factories who constantly hurl themselves down whole flights of stairs with mountains of crockery give me a headache."

Kafka's private life provided little refuge from this nightmare. He regularly patronized various Prague brothels and enjoyed a seemingly endless succession of one-night stands with barmaids, waitresses, and shopgirls— if you can call it enjoyment. Kafka was revolted by sex and suffered from a pronounced Madonna/whore complex. He considered every woman he encountered either a virgin or a slut and wanted nothing to do with them once he was physically gratified. The idea of "normal" married life disgusted him. "Coitus is the punishment for the happiness of being together," he wrote in his diary.

Despite these deficiencies, and a decided lack of self-confidence, Kafka did manage to have a few long-term relationships, though it's an open question whether he had sex with any of the women. In 1912 he met Felice Bauer while staying at Brod's home in Berlin. Kafka wooed her by writing long letters in which he confided his feelings of physical inadequacy—always a winning strategy with the ladies. She helped inspire some of his great works, including *The Judgment* and *The Metamorphosis*. She may have also inspired him to cheat on her with her best friend, Grete Bloch, who claimed many years later that Kafka was the father of her love child. (Most scholars now dispute that assertion.) The relationship with Felice ended in July 1914 with an ugly confrontation in Kafka's office at the Insurance Institute, in which Felice read aloud from his love letters to Grete.

Kafka then conducted an affair by mail with Milena Jesenská-Pollak, the wife of his friend Ernst Pollak. (One wonders what kind of player he would have been had he lived in the age of e-mail.) That relationship ended at Kafka's insistence in 1923. He would later use Milena as the model for one of the characters in his novel *The Castle*.

Finally, Kafka met kindergarten teacher Dora Dymant at a Jewish children's camp in 1923, when he was already dying of tuberculosis. Half his age and from an Orthodox Polish Jewish family, Dora cared for Kafka during the last year of his life. They studied the Talmud together and talked about immigrating to Palestine, where they dreamed of opening a restaurant, with Dora as chef and Kafka as maitre d'. He even wrote to a kibbutz inquiring about a job as a bookkeeper. Those plans were cut short by his death in 1924.

Nobody was surprised that Kafka didn't live to a ripe old age. His friends knew him as the consummate hypochondriac. All his life, he complained about migraines, insomnia, constipation, shortness of breath, rheumatism, boils, blotchy skin, hair loss, failing eyesight, a slightly deformed toe, an acute sensitivity to noise, nearly constant exhaustion, all-over itchiness, and a variety of other ailments, real and imagined. He attempted to counteract these maladies with daily calisthenics and a regimen of naturopathic treatments, including natural laxatives and a strict vegetarian diet.

As it turned out, Kafka had good reason to be concerned. He contracted tuberculosis in 1917, possibly as a result of drinking unpasteurized milk. The last seven years of his life were an unending search for quack cures and the fresh air he desperately needed to relieve his diseased lungs. When he died, he left a note on his desk instructing his friend Brod to burn all his works except *The Judgment*, *The Stoker*, *The Metamorphosis*, *In the Penal Colony*, and *The Country Doctor*. Brod decided to defy the orders. Instead, he readied *The Trial*, *The Castle*, and *Amerika* for publication and helped ensure both his friend's and his own place in literary history.

MR. SAFETY

Did Kafka invent the hard hat? Management professor Peter Drucker makes that claim in his 2002 book *Managing in the Next Society*. Drucker credits Kafka with developing the first civilian safety helmet while working as a claims manager at the Workers' Accident Insurance Institute of Bohemia. It's unclear whether the author invented the headgear or just mandated its use. What is clear is that Kafka was awarded the gold medal of the American Safety Society for his efforts, which helped reduce industrial fatalities and gave us an enduring stereotype of construction workers that we still rely upon today.

JENS AND FRANZ

Ashamed of his scrawny frame and weak muscles, Kafka suffered from what we would today call a negative body image. He wrote often in his diaries about how much he loathed his physical appearance—a theme that turns up repeatedly in his fiction as well. Years before Charles Atlas promised skinny beachgoers that he could bulk up their bodies through weightlifting, Kafka was practicing calisthenics beside an open window under the instruction of his Danish fitness instructor, Jens Peter Müller, a buff exercise guru whose health tips were laced with racist exhortations about the superiority of the Nordic body. Clearly this was not a man a neurotic Bohemian Jew should have been taking life lessons from.

CHEW ON THIS

As a result of his poor self-image, Kafka became a sucker for quack diet schemes. One that really captured his imagination was Fletcherism, a crack-

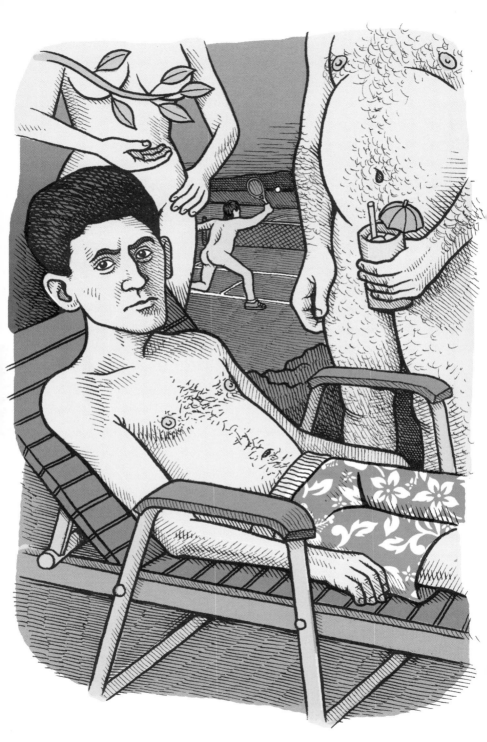

pot chewing regimen devised by a Victorian health food faddist known as "the Great Masticator." Fletcher argued that you should chew a mouthful of food precisely forty-five times before swallowing it. "Nature will castigate those who don't masticate," he warned, and Kafka took it to heart. According to one diary entry, his father was so disgusted by this constant cud chewing that he hid behind a newspaper at the dinner table.

MEAT IS MURDER

Kafka was a strict vegetarian, for both health-related and ethical reasons. (As the grandson of a kosher butcher, this conviction reinforced his father's belief that his son was a complete and utter failure.) One day, while admiring the fish in an aquarium, he declared, "Now I can look at you in peace; I don't eat you anymore!" An early proponent of the raw food diet, Kafka was also involved in the antivivisection movement.

FRANZ KAFKA MADE SEVERAL VISITS TO A NUDIST HEALTH SPA BUT REFUSED TO DROP HIS TROUSERS. OTHER GUESTS REFERRED TO HIM AS "THE MAN IN THE SWIMMING TRUNKS."

THE NAKED TRUTH

For a man who wrote so often about cramped, dark, interior spaces, Kafka sure loved the fresh air. He was known to take long walks around Prague, accompanied by his good friend Max Brod. He also joined the then-faddish nudist movement, cavorting among the clothing-optional crowds at a naturist health spa known as "The Fountain of Youth." It's unlikely Kafka actually dropped trou himself, however. He was extremely skittish about nudity—his own or anyone else's. The other resort residents called him "the man in the swimming trunks." More than once, he was unpleasantly surprised when other residents showed up naked in front of his living quarters or sauntered past him au naturel on the way to the nearby woods.

T. S. ELIOT

SEPTEMBER 26, 1888–JANUARY 4, 1965

NATIONALITY:
AMERICAN

ASTROLOGICAL SIGN:
LIBRA

MAJOR WORKS:
"THE LOVE SONG OF J. ALFRED PRUFROCK" (1915),
"THE WASTE LAND" (1922), *FOUR QUARTETS* (1943)

CONTEMPORARIES & RIVALS:
EZRA POUND

LITERARY STYLE:
OBSCURE, PEDANTIC, AND RICH WITH LITERARY
AND MYTHOLOGICAL ALLUSIONS

WORDS OF WISDOM

"A POET MUST BE DELIBERATELY LAZY. ONE SHOULD WRITE AS LITTLE AS ONE POSSIBLY CAN."

No one ever plumbed the depths of humanity's despair with as much grace and elegance as T. S. Eliot. V. S. Pritchett once described him as "a trim anti-Bohemian with black bowler and umbrella, ushering us to our seats in Hell." Virginia Woolf found his appearance almost irresistibly comical. "Come to lunch," she urged her brother-in-law. "Eliot will be there in his four-piece suit." If Eliot looked like a prim British banker, it's because he was. He toiled for eight years behind the foreign accounts desk at Lloyd's Bank of London, all while working on some of the most revolutionary poems of the twentieth century.

Granted, it was all a bit of a pose. For one thing, Eliot wasn't really British. He adopted British citizenship in 1927, about the time he converted to the Anglican Church. He was born in St. Louis, a descendant of three American presidents: John Adams, John Quincy Adams, and Rutherford B. Hayes. He went to Harvard University, hoping to earn a doctorate in philosophy, but even he admitted his dissertation was "unreadable." When he failed to show up to defend his thesis, the school rejected his Ph.D. application. Instead, Eliot immigrated to England and enjoyed a career as a teacher, banker, editor, critic, and world-class poet.

He remained a virgin until age twenty-six, which will surprise no one who has read his early poems, such as "The Love Song of J. Alfred Prufrock." When he did find someone who could stand him, the results were disastrous. Vivien Haigh-Wood—"Viv" to his "Tom" in the common parlance— was a vivacious, outgoing woman who found the reserved Eliot boring and inhibited. She was also mentally unstable, cheated on him, and may have been an ether addict. But other than that, they got along fine. Eliot described their relationship as evoking "the state of mind out of which came 'The Waste Land'"—not exactly a picture of marital bliss. The couple's mutual friend Aldous Huxley traced "all that dust and despair in Eliot's poetry" to his union with Viv. Amazingly, they kept it together for seventeen years, at which point he'd had enough. After Eliot left her in 1933, Viv descended into madness. She was confined to a mental hospital for the last nine years of her life. Eliot never visited her.

By this time, Eliot had become a famous and respected, if not exactly prolific, poet. He conceived of his poems as "events" that should be parceled out to a breathless public every few years or so. Between such events as "The Hollow Men" and "Ash Wednesday," Eliot wrote critical essays for various literary journals. It was in these essays that readers first glimpsed signs of the latent anti-Semitism that has hindered his critical standing ever since. "Reasons of race and religion combine to make any large number of free-thinking Jews undesirable," he wrote in one such screed. He also had kind words to say about Hitler and Mussolini. Fans were soon sent scrambling back to his earlier poems to find examples of supposedly anti-Jewish caricatures and images. They were there, and they remain a blight on his reputation.

Nevertheless, Eliot was awarded the Nobel Prize in Literature in 1948, and he settled into iconic status as easily as he had once donned a bowler hat. Life still posed hardships, but they were increasingly of the "I'm sorry I can't speak in front of your poetry society" variety. "The years between fifty and seventy are the hardest," Eliot remarked. "You are always being asked to do things, and yet you are not decrepit enough to turn them down."

In fact, Eliot turned down very little. He even reveled a bit in his celebrity. In 1956, more than fourteen thousand attended his lecture at the University of Minnesota—the largest crowd ever assembled for a literary event. The university needed to move the speech into the basketball arena to accommodate the throng. On another occasion, Eliot was made an honorary citizen of Dallas, Texas, as well as an honorary deputy sheriff of Dallas County. Nobody knew why. He didn't go to the movies much, he said, "because they interfere with my daydreams." Yet he was an inveterate jokester who hung a portrait of Groucho Marx in his home alongside the likes of fellow poets W. B. Yeats and Paul Valéry. Eliot even gave marriage another try, achieving happiness late in life in the arms of his erstwhile secretary, Esmé Valerie Fletcher.

A longtime hypochondriac, Eliot was known to check himself into the clinic at the drop of a hat, often for nothing more serious than a case of athlete's foot. But in the winter of 1964 a bad case of emphysema, owing to years of heavy smoking, finally caught up with him and killed him on January 4, 1965. He was honored with a commemorative stone in Poets' Corner of Westminster Abbey.

WORD PLAY

It may not be the most poetic observation, but Eliot's contemporary Dylan Thomas once pointed out that "T. S. Eliot" is an almost perfect palindrome of *toilets*.

OLD POSSUM'S BOOK OF PRACTICAL JOKES

Who knew that the author of "The Waste Land" was such a prankster? Dubbed "Old Possum" by his friend Ezra Pound, Eliot loved to arrange practical jokes for fellow writers who visited him and then lie in wait to catch their reaction. His favorite gags included putting whoopee cushions on people's chairs and the ever-popular exploding cigar. He once broke up a board meeting at his high-toned British publishing house by setting off a bucketful of firecrackers between the chairman's legs.

MY DINNER WITH GROUCHO

J. Alfred Prufrock met Capt. Jeffrey T. Spaulding on the evening of June 3, 1964, as Eliot and Groucho Marx finally broke bread after a long period of pen friendship. The unlikely pals had begun their correspondence a couple years earlier, after Eliot wrote Groucho a fan letter. They exchanged photographs— Groucho had to send him a second picture after Eliot demanded one with his trademark cigar—and soon progressed to the "Dear Tom," "Dear Groucho" level of familiarity. They made plans to have dinner and, in Groucho's phrase, "get drunk together" but never got around to it until one magical spring night in London.

A few days before the chowdown, Eliot wrote to Groucho to confirm that a car was being sent to the comedian's hotel to bring "you and Mrs. Groucho" over for dinner. The star-struck poet also gushed about how Groucho's impending visit had "greatly enhanced my credit in the neighbourhood, and particularly with the green grocer across the street." For his part, Groucho boned up on Eliot's poetry in anticipation of an evening of pretentious literary banter. In case that proved a dry well, he also reacquainted himself with *King Lear*.

After getting over the shock of the seventy-five-year-old Eliot's physical condition (he described him as "tall, lean and rather stooped over ... from age, illness, or both"), Groucho settled in with his wife for what he hoped would be an intellectually stimulating conversation. Wrong. All Eliot wanted to talk about was Marx Brothers movies. He even quoted lines from Groucho's films that the comedian himself had long since forgotten. When Groucho tried to steer the conversation to "The Waste Land," Eliot just smiled wearily. His observations on Shakespeare proved similarly silence-inducing. Almost before the dessert course was served, Groucho and "Mrs. Groucho" were looking for the door. "We didn't stay late," the comic legend later recalled, "for we both felt that he wasn't up to a long evening of conversation—especially mine."

> T. S. ELIOT MAY HAVE LOOKED LIKE A STAID BANKER, BUT HE LOVED PRACTICAL JOKES, PARTICULARLY WHOOPEE CUSHIONS AND EXPLODING CIGARS.

STEAL THIS POEM

The true provenance of Eliot's greatest poem, "The Waste Land," has long been the subject of controversy. Until recently, scholars confined themselves to arguing about how much credit Ezra Pound, who edited Eliot's original version, should receive for the finished product. Then in 1995 a Canadian academic named Robert Ian Scott claimed that both the title and some of the images in Eliot's "Waste Land" were lifted from the work of an obscure Kentucky poet named Madison Cawein. The evidence was thin, and Cawein's down-home barroom verse was about as far from Eliot's work as Amontillado is from moonshine, but it was added grist for those who claim that Eliot was nothing more than a high-minded plagiarist. As if anticipating such charges, Eliot once observed that "immature poets imitate, mature poets steal; bad poets deface what they take, and good poets make it into something better."

THE TOAST OF BROADWAY

How many poets can boast of having won even one Tony Award? Eliot has four: two for his 1950 play *The Cocktail Party* and two, posthumously, for the musical *Cats*, based on his feline-themed book of verse, *Old Possum's Book of Practical Cats*. Although theater snobs may rue the day the Rum Tum Tugger took over Broadway, Eliot would have delighted in the long-running show's success. He was a fanatic about musicals. In fact, after learning that Eartha Kitt had dropped his name in a line from one of her songs in *New Faces of 1952*, he sent a bouquet of roses to her dressing room. When Eliot saw the original Broadway production of *My Fair Lady* for the first time, he overcame his longstanding antipathy for its source material. "Shaw," he remarked, "has been greatly improved by music."

YOU'RE ON YOUR OWN

English majors have long complained about the deliberately obscure nature of Eliot's poetry. While alive, the poet offered little help to anyone attempting to parse its true meaning. At a meeting of the Oxford Poetry Club, a student asked Eliot to explain the line "Lady, three white leopards sat under a juniper-tree," from his poem "Ash Wednesday." "I mean," Eliot replied, "'Lady, three white leopards sat under a juniper-tree.'" On another occasion, an American undergraduate offered a long and thoughtful interpretation of a passage from one of Eliot's "Four Quartets." "Isn't that what it means?" the student asked at the end of his analysis. "It may very well mean that," was all Eliot said. Of his most vexing poem, "The Waste Land," Eliot famously admitted, "I wasn't even bothering whether I understood what I was saying."

Eliot's willful obscurantism extended into the arena of personal advice. One time the young poet Donald Hall visited him in London, seeking counsel on making the transition from Harvard to Oxford. "Now, what advice can I give you?" Eliot asked portentously. After a suitably grand pause he supplied his own response: "Have you any long underwear?"

NOBEL DUMBBELL

On his way to Stockholm to pick up his Nobel Prize in 1948, Eliot submitted to an interview with a none-too-well-read reporter. Asked for which of his works he was being honored, Eliot replied that the Nobel was for "the entire corpus." "And when did you publish that?" asked the dimwitted journalist. Eliot later remarked that *The Entire Corpus* would have made a good title for his first mystery novel.

SOLITARY MAN

Eliot was an inveterate card player, although he always played for low stakes. "I never bet because I never win," he admitted. His favorite games included poker, rummy, and hearts. W. H. Auden once walked in on him during a particularly engrossing game of solitaire. When Auden asked why he wasted his time with such trivial pursuits, Eliot replied, "Well, I suppose it's the nearest thing to being dead."

AGATHA CHRISTIE

SEPTEMBER 15, 1890–JANUARY 12, 1976

NATIONALITY:
ENGLISH

ASTROLOGICAL SIGN:
VIRGO

MAJOR WORKS:
THE MYSTERIOUS AFFAIR AT STYLES (1920),
THE MURDER OF ROGER ACKROYD (1926),
MURDER ON THE ORIENT EXPRESS (1934)

CONTEMPORARIES & RIVALS:
DOROTHY L. SAYERS, NGAIO MARSH,
MARGERY ALLINGHAM

LITERARY STYLE:
STRAIGHTFORWARD, WITH A FLAIR
FOR THE UNEXPECTED TWIST

WORDS OF WISDOM ➤ *"NEVER DO ANYTHING YOURSELF THAT OTHERS CAN DO FOR YOU."*

I'm an incredible sausage machine," Agatha Christie once remarked to an interviewer. She was talking about her prolific output and not—we think—the quality of her work. On that subject, readers have spoken—to the tune of more than two billion books sold. Talk about killing them softly. The "Queen of Crime" managed to make herself fabulously wealthy without harming a single soul.

The consummate British mystery writer had an American father. Born Agatha Mary Clarissa Miller, she enjoyed a very proper English upbringing in the seaside town of Torquay, where Sir Arthur Conan Doyle, one of her biggest literary influences, is said to have written *The Hound of the Baskervilles*. Her mother spurred her interest in writing, once daring her to compose a story to while away the hours on a rainy day.

Agatha married Archibald Christie, a pilot in the Royal Flying Corps, in 1914. During World War I, she worked in a hospital dispensary. While there she developed her intimate knowledge of poisons and what they could do to a human body. "Give me a nice deadly phial to play with and I am happy," she once observed. Indeed, about half the murders in her crime novels can be attributed to poisoning.

Returning from the war, Christie spent nearly a year and a half cranking out her first novel, *The Mysterious Affair at Styles*. The book introduced readers to the rotund Belgian detective Hercule Poirot, but it sold so sluggishly that its author earned not a penny in royalties. All that changed with the publication of *The Murder of Roger Ackroyd*, six years later. That book's ingenious plot twists and surprising solution revolutionized the staid mystery genre. After that, it was off to the races. Christie published ninety-three books and seventeen plays, including six romance novels written under the pseudonym Mary Westmacott. Her works were translated into 103 languages (even more than Shakespeare). Besides Poirot, her best-known characters included Miss Jane Marple, the indomitable English spinster; the enigmatic Colonel Race; and the irrepressible husband-and-wife detective team of Tuppence and Tommy Beresford.

Christie's tales of crime and detection were always wrapped up with a tidy bow at the end, but her personal life was not nearly so neat. Her first marriage ended in divorce in 1928, after she discovered that Archie was cheating on her. In 1930 she remarried, this time to archaeologist Max Mallowan, who also cheated on her. They did manage to keep it together for more than forty-five years, however, during which time she often accompanied him on his digs in Iraq and Syria. Exotic Middle Eastern locales became a staple of her books during this period.

In 1955 Christie became the first recipient of the Grand Master Award from the Mystery Writers of America. She was made a Dame Commander of the Order of the British Empire in 1971. Many of her novels were adapted for film and television, the majority of which Dame Agatha professed to loathe. She did endorse the 1974 movie version of *Murder on the Orient Express*, which earned Albert Finney an Academy Award nomination for his portrayal of Hercule Poirot. No doubt she would have been somewhat puzzled by *Agatha Christie's Great Detectives*, a Japanese animated televised series that ran on Japan's NHK network in 2004, pairing her two most famous sleuths, Poirot and Miss Marple. If nothing else, the show, which reimagined several Christie characters and invented some new ones (including a talking duck), proves that the Queen of Crime has not faded from public consciousness.

Christie went to her grave in 1976 as the world's most famous mystery writer. The Guinness Book of Records has recognized her as the best-selling fiction author of all time. Her play *The Mousetrap*, still going strong in London, is the world's longest running theatrical production. Not bad for the self-described "sausage machine" who turned to mystery only because she "thought it would be fun to try and write a detective story."

!

THE QUEEN OF CARPAL TUNNEL?

Although she ranks as one of literary history's most prolific authors, Agatha Christie never once set pen to paper. She was afflicted with a learning disability called dysgraphia, which prevented her from writing legibly. As a result, she had to dictate all her novels. Here's hoping the poor typist got combat pay!

AND PETA'S "WOMAN OF THE YEAR AWARD" FOR 1907 GOES TO . . .

As a young woman, Christie prided herself on being handy about the house. In her autobiography, she admits that she once successfully chloroformed a hedgehog that had gotten tangled up in her tennis net in order to set it free.

AGATHA AND THE "N" WORD

One of Dame Agatha's most popular books, *And Then There Were None*, has been adapted for stage and screen several times. It's also inspired a video game, a musical spoof, and a song by 1970s singer-songwriter Harry Nilsson. You have to wonder how it would have been received had Christie's publisher stuck with her original title. Originally called *Ten Little Niggers*, the novel was later retitled *Ten Little Indians* and, when that too became politically incorrect, finally reissued as *And Then There Were None*.

MISERABLE FAT BELGIAN BASTARD

The unflappable Hercule Poirot (whose last name comes from the French word for "leek") is one of Christie's most beloved characters. But don't count his creator among his fans. After rolling out the pompous Belgian sleuth in 1926's *The Murder of Roger Ackroyd*, Dame Agatha quickly grew tired of him. As early as the 1930s she claimed to find Poirot "insufferable." In the 1960s she derided him as "an egocentric creep." Still, he kept paying the rent. "I can't bear him," she once declared. "But he has to go on because people ask for him so much."

Despite her distaste, Christie remained fiercely protective of the Poirot franchise. When *The Murder of Roger Ackroyd* was being adapted for the stage, she resisted the director's attempt to makeover the character, vetoing his suggestion "to take about twenty years off Poirot's age, call him Beau Poirot, and have lots of girls in love with him."

MAYBE SHE GOT A LOOK AT THE SCRIPT?

Christie's other great protagonist, spinster sleuth Miss Jane Marple, was more to her liking. Both Hercule Poirot and Miss Marple were memorably parodied as Milo Perrier and Jessica Marbles in Neil Simon's 1976 big-screen mystery spoof *Murder by Death*. Sadly, the great mystery writer died just a few months before the film premiered.

ITCHING ON THE ORIENT EXPRESS

Dame Agatha wrote one of her most famous novels, *Murder on the Orient Express*, in room 411 of the Hotel Pera Palace in Istanbul, Turkey. Dubbed "The Agatha Christie Room," it has been preserved in her honor. One aspect of the Orient Express journey that she may not have wanted to commemorate was her sleeping car on the Paris to Istanbul train. She was bedeviled by bedbugs throughout the ride.

I NEVER SAID THAT!

Although she had a flair for the pithy remark, Christie never actually uttered the one that is most frequently attributed to her: "The very best husband a woman can have is an archaeologist, because the older she becomes the more interested he is in her." Her second husband, archaeologist Max Mallowan, apparently wasn't all that interested. He took a succession of mistresses, one of whom he married the year after Agatha's death.

AGATHA CHRISTIE HAD A LEARNING DISABILITY CALLED DYSGRAPHIA, WHICH PREVENTED HER FROM WRITING LEGIBLY. ALL HER NOVELS WERE DICTATED.

THE CASE OF THE DISAPPEARING AUTHOR

Christie's greatest mystery may have been the one she acted out in real life. In December 1926, the then thirty-six-year-old writer mysteriously disappeared for eleven days. Police suspected foul play, although her philandering first husband, Archibald Christie, seemed to have an airtight alibi: He was canoodling with his mistress at the time of her disappearance. Tipped off by a nosy waiter, the authorities eventually found Agatha holed up in a Yorkshire hotel under an assumed name. She initially claimed to be suffering from amnesia, although years later it was revealed that the entire incident was part of a plot dreamed up by an enraged Agatha to force Archie to give up his mistress. Whatever her intentions, the scheme didn't work. The couple divorced two years later. The 1979 film *Agatha*, starring Vanessa Redgrave as Agatha and Timothy "007" Dalton as Archie, was a fictionalized reenactment of this bizarre episode.

THANKS FOR CLEARING THAT UP

Dame Agatha listed her likes and dislikes in her autobiography. For the record, her major turnoffs included "crowds, being jammed up against people, loud voices, noise, protracted talking, parties, especially cocktail parties, cigarette smoke and smoking generally, any kind of drink except in cooking, marmalade, oysters, lukewarm food, grey skies, the feet of birds or indeed the feel of a bird altogether," and, finally and most emphatically, "the taste and smell of hot milk."

J. R. R. TOLKIEN

JANUARY 3, 1892–SEPTEMBER 2, 1973

NATIONALITY:
ENGLISH

ASTROLOGICAL SIGN:
CAPRICORN

MAJOR WORKS:
THE HOBBIT (1937), *THE FELLOWSHIP OF THE RING* (1954), *THE TWO TOWERS* (1954), *THE RETURN OF THE KING* (1955)

CONTEMPORARIES & RIVALS:
C. S. LEWIS, W. H. AUDEN

LITERARY STYLE:
DENSE AND MYTHOPOETIC

"BEING A CULT FIGURE IN ONE'S OWN LIFETIME, I AM AFRAID, IS NOT AT ALL PLEASANT."

WORDS OF WISDOM

J. R. R. Tolkien didn't just write *The Hobbit*. Deep down, he believed he *was* one. "I am in fact a Hobbit (in all but size)," he wrote to one of his millions of fans. "I like gardens, trees, and unmechanized farmlands; I smoke a pipe, and like good plain food (unrefrigerated), but detest French cooking; I like and even dare to wear, in these dull days, ornamental waistcoats. I am fond of mushrooms (out of a field); have a very simple sense of humor (which even my appreciative critics find tiresome); I go to bed late and get up late (when possible). I do not travel much."

It should come as no surprise to readers of Tolkien's books that he modeled himself after his own fictional creations. After all, the hobbits—whom he initially conceived as analogs to the common soldiers with whom he served in World War I—were as real to him as the very real Frenchmen he despised. One of the reasons Tolkien attracted such a devoted following was his uncommon willingness to commit himself to his own mythology—body, mind, and soul. Heck, even Faulkner took a break from writing about Yoknapatawpha County every now and then. Tolkien practically lived and breathed Middle Earth for more than thirty-five years.

To date, Tolkien's *Lord of the Rings* trilogy has sold more than one hundred million copies worldwide. It is the best-selling work of fiction of all time and the third best-selling book, behind the Bible and the quotations of Mao Zedong. Not bad for a tweed-coated, pipe-smoking Oxford don whose first forty-odd years were taken up with the study of languages. As a child, Tolkien's mother taught him Latin, French, and German. On his own initiative, he picked up Greek, Middle English, Old English, Old Norse, Gothic, modern and medieval Welsh, Finnish, Spanish, and Italian. He could also get by in Russian, Swedish, Danish, Norwegian, Dutch, and Lombardic (whatever that is). When he got bored with existing languages, Tolkien simply invented new ones—fourteen to be precise, with complete alphabets for each. He even took to writing his own diary using made-up letters. Alphabets led to full-blown mythologies, and with that Middle Earth was born.

It was hardly an uncomplicated birth. The London *Times* described *The Lord of the Rings* as having "all the earmarks of a publishing disaster." Tolkien himself bitterly opposed his publisher's decision to issue the tale in three parts. In a separate dispute, the famously persnickety author demanded that the books be printed in several different colored inks. He lost that fight, but publication was delayed while the two sides wrangled. "My work has escaped from my control," Tolkien later confessed, "and I have produced a monster: an immensely long, complex, rather bitter, and rather terrifying romance, quite unfit for children (if fit for anybody)."

It may not have been fit for children, but *The Lord of the Rings* was tailor-made for Hollywood, as Peter Jackson's epic film adaptations would prove. But if it were up to Tolkien the movies never would have been made. He regarded his works as unfilmable and vehemently opposed any attempt at adaptation that intercut his intricate linear storylines. He also feared that major Hollywood studios would do a Mickey Mouse job of bringing Middle Earth to the big screen. "It might be advisable," he wrote, "to let the Americans do what seems good to them—as long as it was possible to veto anything from or influenced by the Disney studios (for all whose works I have a heartfelt loathing)." Lucky, Tolkien's control over his properties never extended to musical homages, else we might never have heard such nuggets of rock and roll lyrical excess as Led Zeppelin's "Ramble On" (which name-drops Gollum and the "depths of Mordor") or Rush's "Rivendell."

Never one to court celebrity, Tolkien lived the life of a slightly daft English philology professor until his death in 1973. He and his wife, Edith, are buried side by side in a single grave near his beloved Oxford. Fittingly, the headstones bear the names of Lúthien and Beren, fictional lovers Tolkien created for one of his Middle Earth fantasies.

!

HITLER AND THE HOBBIT

The Hobbit was banned in Germany until 1945—due to its author's unwillingness to kowtow to the Nazis. When German publishers were considering publishing a German-language edition of the fantasy masterwork in 1937, a government official from the Third Reich contacted Tolkien to inquire whether he was of Aryan descent. "I can only assume that you are asking if I am Jewish," Tolkien replied. "I regret to respond that I have no ancestors among that gifted people." That quip put him permanently on the bad side of the Nazi authorities.

C.S.: I LOVE YOU

Tolkien maintained a long friendship with his friend and fellow fantasist, C. S. Lewis. While at Oxford, they were founding members of the writer's group known as the Inklings, which met twice weekly over pipes of tobacco and pints of beer to read aloud from its members' latest works. In due course, Lewis joined Tolkien as both an acclaimed author and a devout Christian. Tolkien viewed Lewis as an equal, "a man at once honest, brave, intellectual—a scholar, a poet, and a philosopher—and a lover, at least after a long pilgrimage, of Our Lord."

Despite their strong personal bond, however, the two men didn't have much use for each other's work. When Tolkien told Lewis about a character he was creating for *The Lord of the Rings*, Lewis was less than supportive. "Not another fucking dwarf!" he cried in exasperation. For his part, Tolkien found Lewis's masterwork, *The Chronicles of Narnia*, a crushing bore. "It is sad that *Narnia* and all that part of C. S. L.'s work should remain outside the range of my sympathy," he reflected, "as much of my work was outside his."

> J. R. R. TOLKIEN WAS A NOTORIOUSLY BAD DRIVER AND OFTEN NAVIGATED ONE-WAY STREETS IN THE WRONG DIRECTION. EVENTUALLY HIS WIFE REFUSED TO RIDE WITH HIM.

ROAD HOG

Distrustful of all modern conveniences, Tolkien hated automobiles and gave up driving at the onset of World War II. That was good news for his neighbors. A notoriously reckless driver lacking concern for other motorists, Tolkien was well known among the locals for attempting to ram the other vehicles on Oxford's main roadway. "Charge 'em and they scatter!" he would bellow as he barreled into traffic. Things got so bad Tolkien's wife refused to ride in the car with him.

SNOOZE CONTROL

Tolkien's snoring became such a nuisance that he and his wife hit upon an unusual sleeping arrangement: She spent the night in the bedroom, and he spent the night in the bathroom. Sleeping quarters may not have been very comfortable, but it made for easy access to the morning showers.

FRENCH DISS

Tolkien's Gallophobia knew no bounds, and it had started early in his life. On a visit to Paris in his early twenties, he decried "the vulgarity and the jabber and the spitting and the indecency" of the French people. He grew to despise not only French food and culture but the Norman Conquest as well. He believed that William the Conqueror's subjugation of Britain in 1066 had snuffed out a golden age of Anglo-Saxon culture, replacing it with European influences inimical to the flowering of English literature.

GRAMMATICALLY INCORRECT

Today, we call them "little people," but even in Tolkien's day his use of the term *dwarves* caused an uproar. After *The Hobbit* was published in 1937, grammarians assailed him for not using *dwarfs*, which is the preferred plural form according to the *Oxford English Dictionary*. Luckily for Tolkien, he had a persuasive defense: He had edited the dictionary.

I CALL THIS ONE "THE LORD OF ALL THINGS"

If you like the way your Good Book reads, you can tip your hat to the creator of Middle Earth. Tolkien was one of the original translators of the Jerusalem Bible, a version of the Christian Scriptures highly regarded for its literary quality. Those looking for a Tolkien translation of the Apocalypse will be disappointed, however. His contributions are said to be limited to the Old Testament books of Jonah and Job.

AVA WHO?

Tolkien was never one to cultivate his own fame. "There are lots of people in Oxford who have never heard of me," he remarked with pride. He proved it in 1964 when author Robert Graves visited the university to deliver a lecture. At the reception, Graves introduced Tolkien to a beautiful, amply endowed young woman who was being trailed by a phalanx of reporters and photographs. The two chatted pleasantly for several minutes before Graves realized that Tolkien had no idea who the woman was. Told it was movie star Ava Gardner, Tolkien still drew a blank. That was okay, for she had no idea who he was either. They went their separate ways, and literary history lost a chance at the most misbegotten love match since Arthur Miller and Marilyn Monroe.

YOU *CAN* JUDGE A BOOK BY ITS COVER

Tolkien was mortified by the cover illustration that adorned the first American paperback edition of *The Hobbit* in 1965. The lurid painting—which featured a lion, two emus, and a tree with bulbous fruit—seemed to have little or nothing to do with the book's content. "I think the cover ugly," the peeved fantasist wrote to his publisher, "but I recognize that a main object of a paperback cover is to attract purchases, and I suppose that you are better judges of what is attractive in USA than I am. I therefore will not enter into a debate about taste (meaning though I did not say so: horrible colors and foul lettering), but I must ask this about the vignette: What has it got to do with the story? Where is this place? Why a lion and emus? And what is the thing in the foreground with pink bulbs? I do not understand how anybody who had read the tale (I hope you are one) could think such a picture would please the author."

Tolkien received no response to his complaint. In a subsequent phone call, he reiterated his objections about the artist, prompting the publisher's representative to reply, "But the man hadn't *time* to read the book!"

LANGUAGE POLICE

As you might expect, Tolkien—a philologist by trade—had very particular opinions when it came to language. He once said that the words "cellar door" made up the most beautiful phrase in the English language. He also knew what he *didn't* like. Of American English, he once observed: "[It] is essentially English after having been wiped off with a dirty sponge."

TAX *THIS!*

Tolkien was a notorious skinflint. He kept a detailed record of every last penny he spent, right down to postage stamps and razor blades. He was especially stingy when it came to his tax dollars. When the British government hatched a scheme to use public funds to finance the new supersonic jetliner, Tolkien hit the ceiling. The words "Not a penny for Concorde!" were found scrawled across his income tax form.

F. SCOTT FITZGERALD

SEPTEMBER 24, 1896–DECEMBER 21, 1940

NATIONALITY:
AMERICAN

ASTROLOGICAL SIGN:
LIBRA

MAJOR WORKS:
THE GREAT GATSBY (1925),
TENDER IS THE NIGHT (1934)

CONTEMPORARIES & RIVALS:
ERNEST HEMINGWAY, WILLIAM FAULKNER,
NATHANIEL WEST

LITERARY STYLE:
SUPPLE, LUMINOUS, AND WITTY

*"FIRST YOU TAKE A DRINK,
THEN THE DRINK TAKES A
DRINK, THEN THE DRINK
TAKES YOU."*

WORDS OF WISDOM

Drunk at 20, wrecked at 30, dead at 40," F. Scott Fitzgerald once wrote in his notebooks, in one of his occasional impious attempts at concise autobiography. He wasn't too far off. Dead at age forty-four, Fitzgerald spent many years in an inebriated haze and nearly a decade deep in debt and out of favor with the literary establishment. That we remember him at all is a testament to the undeniable style and grace of his writing.

He was well born, an indirect descendant and namesake of Francis Scott Key, author of "The Star-Spangled Banner." Wisely, he elected not to call himself by his full name, Francis Scott Key Fitzgerald. Not that it would have cost him anything in terms of popularity. He had none. When he turned six years old, Fitzgerald's parents threw him a birthday party. No one showed up. Scott, as he was known, ended up eating the entire cake, candles and all. It wouldn't be his last disastrous social gathering. "Parties," he later wrote, "are a kind of suicide."

Good looks helped improve Fitzgerald's prospects. At Princeton, he was voted the prettiest boy in his class. Looking good was just about all he was good at. As a freshman, he failed math, Latin, and chemistry. Lucky for him a war was on, so this indifferent student signed up for the U.S. Army. He hoped to get killed in World War I, leave behind a good-looking corpse and an unfinished novel, and thereby achieve literary immortality. But that was not to be. He never saw combat and was forced to find another way to make his mark. His chance arrived with the publication of his acclaimed debut novel, *This Side of Paradise*, in 1919.

By then he had already met Zelda Sayre, the Alabama spitfire who became his wife and "accomplice" for the next two decades. Together they blazed a drunken path through Jazz Age America. They plunged into the fountain of New York's Plaza Hotel, rode on the hoods of Manhattan taxicabs, and threw themselves into the sea from a thirty-five-foot precipice after returning plastered from a late-night shindig at Gerald and Sara Murphy's place on the Riviera. Zelda told her hostess afterward, "But, Sara, didn't you know? We don't believe in conservation."

All this forced gaiety masked a desperate reality. Despite critical success, Fitzgerald lived well beyond his means. *The Great Gatsby* sold only thirty thousand copies, and the follow-up, *Tender Is the Night*, managed barely half that number. Even in his 1920s heyday, Fitzgerald never made a lot of money, and what he did make he spent like a drunken sailor. As a result, he was constantly in debt to friends, editors, and agents. Zelda fared no better. Long considered a charming eccentric (Ring Lardner called her a "novelty"), she was diagnosed with schizophrenia in 1930. She spent the rest of her life in and out of various institutions before perishing horribly in an asylum fire in 1947.

With the Jazz Age killed off by the Great Depression, Fitzgerald did what he must to earn a living: He went to Hollywood. Dialogue was never his strong suit, however, and the few films he worked on are not highly regarded. He spent two weeks working on a rewrite of the screenplay for *Gone with the Wind* but was fired before he could damage it much. He did find a new lover in gossip columnist Sheilah Graham. She would remain steadfastly by his side for his slow descent into alcoholism and irrelevance.

In August 1940, Fitzgerald received what would be his final royalty statement. It reported total sales of all of his books of only forty copies. The "amount due to author" was $13.13. Destitute, but at long last on the wagon, Fitzgerald immersed himself in his last, unfinished novel, *The Love of the Last Tycoon*. He was working on the manuscript on December 21, 1940, when he took time out to eat a Hershey bar and read an article about the Princeton football team in his alumni newsletter. Stricken with the latest in a series of heart attacks, he collapsed onto the floor of Graham's home and died instantly. At the time of his death, Fitzgerald had $706 to his name, $613.25 of which went to cover his funeral expenses. Fortunately he had left provision in his will for "the cheapest funeral" possible.

!

FOOT FANCIER

Fitzgerald had a serious foot fetish, and his tendency to link feet with sex dated from early childhood. All his life, he refused to let others see his unshod feet, which he associated in his mind with his own nakedness. Swimming was out of the question, and he was known to wear shoes and socks even while on the beach. "The sight of his own feet filled him with embarrassment and horror," noted a 1924 interviewer. When it came to women's tootsies, however, Fitzgerald was positively batty. He confessed to a prostitute that the sight of a woman's feet had always excited him and made caressing her feet a part of their lovemaking ritual. A bizarre passage in *This Side of Paradise*, in which the main character is revolted by the sight of a chorus girl's feet, may have been Fitzgerald's attempt in his writing to come to grips with these impulses.

SIGN OF THE CROSS

Fitzgerald was no fan of crossword puzzles, which first gained popularity during the Jazz Age. He cited America's passion for the puzzles as a sign of the "widespread neurosis" then gripping the nation.

> NOTHING JAZZED UP A DULL PARTY LIKE SCOTT AND ZELDA FITZGERALD ARRIVING DRUNK AND ON ALL FOURS, BARKING LIKE WILD DOGS.

PARADISE LOST

This Side of Paradise helped make Fitzgerald's reputation as a chronicler of the Jazz Age, but early success brought him little satisfaction. Later in his career, when a fan approached and effusively praised his debut novel, Fitzgerald exploded. "Mention that book again and I'll slug you!" he thundered.

PAPA DON'T PREACH

Fitzgerald had a long and complicated relationship with his protégé Ernest Hemingway (see page 207). In a nutshell: Fitzgerald was nice to Hemingway, but Hemingway treated Fitzgerald like dirt. In public, Fitzgerald refrained from returning fire, but in private, he let others know how he really felt. "[Hemingway] was always willing to lend a hand," he once observed, "to those above him." Zelda had an even lower opinion of her husband's chief rival. Hemingway, she remarked, was "all bullfighting and bullshit."

PARTY ANIMALS

Decades before Diddy, long before Lindsay Lohan, Scott and Zelda Fitzgerald were the king and queen of the celebrity party circuit, astounding guests with their outrageous, drunken behavior. At a party hosted by Hollywood mogul Samuel Goldwyn, the couple showed up at the front gate, uninvited, crouching on all fours and barking like dogs. Having somehow been granted admittance despite this display, Zelda immediately vanished upstairs for a luxurious bath in Goldwyn's tub. At another affair—this time one to which they had been invited—the pair took the words "Come as you are" literally, showing up in their pajamas. Zelda's PJs didn't stay on long. After a few belts, she discarded them entirely and started dancing naked. Exhibitionism was a staple element in her repertoire. She was so bored at one staid literary affair that she removed her panties and threw them at the assembled throng. On a visit to see publisher William Randolph Hearst at his San Simeon mansion, Scott got into the act, borrowing one of Zelda's bras and using it to cover up a nude sculpture in Hearst's garden. On other occasions, the tag-team pranksters enjoyed playing with fire. In the days when he was still flush with cash, Scott was famous for lighting his cigarettes with $5 bills. Zelda once called the fire department to come to a party at a posh seaside resort. When they showed up and demanded to know where the fire was, she pointed at her own heart. Perhaps the Fitzgeralds' most inventive prank occurred at a party hosted by actress Lois Moran. With great earnestness, Scott went around to each party guest, collecting their wristwatches and jewelry. He then disappeared into the kitchen, where he boiled them in a saucepan of tomato soup. Mm-mm good.

--- A WISE EDITORIAL DECISION ---

A title can make or break a book, and Fitzgerald had a devil of a time coming up with a good one for his greatest novel. He originally planned to call *The Great Gatsby* by the title *Trimalchio in West Egg* (a too-clever reference to a character in Petronius's *Satyricon*). His editor, Maxwell Perkins, thought better of that and persuaded him to change it. For a while, Fitzgerald was hot on *The High-Bouncing Lover* before hitting on the classic, succinct title we know today. Even then, Fitzgerald had his doubts. Just before the book was to be printed, he cabled Perkins with the suggestion that they change the name to *Under the Red White and Blue*. What would be the consequences of delaying publication, Fitzgerald asked. Perkins's cabled, one-word reply: "Fatal."

A GREAT STRETCH

In one of the more imaginative interpretive leaps in literary history, an American literary scholar named Carlyle Thompson once promulgated the theory that Jay Gatsby was a black man. His evidence? Flimsy. Thompson cites Fitzgerald's description of Gatsby's "brown body," "tanned skin," and "close-cropped hair" as signs that he was "passing" as white. In addition, Gatsby's estate is said to rest on forty acres, a supposed reference, according to Thompson, of the "40 acres and a mule" freed slaves were promised in the aftermath of the Civil War. Finally, Gatsby's military medal from Montenegro is offered as the final piece of the puzzle since the word *Montenegro* means "black mountain" in Spanish. "Is Fitzgerald calling Gatsby a black mountain?" Thompson wonders. Does somebody have a little too much free time?

ALL JOYCED UP

Fitzgerald's literary idol was James Joyce, whom he considered the master of the modern novel. When they first met at a dinner party in Paris, Fitzgerald was beside himself with glee. He even offered to prove his admiration for the Irish author by throwing himself out a nearby window. After the party, Fitzgerald presented Joyce with a signed copy of *The Great Gatsby*—complete with a drawing of himself on his knees worshipping at the feet of a beatific, haloed Joyce.

DISSES WITH WOLFE

One writer Fitzgerald had no use for was his contemporary Thomas Wolfe. When editor Maxwell Perkins sent to Fitzgerald a galley of Wolfe's first novel, *Look Homeward, Angel*, complete with a dedication to Perkins, Fitzgerald's reply was terse. "Dear Max," he wrote, "I liked the dedication, but after that I thought it fell off a bit."

DEAD END

Fitzgerald's funeral was a sad, sorry spectacle. The undertaker botched his work, overly rouging the cheeks so that Fitzgerald looked, in the words of one mourner, "like a cross between a floor walker and a wax dummy." The wake drew a sparse crowd of gawkers and hangers-on. Nathaniel West, one of Fitzgerald's few close friends and author of *Day of the Locust*, actually died in a car accident on the way to the service. One literary figure who did show up was acid-tongued Dorothy Parker. Looking down at Fitzgerald's hideously made-up corpse, she quipped, "The poor son-of-a-bitch!" Few people recognized her remark as a quote from *The Great Gatsby*. They probably just assumed she was expressing the consensus held by the American literary community. In a final, posthumous insult, Ernest Hemingway devoted several pages of his tell-all memoir *A Moveable Feast* to a savagely unflattering portrait of Fitzgerald as an impotent, insecure buffoon.

WILLIAM FAULKNER

SEPTEMBER 25, 1897–JULY 6, 1962

NATIONALITY:
AMERICAN

ASTROLOGICAL SIGN:
LIBRA

MAJOR WORKS:
THE SOUND AND THE FURY (1929),
LIGHT IN AUGUST (1932), *ABSALOM, ABSALOM!* (1936)

CONTEMPORARIES & RIVALS:
**ERNEST HEMINGWAY, F. SCOTT FITZGERALD,
JOHN DOS PASSOS**

LITERARY STYLE:
STREAM OF CONSCIOUSNESS MEETS SOUTHERN GOTHIC

*"THE PAST IS NEVER DEAD.
IT'S NOT EVEN PAST."* ◄ WORDS OF WISDOM

He was born into a distinguished family. He lived in the shadow of a famous relative, whose career achievements he sought to outdo. He volunteered for wartime flight training but never saw combat. His military record became the subject of controversy.

Alas, the similarities between William Faulkner and George W. Bush end there. Only one of the two went on to become arguably the greatest novelist in American history. The other went on to become arguably . . . well, you fill in the blank according to your own political persuasion.

William Faulkner was born without a "u" in his name on September 25, 1897, in New Albany, Mississippi. He grew up in nearby Oxford, where the locals regarded him as an aloof, affected eccentric. His great-grandfather, William Clark Falkner, who died eight years before young William was born, was a decorated Civil War veteran who saw action at the Battle of First Manassas. Known as "the Old Colonel," W. C. Falkner also wrote a bestselling novel, *The White Rose of Memphis*, and became one of Oxford's most prominent citizens. It's said that when Faulkner entered the third grade, he was asked what he wanted to be when he grew up. "I want to be a writer like my great-granddaddy," he replied, the start of a lifelong effort to live up to the Old Colonel's name.

Faulkner was a poor student. One of his classmates called him "the laziest boy I ever saw . . . almost inert . . . he would do nothing but write and draw." Although Faulkner received less than admirable marks in grammar and language, he did not, as legend has it, fail English. Nor did he graduate high school, although he was later allowed to attend Ole Miss as a returning World War I veteran. Faulkner's brief stint in Canada's Royal Air Force—during which he saw no combat but bragged that he had been severely injured in a crash—saw to that. He received a D in English during his first semester at college but was not dissuaded from pursuing a writing career. Writing poetry (his specialty at that point) was also a good way to impress the ladies—especially his childhood sweetheart, Estelle Oldham, whom he later married and serially cheated on.

While honing his craft, Faulkner worked at a variety of odd jobs—bookstore cashier, university postmaster, bank clerk. He eventually drifted to New Orleans, where his friend Sherwood Anderson, also a writer, encouraged him to concentrate on fiction. His first novel, *Soldier's Pay*, was published in 1926. His third novel, *Sartoris*, was the first of fifteen set in fictional Yoknapatawpha

County. This stand-in for Faulkner's home county served as the canvas on which the great master painted his most unforgettable portaits: *The Sound and the Fury* (1929), *As I Lay Dying* (1930), *Light in August* (1932), and *Absalom, Absalom!* (1936). A highly original mixture of Southern Gothic atmospherics and Joycean stream of consciousness, his novels won acclaim in literary circles but precious little in financial compensation.

For that, Faulkner turned to Hollywood, where he toiled as a screenwriter for most of the 1940s. The pay was good, and he got to hobnob with the stars and satisfy his cravings for hard liquor and extramarital sex. But he hated having to answer to studio executives and felt like he was wasting his talent on B-movies and bourbon.

"Sometimes I think if I do one more treatment or screenplay, I'll lose whatever power I have as a writer," he told one of his mistresses. He also confessed: "When I have one martini I feel bigger, wiser, taller. When I have a second I feel superlative. After that, there's no holding me." The drinking and carousing began taking a toll on his health, and consequently his work suffered. Though the quality of his novels declined, he managed to snag two Pulitzers and the Nobel Prize in Literature. His Nobel acceptance speech—which some contend he delivered while drunk—was lauded as one of the most eloquent statements of faith in humanity ever delivered.

On July 6, 1962, a few weeks after being thrown from a horse near his farm in Oxford, Faulkner died of a heart attack in his hospital bed. Although the *New York Times* obituary remarked on his "obsession with murder, rape, incest, suicide, greed, and general depravity," Faulkner is remembered today as one of the most innovative stylists in all American fiction, an author whose garish subject matter was years ahead of its time.

COUNT NO 'COUNT

Faulkner wasn't exactly a beloved figure in his hometown of Oxford, Mississippi. In fact, local residents considered him something of a pretentious fop. When his back was turned, people referred to him as "Count No 'Count," a reference to what they considered to be his shiftlessness and inability to hold down a steady job. In fact, Oxford's main department store, J. E. Neilson's, still displays a framed copy of Faulkner's peevish reply to one of his many creditors, who wrote seeking satisfaction on a long overdue bill: "If this [$10 payment] dont suit you, the only alternative I can think of is, in the old Miltonic phrase, sue and be damned."

GOING POSTAL

One of the few jobs Faulkner did manage to hang onto was postmaster of the University of Mississippi post office, from 1921 to 1924. Not surprisingly, the effete, haughty genius proved to be the very model of a toxic employee. Faulkner was rude to customers (when he wasn't ignoring them) and oblivious to his responsibilities. He spent most of his workday writing or playing bridge and mah-jongg with cronies he hired as clerks. He was often caught throwing people's mail into the garbage. When a postal inspector was assigned to investigate him, Faulkner agreed to resign. He later summed up his experience: "I reckon I'll be at the beck and call of folks with money all my life, but thank God I won't ever again have to be at the beck and call of every son of a bitch who's got two cents to buy a stamp."

WHAT DID YOU DO IN THE WAR?

Like a lot of writers of his generation, Faulkner longed to prove himself on the battlefield. Alas, his attempts to enlist in the U.S. Army proved fruitless because of his small stature. Not to be deterred, Faulkner joined the Royal Air Force in Canada. He even affected a British accent (long before Madonna made such efforts fashionable) and started spelling his last name with a "u" to make himself seem more aristocratic.

Sadly, World War I ended before Cadet Faulkner could complete his preflight training. He returned home to Oxford in December 1918, never having seen combat. That hardly stopped him from pretending he had, however.

Enamored with the idea of being a bitter, disillusioned vet, Faulkner paraded around town in an R.A.F. lieutenant's uniform (although he had never achieved that rank), telling everyone about his combat exploits flying over Europe. He even claimed to have suffered a fractured skull, which required that his head be fitted with a steel plate. It was all a grand, bald-faced lie.

Many years later, Faulkner's tall tales about his war heroics came back to haunt him. When editor Malcolm Cowley was doing research for *The Portable Faulkner* in 1946, he asked the middle-aged author about his military service. "You're going to bugger up a fine dignified distinguished book with that war business," Faulkner informed him. When it was finally published, the book's "About the Author" section contained only a vague reference to Faulkner's having served in the R.A.F.

YOKNAPATAWPHA? I HARDLY KNEW HER!

The first question many readers ask upon diving into Faulkner's convoluted mythos is "What the heck is Yoknapatawpha?" Faulkner claimed it meant "slow water running through the flatland," and most assume the author simply made it up. However, there really once was a Yoknapatawpha, or "Yockney-Patafa" as early maps called it. Named after the Yocona River in Lafayette County, Mississippi, where Faulkner lived, the word may derive from a Chickasaw Indian term meaning "split land."

GO DOWN, MICKEY

Faulkner spent several years working in Hollywood, writing scripts for such classic films as *The Big Sleep* and *To Have and Have Not* (as well as clunkers, like *Submarine Patrol* and *God Is My Co-Pilot*). If he'd had his way, however, he might have produced a stream-of-consciousness sequel to *Steamboat Willie*. Upon arriving in town, he told the head of MGM's Story Department that he was qualified to write only newsreels and Mickey Mouse cartoons.

FAULKNER, MEET RHETT BUTLER

One day Faulkner took a break from the Hollywood back lot and went dove hunting with director Howard Hawks and a rather famous actor. The lantern-jawed star kept silent while Faulkner and Hawks chitchatted about great literature. At long last, the actor—Clark Gable—asked Faulkner who, in his opinion, were the greatest living authors. Faulkner replied with a list of favorites that included Hemingway, Dos Passos, and, of course, himself. "Oh, do you write?" Gable inquired, revealing he had no idea with whom he was hunting. "Yes, Mr. Gable," Faulkner shot back. "What do you do?"

WILLIAM FAULKNER WORKED AS A POSTMASTER FROM 1921 TO 1924 BUT LOST THE JOB AFTER HE WAS CAUGHT (ON MULTIPLE OCCASIONS!) THROWING MAIL INTO THE GARBAGE.

AND WHEN I SAY "WORK," I MEAN "DRINK"

Long before technological advances made telecommuting possible, Faulkner came up with his own novel approach. According to legend, he once asked the head of MGM if he could work from home for the day. The chief agreed, and Faulkner walked off the lot. Someone tried to reach him later at his Hollywood apartment and realized he'd gone back to Mississippi. When Faulkner said "home," he wasn't kidding.

PIPE DOWN

Ever the eccentric, Faulkner would accept only one type of Christmas gift: pipe cleaners. Around the holiday, his tree would be festooned with pipe cleaners in various colors, each one bearing a tiny tag with the name of the gift-giver. Dill-brand pipe cleaners were his favorite. In fact, if anyone gave him anything *but* a pipe cleaner for Christmas, Faulkner would bring the package into his office and let it sit there unopened.

KEEP YOUR PRIZE, JUST GIVE ME THE SUIT

Faulkner wasn't exactly thrilled about receiving the Nobel Prize. His wife had to cajole him into traveling to Stockholm to accept it, convincing him that his

daughter Jill really, *really* wanted to go to Sweden (she didn't). Finally, after kvetching to a Swedish reporter that he was a "farmer" and couldn't tear himself away from his crops long enough to fly overseas, Faulkner agreed to go, on one condition: that he not have to buy a new suit. But apparently the one he rented grew on him; after accepting his award, he refused to give up the outfit. He told his editor, Bennett Cerf: "I might stuff it and put it in the living room and charge people to come in and see it, or I might rent it out, but I want that suit." Cerf relented and had Random House pick up the tab.

O FAULKNER, WHERE ART THOU?

As one of America's greatest novelists, Faulkner lives on in the imaginations of readers everywhere. But he also had an interesting cinematic afterlife—in the films of sibling auteurs Joel and Ethan Coen. The writer/director tandem who gave us such classics as *The Big Lebowski* and *Fargo* like to slip sly references to Faulkner into their movies. In 1987's *Raising Arizona*, the escaped convicts played by John Goodman and William Forsythe are named Gale and Evelle Snoats, an allusion to the Snopes brothers featured in numerous Faulkner stories and novels. The character of Vernon Waldrip in the Coens' *O Brother, Where Art Thou?* corresponds to a character of the same name in Faulkner's short story "If I Forget Thee, Jerusalem." And, most notably, the character of W. P. Mayhew (played by *Frasier's* John Mahoney) in 1991's *Barton Fink* was clearly based on Faulkner himself. Like Faulkner, Mayhew is a brilliant Southern novelist turned raging alcoholic who sells out to Hollywood and carries on an affair with a studio employee.

ERNEST HEMINGWAY

JULY 21, 1899–JULY 2, 1961

NATIONALITY:
AMERICAN

ASTROLOGICAL SIGN:
CANCER

MAJOR WORKS:
THE SUN ALSO RISES (1926), *A FAREWELL TO ARMS* (1929), *FOR WHOM THE BELL TOLLS* (1940), *THE OLD MAN AND THE SEA* (1952)

CONTEMPORARIES & RIVALS:
WILLIAM FAULKNER, F. SCOTT FITZGERALD, JOHN DOS PASSOS, GERTRUDE STEIN

LITERARY STYLE:
TERSE, SPARE, SUCCINCT

"ALWAYS DO SOBER WHAT YOU SAID YOU'D DO DRUNK. THAT WILL TEACH YOU TO KEEP YOUR MOUTH SHUT."

WORDS OF WISDOM

Ernest Hemingway spent more than thirty years in the spotlight as America's foremost literary celebrity. He survived five wars, four automobile accidents, and two airplane crashes. He wrote about himself, and his own experiences, more than any other author of his time. Yet biographers still struggle to get a handle on the man about whom fellow writer Morley Callaghan once noted, "We can never be sure whether he is telling the truth or whether he is being seduced by his imagination into believing the legends he created for himself."

These few things we know for sure: He was born in 1899 in Oak Park, Illinois. As a child, he rebelled against his neurotic mother—who sent him to dance classes and did her best to emasculate him—by adopting a macho facade that was expressed in his lifelong love of hunting, fishing, and physical activity. He caught the writing bug in high school and developed his trademark declarative style while working as a cub reporter for the *Kansas City Star*.

When war broke out in Europe in 1914, Hemingway was drawn to the action. He joined the army and became an ambulance driver on the Italian front. His experiences there would form the basis for his classic novel *A Farewell to Arms*. On July 8, 1918, Hemingway's vehicle came under heavy mortar fire, and he took shrapnel in both legs. Plugging his gaping wounds with cigarette butts, he was able to drag one of his fellow soldiers to safety, an act of bravery that earned him a medal from the Italian government and a ticket out of the combat zone.

Between the wars, Hemingway experienced the first blush of literary fame. He settled in Paris, becoming part of an expatriate circle that included Ezra Pound, F. Scott Fitzgerald, and Gertrude Stein. In 1926 he published *The Sun Also Rises*, a jagged, jarring novel about a maimed, impotent war veteran, his sexually voracious lover, and their expatriate friends in—you guessed it—1920s Paris. The novel and a subsequent short-story collection helped catapult Hemingway into the front ranks of literary celebrity, a position he relished and cultivated for the rest of his life.

Fame and fortune freed Hemingway—or "Papa" as he now preferred to style himself—to pursue new and violent experiences wherever he found them. He attended bullfights, went on safaris in Africa, and covered the Spanish Civil War for newspapers—turning each episode into another classic story, novel, or autobiographical treatise. When World War II erupted,

Hemingway defied his advancing age—and a suspicious FBI chief J. Edgar Hoover—and went hunting for German submarines off the coast of Cuba. Some claim this escapade was merely an excuse to get drunk and go fishing, just as they dismissed his later attempts to take part in the liberation of Paris as nothing more than a visit to the Ritz Hotel bar. Nevertheless, Hemingway could claim he was there, at the center of the action, as always.

Hemingway's literary output declined in the postwar years, even as he remained a worldwide celebrity. He didn't write a significant novel after *For Whom the Bell Tolls*, in 1940. Most of his time was spent burnishing his own legend or settling old scores by attacking fellow writers in print. Privately, Hemingway fumed at never having been awarded the Nobel Prize in Literature. We can only imagine his glee when his 1952 novella *The Old Man and the Sea* scored him not only that award but a Pulitzer to boot. Perhaps Papa still had some gas in the tank, after all.

Sadly, even this late comeback could not cure Hemingway of the one affliction that dogged him his entire adult life: depression. During the last decade of his life, his naturally dark mood was clouded even further by a series of health crises. He survived two separate airplane crashes, each time emerging with severe internal injuries. He was seriously burned in a bushfire accident, developed high blood pressure and liver problems related to his alcoholism, and underwent electroshock therapy that wiped out much of his memory. In his final days, he was kept under near-constant sedation to prevent him from taking his own life. His wife, Mary, went so far as to lock up his guns in the basement of their home in Ketchum, Idaho. Unfortunately, a despondent Hemingway found the keys, and on the morning of July 2, 1961, he put both barrels of a shotgun to his forehead and pulled the trigger. The man who had once observed that "a man can be destroyed but not defeated" had succeeded in destroying himself at last.

MAMA'S BOY

As an adult, Hemingway was the embodiment of masculine virtue. How surprising, then, that he began life as a small girl. Hemingway's eccentric mother so desired a twin for his older sister Marceline that she dressed young Ernest in girl's clothes, gave him a girl's haircut, and passed him off to neighbors as her "daughter" Ernestine.

THE ODD COUPLE

Ernest Hemingway and F. Scott Fitzgerald were the Oscar and Felix of America's lost generation. Born only three years apart, they formed one of the most unusual friendships in literary history. Hemingway was brash, blustering, and self-confident; Fitzgerald was insecure, mannered, and somewhat foppish. Yet they were inseparable for a brief period and have been linked in the popular imagination ever since.

They first met in 1925, at the fabulously named Dingo Bar in Paris. Hemingway was only twenty-five years old at the time, a virtual unknown, whereas Fitzgerald, three years his senior, had just published *The Great Gatsby* and was well on his way to literary superstardom. Nevertheless, the two became fast friends. In fact, their relationship became surprisingly intimate. When Fitzgerald's wife, Zelda, reportedly mocked the size of her husband's genitalia, Hemingway conducted an impromptu men's room inspection to reassure his friend about the adequacy of his endowment. "You're perfectly fine," Papa told Fitzgerald. "You are OK. There's nothing wrong with you."

Despite such heartwarming moments, the friendship cooled considerably after 1926. The estrangement was due, in part, to simple jealousy. Hemingway's star was rising while Fitzgerald was entering a long, slow, steep artistic decline. Hemingway also developed a nasty habit of mocking his old friend in print. He created a thinly veiled, unflattering caricature of Fitzgerald in *The Sun Also Rises* and slogged him by name in the short story "The Snows of Kilimanjaro," prompting Fitzgerald to beg him not to make fun of him again. For a while Hemingway complied. But he couldn't resist the chance to get in the last word. Long after Fitzgerald died, Hemingway trashed his erstwhile mentor one last time in his posthumously published memoir, *A Moveable Feast*, depicting the *Great Gatsby* author as a fey, impotent coward.

A HAIRY SITUATION

Hemingway didn't take kindly to slights against his manhood. In fact, he nearly blew a gasket after critic Max Eastman belittled him in a scathing review of his 1932 bullfighting treatise, *Death in the Afternoon*. Eastman wrote that Hemingway "lacks the serene confidence that he is a full-sized man" and compared his writing style to a man "wearing false hair on his chest."

Several years later, Hemingway ran into Eastman in the offices of editor Maxwell Perkins. After shaking Eastman's hand, a grinning Hemingway ripped open both Eastman's shirt and his own—revealing the luxurious man-pelt that proved that he, Hemingway, was by far the fuzzier bear of the two. "What do you mean accusing me of impotence?" Hemingway demanded. He then proceeded to rub a copy of Eastman's own review in his face and wrestled the mortified critic to the floor. It was the last time Eastman ever gave Papa a bad review—at least in such personal terms.

A LOAD OF BULL

Hemingway never ran with the bulls at Pamplona, though many associate him with the annual Spanish spectacle because he wrote about it in *The Sun Also Rises*. In fact, Hemingway never ran at all due to the leg wounds he suffered during World War I. Never mind the charging bulls—the cobblestone streets of Pamplona would surely have been too much for him.

JUST BECAUSE YOU'RE PARANOID . . .

. . . doesn't mean they're not out to get you. For years, Hemingway told anyone who'd listen that the FBI was following him. Most just dismissed it as another of Papa's crackpot theories, but it turns out he was on to something. Files released after Hemingway's death reveal the feds were monitoring the writer's activities, starting from World War II until his death. Score one for paranoids everywhere!

THE SON ALSO FALLS

If Hemingway's youngest son, Gregory, had lived long enough to write his autobiography, he might have titled it *From Elephant Hunter to Exhibitionist*. Always his father's favorite, Gregory shared many of Papa's macho mannerisms and was a crack shot who once killed eighteen elephants while on safari in Africa. But he lived a double life as a transvestite (Hemingway once caught him trying on his stepmother's nylons) and eventually opted for sex-reassignment surgery. Rechristening himself "Gloria," he suffered frequent blackouts due to manic depression and was arrested several times for assaults against police officers. The last such altercation occurred in September 2001, when Gregory/Gloria, apparently intoxicated, was spotted walking naked through the streets of Key Biscyane, Florida. Police picked him up for indecent exposure as he frantically tried to pull a flowered thong over his exposed genitals. Six days later, he had a heart attack and died in his cell at the Miami-Dade Women's Detention Center.

Few explanations were offered for yet another Hemingway's slow descent into the abyss. As Gregory himself once mused in an interview, "What is it about a loving, dominating, basically well-intentioned father that makes you end up going nuts?" We may never know.

> AFTER ONE CRITIC GAVE HIM A BAD REVIEW, ERNEST HEMINGWAY LITERALLY WRESTLED THE MAN TO THE FLOOR.

WHAT A WAY TO "GAUX"

Is there a Hemingway curse? As if the strange saga of Gregory Hemingway weren't proof enough, there's also the sad end of Margaux Hemingway, Papa's granddaughter. The statuesque older sister of actress Mariel Hemingway was once one of the hottest models in New York. Then depression, substance abuse, and eating disorders took their toll. By the 1990s, she had hit the skids, posing nude for *Playboy*, appearing in infomercials for crackpot baldness cures, and lending her voice to a celebrity psychic hotline. (The ads boasted: "Margaux Hemingway: The name holds its own mystery.") On July 2, 1996—exactly thirty-five years after her grandfather took his own life—she joined him on the roll call of family suicides, along with Ernest's father, Clarence; his sister Ursula; and his brother Leicester. The forty-one-year-old took a lethal overdose of phenobarbital in her Santa Monica, California, apartment.

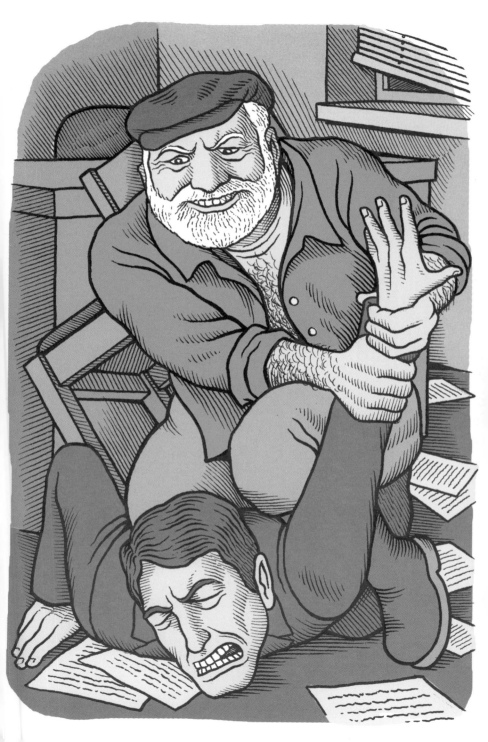

THE SINCEREST FORM OF FLATTERY

Each year, Harry's Bar & American Grill in Century City, California (a stateside replica of one of Hemingway's favorite Italian watering holes), sponsors the International Imitation Hemingway Competition, better known as the Bad Hemingway Contest. Competitors must submit an original one-page passage parodying the author's trademark style, with the stipulation that they include a complimentary reference to the host restaurant. Recent entries, which have been collected and published in book form, have included "A Farewell to Lunch," "The Snooze of Kilimanjaro," "The Old Man and the Seal," and the Hemingway-meets-Monica-Lewinsky classic "Across the Potomac and into Her Pants." The grand prize is an all-expense-paid trip for two to the real Harry's in Florence, Italy. Somewhere, Papa is smiling.

AYN RAND

FEBRUARY 2, 1905–MARCH 6, 1982

NATIONALITY:
AMERICAN (RUSSIAN BORN)

ASTROLOGICAL SIGN:
AQUARIUS

MAJOR WORKS:
WE THE LIVING (1936), *THE FOUNTAINHEAD* (1943),
ATLAS SHRUGGED (1957)

CONTEMPORARIES & RIVALS:
LILLIAN HELMAN, HOWARD FAST

LITERARY STYLE:
WEIGHTY, TENDENTIOUS SPEECHIFYING

"MONEY IS THE BAROMETER OF SOCIETY'S VIRTUE."   WORDS OF WISDOM

Give Ayn Rand credit. (On second thought, give her cash; the U.S. dollar was virtually a sacred object to her.) From humble beginnings, she managed to found her own philosophical movement and become one of the most-read, most widely admired authors of the twentieth century. Heads of state and high achievers, from Billie Jean King to Alan Greenspan, are counted among her acolytes. And she stuck with the same weird hairstyle for more than half a century—an achievement unto itself.

Born Alisa Zinovievna Rosenbaum in pre-Soviet Russia, Rand immigrated to the United States in 1926. She arrived in New York by way of Hollywood, where she appeared in Cecil B. DeMille's religious epic *King of Kings* and worked her way up to head of the RKO wardrobe department. Fueled by anti-Communism, she began writing screenplays, and then novels, that reflected her me-first, radically individualist philosophy. *The Fountainhead*, published in 1943, made a hero out of an imperious architect named Howard Roark (a thinly veiled Frank Lloyd Wright) and began attracting adherents to Rand's school of thought, now known as Objectivism.

In 1947 Rand appeared before the House Un-American Activities Committee, not to name names but to denounce Hollywood for its positive portrayals of life in the Soviet Union. She seemed to relish her role as a gadfly and as the hub of a philosophical movement (some would say *cult*) promulgated by her lover/disciple Nathaniel Branden in the 1950s and 1960s. The publication of her magnum opus, *Atlas Shrugged*, in 1957 only cemented her reputation as the foremost proponent of "rational egoism." Many combative talk show appearances followed.

Never a favorite of the literary establishments, Rand took a regular licking from publishers and critics alike. One publisher rejected *The Fountainhead* with the note, "It is badly written and the hero is unsympathetic." Another groused, "I wish there were an audience for a book of this kind. But there isn't. It won't sell." *Atlas Shrugged* was deemed "unsaleable and unpublishable." Reviewing the thousand-page novel for *The National Review*, Whittaker Chambers (yes, *that* Whittaker Chambers) decried its "dictatorial tone," noting that "out of a lifetime of reading, I can recall no other book in which a tone of overriding arrogance was so implacably sustained. Its shrillness is without reprieve. Its dogmatism is without appeal."

Dogmatism aside, Ayn Rand had a softer side the public rarely saw. She collected stamps and agate rocks. She was a Scrabble freak. When no one was around, she liked to crank up her phonograph and play what she called "Tiddlywink Music"—early twentieth-century popular songs such as "Mairzy Doats" and "It's a Long, Long Way to Tipperary." She was even known to pick up a baton, dance in circles, and conduct along with the records. Although she had no interest in the natural world—she claimed to hate looking up at the stars—she was beguiled by human-made objects such as skyscrapers. "I would give the greatest sunset in the world for one sight of New York's skyline," she said. "I feel that if a war came to threaten this, I would throw myself into space, over the city, and protect these buildings with my body."

One wonders if she felt the same way about Aaron Spelling's house. In a 1980 interview with Phil Donahue, Rand admitted she was a huge fan of the television show *Charlie's Angels*. She called the 1970s jigglefest "the only romantic television show today. It's about three attractive girls doing impossible things. And because they're impossible, that's what makes it interesting. It shows three young girls who are better than so-called real life."

Ayn Rand's own so-called life ended on March 6, 1982, when she died of heart failure. She is buried in the Kensico Cemetery in Valhalla, New York, one grave over from big-band conductor Tommy Dorsey.

!

WHAT'S IN A NAME?

So how did Alisa Zinovievna Rosenbaum become Ayn Rand? Not, as is commonly believed, by adopting the name of her preferred typewriter brand. The Remington-Rand typewriter company did not exist in 1926, when she changed her handle, so that was not her inspiration. Some have claimed she named herself after the currency of South Africa, but no evidence supports this theory, either. The most likely explanation is that the English word *rand* closely resembles Rosenbaum when written in her native Russia's Cyrillic alphabet. As for Ayn (pronounced "ine"): It's the first name of a Finnish writer she admired.

SPEED DEMON

From age twenty-eight until her mid-seventies, Rand had a—shall we say—long-term relationship with the diet drug Dexedrine. The weight-loss pill, which contains the powerful stimulant dextroamphetamine, was often featured in TV after-school specials warning teenagers about the dangers of becoming addicted to speed. Reportedly, Rand popped two of the little green pills a day for more than forty years, until her doctor advised her to stop. That could certainly account for some of the mood swings and angry outbursts for which she became famous.

STAMPING GROUND

When she wasn't whacked out on greenies, Rand indulged another of her favorite pastimes: stamp collecting. She first picked up the philatelic bug in childhood and then returned to it in her sixties. In typical Randian fashion, she explains the philosophical underpinnings of her hobby in a 1971 essay, appropriately titled "Why I Like Stamp Collecting."

BOY TOY

Rand tended to attract acolytes, and none was more devoted than Nathan Blumenthal, the Canadian college student who became by turns her protégé, intellectual heir, and personal stud service. They first met in 1950, after the then nineteen-year-old Blumenthal wrote a fan letter to her. To his surprise, the famous author invited him to her home in Manhattan to take part in one of the floating philosophical bull sessions she called "The Collective." Blumenthal (who would soon restyle himself as Nathaniel Branden) quickly ingratiated himself into her inner circle. Rand even served as the maid of honor at his wedding. By 1955 their relationship had turned physical. Rand was now fifty; Branden was twenty-five. She bragged to friends that she needed to have sex with him at least two times a week to ward off writer's block.

How did their spouses react to this unique arrangement? Rand's husband, Frank O'Connor, seemed fine with it. Branden's wife put up with it for a few years (Rand had been kind enough to inform her beforehand that she planned to start diddling her husband) but eventually divorced him. Branden parlayed his intimate access to the Objectivist visionary to found the Nathaniel Branden Institute, a think tank devoted to spreading Rand's selfishness-based gospel. By 1968 the bloom was off the rose, however, and Branden started secretly seeing another of Rand's disciples, who happened to be a beautiful young model. When Rand discovered the infidelity, she went ballistic and vowed to destroy him. In a public declaration, she officially cast him out of the Objectivist movement. Today, Branden works in Beverly Hills, California, as a psychotherapist specializing in self-esteem issues. He published a tell-all memoir, *My Years with Ayn Rand*, in 1999.

YOU'RE DA-DA-DA-DEAD TO ME!

Rand hated all Romantic classical music, especially Beethoven and Brahms. In fact, she was known to terminate friendships with people if she discovered they liked Beethoven!

GOLDWATER GIRL

Rand is usually associated with political conservatism. However, her own views were not so easily pigeonholed. Although she often supported Republican presidential candidates, she voted for Franklin Delano Roosevelt in 1932 (although she later regretted doing so) and refused to endorse Ronald Reagan in 1980. (She denounced his "mixture of capitalism and religion" and called him "the representative of the worst kind of conservatism.") The candidate who most nearly embodied her political philosophy was Senator Barry Goldwater, the GOP maverick from Arizona. Endorsing him in her *Objectivist Newsletter* in 1964, Rand wrote: "In an age of moral collapse, like the present, men who seek power for power's sake rise to leadership everywhere on earth and destroy one country after another. Barry Goldwater is singularly devoid of power lust. . . . In a world ravaged by dictatorships, can we afford to pass up a candidate of that kind?" Apparently, we could. Despite Rand's backing, Goldwater lost the presidential election to Lyndon Johnson by more than fifteen million votes.

SO THAT'S WHAT 2112 WAS ALL ABOUT!

And the Grammy for unlikeliest Ayn Rand disciple goes to . . . Neal Peart of the Canadian rock band Rush. The drummer and lyricist behind such progressive rock classics as "Tom Sawyer" and "New World Man" became enamored with Rand's Objectivist philosophy while living in London in the early 1970s. Attentive listeners can find references to Rand's writings sprinkled throughout Rush's lyrics.

> AYN RAND WAS AMONG THE MANY FANS OF THE 1970s JIGGLEFEST *CHARLIE'S ANGELS*. SHE ONCE DESCRIBED IT AS "THE ONLY ROMANTIC SHOW [ON] TELEVISION TODAY."

THE TENNIS CONNECTION

Along with attracting such diverse characters as rocker Neal Peart, former Federal Reserve chairman Alan Greenspan, and former British prime minister Margaret Thatcher, Rand seems to have touched a chord with an unusually large number of female tennis legends. Billie Jean King, Chris Evert, and Martina Navratilova have all spoken at length about the impact of Rand's novels on their lives. When asked to name her favorite book, Navratilova picked *The Fountainhead*, crediting it with teaching her the importance of "striving for excellence, sticking to your beliefs and ideals even if it means going against the popular tide." King claimed that *Atlas Shrugged* helped turn around her career in the early 1970s.

ALMIGHTY DOLLAR

In a speech at Yale University in the early 1960s, Rand declared: "The cross is the symbol of torture. I prefer the dollar sign, the symbol of free trade, therefore of the free mind." At her 1982 funeral, that preference was on full display. She was laid to rest beside a six-foot-tall floral arrangement in the shape of a dollar sign.

JEAN-PAUL SARTRE

JUNE 21, 1905–APRIL 15, 1980

NATIONALITY:
FRENCH

ASTROLOGICAL SIGN:
GEMINI

MAJOR WORKS:
NAUSEA (1938), *NO EXIT* (1944)

CONTEMPORARIES & RIVALS:
ALBERT CAMUS, SIMONE DE BEAUVOIR,
ANDRÉ MALRAUX

LITERARY STYLE:
TENDENTIOUS, DOGMATIC, CLAUSTROPHOBIC

WORDS OF WISDOM ➤ *"LIFE BEGINS ON THE OTHER SIDE OF DESPAIR."*

Jean-Paul Sartre has the dual distinction of being both a revered national hero *and* the subject of numerous satirical Monty Python sketches. An almost perfect blend of serious, committed thinker and tedious, self-righteous windbag, Sartre was easy to make fun of but hard to ignore. In 1960, when he outraged bourgeois French society by publicly urging the nation's soldiers stationed in Algeria to desert, President Charles de Gaulle was asked why he didn't have his nemesis thrown in prison. "One does not arrest Voltaire," de Gaulle replied—as good an indicator as any of Sartre's uniquely exalted place in French society.

Sartre was the son of a French naval officer, who died when he was a baby, and a German Alsatian woman whose cousin was Albert Schweitzer, the great physician and humanitarian. His distinctive walleyed appearance was the result of a bad childhood cold that left him nearly blind in his right eye. Saddled with trollish looks and an attendant fear of physical intimacy, Sartre seemed bound from an early age for a career in philosophy. He studied at the Sorbonne, where he met his lifelong inamorata Simone de Beauvoir, a woman eerily attracted to him despite his ugliness, short stature, and revolting personal hygiene. She even put up with his weird habit of writing her detailed descriptions of his erotic adventures with other women. They remained lovers—though hardly monogamous ones—for the rest of his life.

During World War II, Sartre worked as a meteorologist for the French army. He was captured by the Nazis and thrown in a prison camp, where he found the environment strangely conducive to writing plays. He won his release after convincing the German authorities that he was partially blind and immediately headed to occupied Paris and a cushy teaching position that conveniently became available when a Jewish educator was—ahem— sent to the east. If the circumstances of his employment grated on Sartre's conscience, he never showed it. In fact, the philosopher, novelist, and playwright did quite well under the Nazis. Hopped up on speed, he wrote his existentialist treatise *Being and Nothingness* in 1943; his play *No Exit* was a smash in 1944. And though Sartre gave lip service to joining the French Resistance, he did little or nothing to thwart the Nazi occupation.

After the liberation of France, all was forgiven and Sartre found himself hailed as a national hero. His existentialist belief system, grounded in the experience of despair and the need to carve out meaning for oneself through engagement with the world around us, became all the rage in his homeland

and throughout Europe. Politically, Sartre drifted left, aligning himself with the French Communist party and becoming an outspoken champion of third-world liberation movements. As though to prove the old saw that the personal is the political, he even took an Algerian mistress, Arlette Elkaim, whom he secretly adopted in 1965. (Amazingly, it was she, and not de Beauvoir, who became the executor of his estate after his death in 1980.) He kept up a steady literary output throughout the 1960s, only ceasing when blindness overtook him in 1973. His final years were plagued by illness, in large measure due to his diet of alcohol, tobacco, and amphetamines.

As his days on Earth dwindled, Sartre began to rethink his lifelong commitment to atheism. In an interview with his good friend Benny Lévy in early 1980, he confessed to having second thoughts about the existence of God. "I do not feel that I am the product of chance, a speck of dust in the universe," Sartre admitted, "but someone who was expected, prepared, prefigured. In short, a being whom only a Creator could put here; and this idea of a creating hand refers to God." One can excuse a dying man for expressing such a hope in his final hours, but, in a more troubling revelation, Sartre went on to recant virtually the entire foundation of his philosophy. "I talked about despair, but it's nonsense," he told Lévy. "I talked about it because it was being talked about; it was fashionable. . . . I've never experienced despair, nor seen it as a quality that could be mine."

Lest Sartre's legions of followers lose heart at this "Sorry, folks, I was only pulling your leg" admission, de Beauvoir was quick to disavow her old lover's astounding volte face, calling it "the senile act of a turncoat." His coat sufficiently turned, Sartre died in his sleep on April 15, 1980, bound for who knows where. A crowd of fifty thousand lined the streets of Paris for his funeral procession.

NICE BEAVER!

Sartre came up with a unique pet name for Simone de Beauvoir. He called her "le castor," the French word for beaver, because her name sounded like *beaver* in English.

HERE'S TO NOTHINGNESS!

The image of French intellectuals sitting around gabbing in sidewalk cafés is a stereotype we owe mostly to Sartre. At the height of his fame, he could be frequently seen holding court with longtime lover Simone de Beauvoir and others in his existential circle. Truth be told, they were not the most conscientious revelers. Sartre and his posse were once whooping it up over bottles of champagne in a Paris café. Every time they poured another glass, they raised a toast to the absurdity of existence. The toasts became increasingly boisterous, and before long a woman leaned out the window above and demanded they keep it down. In response, Sartre and his friends just got louder.

Enraged, the woman disappeared inside her apartment and returned soon after with a bucket full of feces. She proceeded to dump it over the windowsill, aiming at Sartre and company. Whether her aim was bad or the prevailing winds were blowing the wrong way, she missed her mark and instead ended up dousing another patron on the way out of the restaurant. Convinced this was proof of the validity of their philosophy, the drunken existentialists went right back to toasting the absurdity of the universe.

GONE TRIPPIN'

"Psychedelic" and "Sartre" might seem like an odd combination, but give the man credit for being way ahead of the times. Sartre was experimenting with mind-altering substances in the 1930s, long before Timothy Leary helped make them fashionable among the 1960s counterculture. Determined, as he put it, to "break the bones in his head" and unlock his imagination, Sartre first took mescaline in 1935, under the supervision of a medical intern he had befriended. At first, the effects were mild. After a couple days, however, Sartre began to experience more and more unpleasant hallucinations. In one, he believed he was being pursued by a giant lobster. He also reported seeing orangutans, a clock face with the features of an owl, and houses gnashing their jaws. Weird visions continued to haunt him for the better part of a year. Sartre later wrote some of his psychedelic perceptions into his novel *Nausea*, in the scenes in which the protagonist, Roquentin, feels as if he is "merging" with the natural environment that surrounds him.

PUFF DADDY

When not experimenting with hard drugs, Sartre stuck with his old favorite: nicotine. He smoked two packs of cigarettes and several pipefuls of tobacco a day. Even in tobacco-mad France, that's a lot—and bad form for a national icon. In fact, when the French National Library issued a commemorative poster on the hundredth anniversary of Sartre's birth, officials were forced to airbrush the cigarette out of his hand in compliance with laws prohibiting the advertisement of tobacco.

DETERMINED, AS HE PUT IT, TO "BREAK THE BONES IN HIS HEAD" AND UNLOCK HIS IMAGINATION, SARTRE BEGAN DABBLING WITH MESCALINE—AND EXPERIENCED BIZARRE HALLUCINATIONS FOR NEARLY A YEAR.

HOLD THE CRAWFISH

Maybe it had something to do with his drug-induced vision of a giant rampaging lobster, but Sartre had a lifelong fear of sea creatures, particularly shellfish. He was terrified of being caught in a crab's claws or attacked by an octopus and dragged underwater.

228 · SECRET LIVES OF GREAT AUTHORS

MY TERROR BUDDIES

Sartre's radical politics put him in touch with some unsavory characters. In 1960 he traveled to Cuba to schmooze about revolution with Fidel Castro and Ernesto "Che" Guevara. Sartre was so snowed, he dubbed the murderous Che "the most complete human being of our age." When Palestinian terrorists killed eleven Israeli athletes at the 1972 Munich Olympics, Sartre was quick to defend them, saying terrorism was a "terrible weapon, but the oppressed poor have no others." He also declared that it was "perfectly scandalous that the Munich attack should be judged by the French press and a section of public opinion as an intolerable scandal." In 1974 he visited Andreas Baader, leader of the infamous Baader-Meinhof gang, in his cell at Stammheim Prison in Stuttgart, Germany. Although he later dismissed Baader as "incredibly stupid" and "an asshole," immediately after the meeting he went on German television to advocate for the creation of an international committee to protect the interests of "political prisoners." (Baader's crimes included multiple bank robberies and blowing up a Frankfurt department store.)

THE LADIES MAN

Despite his ungainly appearance, Sartre was a notorious womanizer who ran through mistresses as ravenously as he did packs of Boyard cigarettes. He even tried to hit on a comely young Brazilian journalist while Simone de Beauvoir was in the hospital recovering from a bout of typhoid. He justified his infidelity by likening it to masturbation and refused to climax alongside his partners—not to forestall pregnancy but simply to deny them any unnecessary intimacy.

SMOKE 'EM IF YOU GOT 'EM

He may not have done much to aid the French Resistance, but Sartre objected to at least one aspect of Nazi occupation. Wartime tobacco shortages seriously cramped his two-pack-a-day habit. Not to be denied, the resourceful philosopher could often be seen scrounging for butts on café floors, stuffing the tobacco into his pipe. Sartre's nicotine jones was so strong he let his students smoke in class. He quit only after doctors threatened to amputate his legs to cure his circulatory problems.

RICHARD WRIGHT

SEPTEMBER 4, 1908–NOVEMBER 28, 1960

NATIONALITY:
AMERICAN

ASTROLOGICAL SIGN:
VIRGO

MAJOR WORKS:
NATIVE SON (1940), *BLACK BOY* (1945)

CONTEMPORARIES & RIVALS:
RALPH ELLISON, JAMES BALDWIN, FRANTZ FANON

LITERARY STYLE:
SPARE, DIRECT, AND POWERFUL

"MEN CAN STARVE FROM A LACK OF SELF-REALIZATION AS MUCH AS THEY CAN FROM A LACK OF BREAD."

WORDS OF WISDOM

e came like a sledgehammer," historian John Henrik Clarke wrote of Richard Wright, "like a giant out of the mountain with a sledgehammer, writing with a sledgehammer."

Generations of American high school students know Wright as the sledgehammer who put *Black Boy* on their tenth-grade English reading lists. But it is his earlier book, *Native Son*, and a handful of essays and short stories on which his literary reputation still stands. Wright had a lot in common with the giants of modern American literature. Like Hemingway, he was an avowed expatriate. Like Faulkner, he was a native Mississippian (and, oddly enough, a former postal employee). But the color of Wright's skin, along with his radical political beliefs, prevented him from achieving the stature of those two legends. He spent much of his life looking for a country where he could hang his hat and keeping one step ahead of the FBI.

One of the first African Americans to gain fame through the use of the written word, Wright grew up in the Jim Crow South, where even having a library card marked him as suspect among the white community. Nevertheless, he cooked up a scheme to procure one and used it to pore through the works of his first literary idol, H. L. Mencken. His eyes opened to the possibilities beyond Natchez, Mississippi, Wright high-tailed it out of town as soon as he came of age. He settled in Chicago, where for the next decade he worked in a post office on the South Side and wrote a succession of well-regarded stories and poems for small literary periodicals. In a sign of his growing stature, Wright was named one of the "twelve distinguished Negroes" of 1939 by the Schomburg Collection of Negro Literature and Art in New York City.

The publication of *Native Son* in 1940 proved to be Wright's creative and commercial breakthrough. The story of a "brute Negro" named Bigger Thomas who accidentally kills a white woman and pays a horrific price, the novel elevated Wright to iconic status almost overnight—and not just in the black community. In the ultimate mark of mainstream acceptance, *Native Son* became the first work by an African American writer to be selected by the Book-of-the-Month Club. (To be fair, the club's staid board made him cut some of the novel's more racially charged passages.) Within a few months, the one-time Chicago postal clerk became the wealthiest and most prominent black writer in America.

He also became a Communist. A popular move during the depths of the Great Depression, when leftist agitation was all the rage, it was one that would haunt Wright the rest of his days, as his paranoid fears of surveillance by government authorities turned out to be all too real. Although he renounced Communism in 1944—he even wrote a mea culpa essay entitled "I Tried to Be a Communist" (hint, hint)—the American government never let him live down his erstwhile party membership. From the moment he entered the public eye, Wright was being watched by the FBI. The CIA kept tabs on him as well. Other well-known African Americans were deputized to slander him in the black press. The fact that Wright took two white wives—ballet dancer Dhima Rose Meadman in 1939 and Communist Party organizer Ellen Poplar in 1941—surely didn't endear him to the authorities either.

In 1946, fed up with the way he was being treated in his native country, Wright moved to France and became a permanent expatriate. In Paris, he was welcomed *avec bras ouverts* by such preeminent intellectuals as Gertrude Stein, Simone de Beauvoir, Jean-Paul Sartre, and André Gide. He led a rich life, joining various radical organizations and agitating for the decolonization of developing countries. But his work suffered for being cut off from the land of his birth and the source of his inspiration. These days, few people—in or outside a high school English class—have read *The Outsider*, *Savage Holiday*, or any of the other didactic books and essays Wright wrote in his final years. Even many of his one-time acolytes in the black literati turned against him. By the time of his death from a heart attack in 1960, Wright was deeply in debt and had fallen out of favor with the literary establishment. The lack of an autopsy and the hurried circumstances of his cremation—reportedly with a copy of *Black Boy* at his side—led to the circulation of a number of ghoulish conspiracy theories about his demise. To this day, some insist that Wright, who had no history of heart disease, was murdered by his mistress, bumped off by the CIA, or both. If so, it would have been a more fitting end for a writer who lived his life on the run from real and imagined oppressors.

ANGRY YOUNG AUTODIDACT

Not content with the books he was assigned in school, the teenaged Wright decided to design his own reading program. His first stop was the local branch of the Memphis public library system. But the institution adhered to a strict whites-only lending policy. Infuriated, Wright marched home and immediately composed a fake letter from a mythical Caucasian library patron to the librarian. "Dear Madam," the note read. "Will you please let this nigger boy have some books by H. L. Mencken?" Wright soon had his reading list filled.

RICHARD WRIGHT JOINED THE COMMUNIST PARTY DURING THE GREAT DEPRESSION—A MEMBERSHIP HE WOULD LIVE TO REGRET.

--- PEN PALS ---

When Wright married dancer Dhima Rose Meadman in 1939, fellow African American literary icon Ralph Ellison stood as his best man.

HOORAY FOR HOLLYWOOD

From the moment it was published, *Native Son* began attracting interest from Hollywood producers. Wright long resisted all offers to adapt his novel for the big screen. He feared that his message would get lost as the tragic tale of Bigger Thomas was toned down to appeal to a mass audience. He also fretted about wholesale changes to the plot—and with good reason. In 1947 producer Joseph Fields of MGM approached Wright with the idea of "reimagining" Bigger and all the novel's African American characters as whites. In Fields's version, Bigger would be recast as a member of a white ethnic minority group who applies for a job alongside a Pole, an Italian, a black man, and a Jew. The concept so horrified Wright that he gave up on Hollywood entirely and started fielding offers from European producers instead.

Eventually, Wright found his man in Pierre Chenal, a French filmmaker. Chenal agreed to stick to the novel as written, on the condition that Wright himself play the title character. Casting a forty-year-old man with no acting

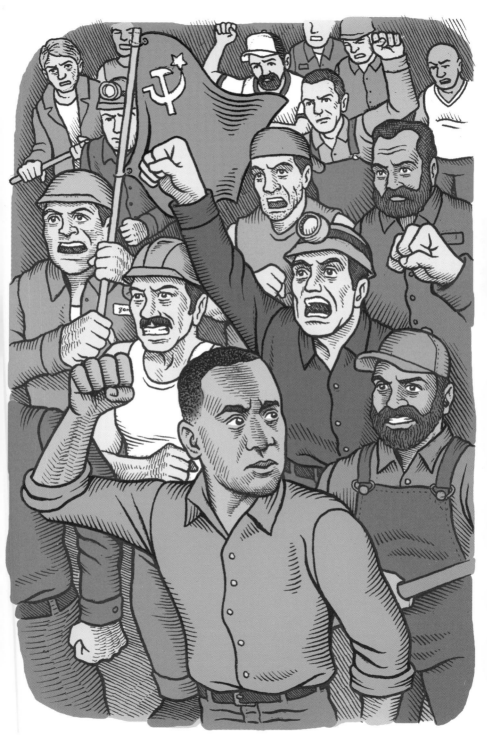

experience in the part of a nineteen-year-old protagonist was just the first in a series of mistakes that would bedevil the low-budget production. When the U.S. government pressured France to distance itself from the project, Chenal was forced to relocate the operation to Argentina. Bureaucratic snafus, shady dealing by the Argentine backers, and Chenal's own ineptitude sent the project soaring off schedule and over budget. Miraculously, the movie wrapped, and a gala premiere was held on board a Pan-American strato-clipper on November 4, 1950.

Hopes were high for a positive reception in Wright's native land, but America was not kind to this *Native Son*. Before the film's debut, the New York State Board of Censors ordered the distributor to cut a half hour's worth of footage that it considered too politically charged for American audiences. This bowdlerized version appalled critics, who reserved special venom for Wright's amateurish performance. In public, the author put on a brave face. "I offer no alibis for this picture," he commented. "Good or bad, it's what I wanted." In private, however, he was deeply embarrassed. Only years later did an uncut version of *Native Son* surface on the European film festival circuit. By that time, it was too late to salvage Wright's cinematic reputation.

WITH FRIENDS LIKE THESE . . .

When living in Paris, Wright practically adopted James Baldwin, an up-and-coming African American writer fourteen years his junior. Baldwin was virtually unpublished and looked to the established author for advice and inspiration. In turn, Wright was generous with his time and counsel. Unfortunately, nobody told Baldwin that gratitude was part of the deal. One of the first things he wrote after settling in Paris was an essay attacking the tradition of "protest" fiction in contemporary black literature. The principal object of his ire? *Native Son*. Immensely hurt, Wright never forgave Baldwin.

CUCKOO FOR HAIKU

Wright caught the haiku bug. During the last decade of his life, while living in France, he composed more than four thousand of the gnomic three-line poems, which he called "spider webs." They were collected and published posthumously.

WILLIAM BURROUGHS

FEBRUARY 5, 1914–AUGUST 2, 1997

NATIONALITY:
AMERICAN

ASTROLOGICAL SIGN:
AQUARIUS

MAJOR WORKS:
JUNKIE (1953), *NAKED LUNCH* (1959)

CONTEMPORARIES & RIVALS:
JACK KEROUAC, ALLEN GINSBERG

LITERARY STYLE:
PARANOID MUSINGS CUT UP AND
RANDOMLY REASSEMBLED

*"IN THE U.S., YOU HAVE
TO BE A DEVIANT OR DIE
OF BOREDOM."*

WORDS OF WISDOM

One of world literature's most celebrated outsiders, William S. Burroughs did not lack for establishment bona fides. His paternal grandfather, William Seward Burroughs I, invented the calculator. His mother, Laura Harmon Lee Burroughs, claimed to be descended from Confederate general Robert E. Lee and had a brother who handled public relations work for John D. Rockefeller (not to mention Adolf Hitler). Burroughs himself attended Harvard University, that bastion of Ivy League rectitude, although he retained no affection for the place. "I hated the university and I hated the town it was in," he said of his alma mater. "Everything about the place was dead. The university was a fake English setup taken over by the graduates of fake English public schools."

Burroughs also served in the U.S. Army, a fact they've probably never highlighted in their recruitment literature. Fans of the "outlaw" Burroughs can take solace in the fact that he was discharged for a very Burroughsesque reason: He was deemed mentally unsuitable for military service after he deliberately cut off the tip of his left pinkie to impress a man on whom he had a crush. He did not lack for gallantry. During World War II, he wedded the delightfully named Ilse Klapper, a German Jew, in a marriage of convenience designed to help her escape from Nazi-controlled Austria. He later married Joan Vollmer, whom he killed during some handgun horseplay (more on that later). Neither wife was unaware where Burroughs's real sexual allegiances lay. He was out and proud and made no bones about it.

Most scholars date the birth of the Beat Generation to the 1943 meeting of Burroughs, Allen Ginsberg, and Jack Kerouac at Columbia University. Before that, Burroughs had worked as an exterminator, fenced stolen goods, and sold drugs to make a living. After that, he wrote, sold drugs, and took drugs to keep from dying. Truth be told, he never needed a real job. Throughout his life, he was propped up by a monthly allowance from his wealthy family—not quite the "Burroughs millions" that some literary mythmakers have claimed, but enough to pay his rent and keep him well stocked with narcotics, which is all he ever really wanted.

Drugs are the one constant in Burroughs's life. They run through his biography like, well, a shot of heroin through a junkie's vein. Controlled substances bedeviled him from an early age. As a teenager, he was kicked out of his posh New Mexico boarding school for taking choral hydrate, a sedative used to anesthetize rats. In the 1950s, he spent several months trolling through South America in search of a mystical psychedelic brew called *yage*, which supposedly imparted telepathic powers. Burroughs even used the $3,000 advance he received for his masterwork, *Naked Lunch*, to score some heroin. Along with smack, he indulged in magic mushrooms, marijuana, hashish, and morphine—whatever was in season, really. He tried numerous cures to help him kick the habit, including Dr. John Yerbury Dent's celebrated apomorphine treatment, but nothing stuck. Ultimately, Burroughs resigned himself to living in places where he could get drugs cheaply and/or legally, and he wrote the addiction experience into his work.

Outrage over Burroughs's drug use and his outré homosexual lifestyle made him an easy target for censors and other public rebukes. In 1962 *Naked Lunch* became the center of the last major obscenity trial in the United States, and the book was ruled indecent by the Commonwealth of Massachusetts; the decision followed a sensational trial during which Allen Ginsberg, Norman Mailer, and others testified in its defense. The ruling was later overturned on appeal. Despite achieving cult status in the 1970s—in part for his dapper taste in chapeaus—Burroughs was never fully embraced by the literary establishment. He was inducted into the American Academy of Arts and Letters only in 1983, after a lengthy lobbying campaign spearheaded by Ginsberg. Burroughs seemed to prefer the company of rock stars, counting Lou Reed, David Bowie, and Patti Smith among his many admirers. After spending most of the 1970s in New York schmoozing with the Studio 54 set, he moved to Lawrence, Kansas, in 1983 to live out his last fourteen years in a drug-addled haze. When he died of a heart attack in 1997 at the improbable age of eighty-three, he had outlived his younger and less chemically indulgent Beat compadres Kerouac and Ginsberg by twenty-eight years and four months, respectively.

THE NEEDLE AND THE DAMAGE DONE

Burroughs's addiction to heroin was powerful and all-consuming. He once sold his typewriter to buy some smack, reducing his literary output to a trickle as he struggled to write out his manuscripts by hand. On another occasion, he confessed to having foregone bathing or changing his clothes for a year, a lifestyle choice that must have endeared him to friends and neighbors. Between fill-ups of horse, Burroughs would sit staring into space for days. "I could look at the end of my shoe for eight hours," he once reported.

DO TELL

Killing your own wife would be a career-ending misstep for most writers—and most people, generally—but it didn't seem to break Burroughs's stride. In 1951, while entertaining at their home in Mexico, Burroughs and his wife, Joan, decided to regale guests with their vaunted "William Tell" routine. Joan balanced a highball glass on her head while Burroughs took aim with his .38 caliber pistol. (The questionable wisdom of a zonked-out heroin addict using a jittery Benzedrine addict for target practice seems not to have occurred to anyone.) Burroughs missed badly, blowing Joan's brains out and killing her instantly. Party over. After a complicated Mexican legal proceeding involving a few carefully placed bribes, Burroughs was allowed to flee the country and convicted of homicide in absentia. He was given a two-year suspended sentence. Where another man might have been wracked by guilt, Burroughs preferred to look on the bright side. "I am forced to the appalling conclusion that I would have never become a writer but for Joan's death," he later wrote. "The death of Joan brought me in contact with the invader, the Ugly Spirit, and maneuvered me into a lifelong struggle, in which I have had no choice except to write my way out."

THANKS FOR LUNCH, JACK

Burroughs's most memorable work boasts one of literary history's most arresting titles: *Naked Lunch*. For that we can thank Jack Kerouac. Burroughs initially planned to call his novel *Interzone*, after the "international zone" in Tangiers where he wrote most of its fragments. He later chose the more sensational *Naked Lust*. One day Kerouac was visiting Burroughs in his Moroccan redoubt and spotted the manuscript from across the room, reading the title erroneously as "Naked Lunch." Burroughs was so amused by it that he kept it that way—and a literary classic was born.

HOWL YA LIKE ME NOW?

Despite a twelve-year age difference, Burroughs and Allen Ginsberg shared a brief, torrid sexual affair in the early 1950s. The coupling went down in flames, however, when Burroughs fell in love with his protégé. "Bill wanted a relationship where there were no holds barred," Ginsberg later wrote, "to achieve the ultimate telepathic union of souls." When it came time to dump Burroughs, Ginsberg was somewhat less eloquent in his word choice: "I don't want your ugly old cock," he told him. It took many years for the two men to repair their broken friendship.

I'LL BE XENU

For a writer so obsessed with mind control, Burroughs seems like an unlikely convert to Scientology. But in the late 1960s he became an enthusiastic adopter of science-fiction writer L. Ron Hubbard's alien-based belief system. Calling Scientology "a real science of communication," Burroughs began preaching its gospel throughout London, where he then lived. He even underwent the so-called Joburg, an exhaustive sexual and criminal "security check" performed on Scientology adepts. After a few months, Burroughs opted to leave, declaring, "Scientology was useful to me until it became a religion, and I have no use for religion. It's just another of those control-addict trips, and we can all do without those."

MEMBER OF THE BAND

With his outlaw persona and his radical aesthetic technique, Burroughs had a natural affinity for the world of rock music. As many now know, the band Steely Dan took its name from the "Steely Dan III from Yokohama," an enormous rubber dildo featured in *Naked Lunch*. The term *heavy metal* is also a Burroughsism. It appears in his novels *The Soft Machine* and *Nova Express* as a metaphor for addictive drugs.

Late in life, Burroughs developed close collaborative relationships with several rock music performers, including Tom Waits, Nick Cave, and Genesis P-Orridge of Throbbing Gristle. His good friend Kurt Cobain even asked him to appear as Jesus Christ in the video for Nirvana's song "Heart-Shaped Box," but Burroughs declined. In 1992 he did record an EP with Cobain entitled "The Priest They Called Him."

One of Burroughs's more like-minded collaborators was Al Jourgensen, front man for the Chicago-based "industrial" metal band Ministry. Burroughs and Jourgensen shared a passion for heroin, which they indulged in together at least once. "Burroughs doesn't live on this planet," Jourgensen said of their memorable smack-shooting session. "Basically, we talked about eradicating the raccoons from his petunia garden. We finally decided on dosing them with methadone. That slowed them down enough for Bill to take out his .38 and scare them away." Once they dealt with the varmint problem they were able to get down to business. Burroughs appears as a guest on the Ministry song "Just One Fix," performing a spoken-word part.

WHEN WILLIAM AND JOAN BURROUGHS ENTERTAINED THEIR PARTY GUESTS WITH A GAME OF "WILLIAM TELL," THE FESTIVITIES WERE INTERRUPTED BY A SUDDEN AND UNEXPECTED MURDER.

LIVE FROM NEW YORK . . . IT'S WILLIAM BURROUGHS!

Burroughs's first-ever television appearance was also one of the most bizarre guest spots in the annals of late-night comedy. It took place on November 7, 1981, when the sixty-seven-year-old literary icon dropped by the *Saturday Night Live* studios on the invitation of head writer Michael O'Donoghue. A huge fan of Burroughs's work, O'Donoghue prevailed upon *SNL* producer Dick Ebersol to let the author do a live reading on that night's show, which was hosted by supermodel Lauren Hutton. At dress rehearsal, the performance—during which Burroughs slurred his way through excerpts from *Naked Lunch* and *Nova Express* to the strains of "The Star-Spangled Banner"—proved so bizarre that Ebersol ordered O'Donoghue to make Burroughs cut it down from six minutes to three. A perturbed O'Donoghue willfully neglected to relay the producer's instructions, and Burroughs was allowed to rave on for the full six minutes. His

surreal rant about nuclear explosions and drunkenly performed appendec-
tomies seemed to bewilder the audience, which tittered nervously, unsure
whether or not it was supposed to be a comedy sketch. All was quickly put
right as musical guest "Super Freak" Rick James and a cast led by Eddie
Murphy and Joe Piscopo reasserted control of the show.

BLADE TO ORDER

Eagle-eyed viewers of Ridley Scott's 1982 sci-fi noir classic *Blade Runner* may
notice Burroughs's name in the credits. The title was a tip of the hat to the
Naked Lunch author, who around that time was circulating a screenplay called
Blade Runner that had nothing to do with Scott's film or the Phillip K. Dick
novel *Do Androids Dream of Electric Sheep?* on which it was based. For the
record, Burroughs's tale concerns a group of teenage smugglers, called Blade
Runners, who provide banned surgical instruments to doctors in a fascistic
future America ruled by secret police.

CARSON MCCULLERS

FEBRUARY 19, 1917–SEPTEMBER 29, 1967

NATIONALITY:
AMERICAN

ASTROLOGICAL SIGN:
AQUARIUS

MAJOR WORKS:
THE HEART IS A LONELY HUNTER (1940),
REFLECTIONS IN A GOLDEN EYE (1941),
THE MEMBER OF THE WEDDING (1946)

CONTEMPORARIES & RIVALS:
FLANNERY O'CONNOR, EUDORA WELTY, HARPER LEE

LITERARY STYLE:
THE FREAKISH LIVES OF SOUTHERN MISFITS
ACHINGLY RENDERED IN FLUID, LYRICAL PROSE

"THERE'S NOTHING THAT MAKES YOU SO AWARE OF THE IMPROVISATION OF HUMAN EXISTENCE AS A SONG UNFINISHED. OR AN OLD ADDRESS BOOK."

WORDS OF WISDOM

Want to start an argument at your next book club meeting? Stand up and ask what everybody thinks of Carson McCullers. This is an author people either love or hate. In the "pro" corner stand Graham Greene (who preferred her to William Faulkner and praised her "original poetic sensibility"), her friend Tennessee Williams (who called her "a genius"), and Gore Vidal (who dubbed her limpid prose "one of the few satisfying achievements of our second-rate culture"). Arguing the case against are Arthur Miller (he called her "a minor author"), her fellow Southern Gothicist Flannery O'Connor ("I dislike her work intensely"), and the influential film critic Stanley Kauffmann (who derided her as "Spanish moss hanging on the tree of American literature"). Though her life was short, and her literary output relatively sparse, this genial bisexual from Columbus, Georgia, had a way of stirring up strong opinions.

Born Lula Carson Smith, the future Carson McCullers was truly destined for literary greatness. Just ask her mother. Marguerite Waters Smith—herself the granddaughter of a Confederate war hero—told anyone who would listen that mysterious portents indicated that her unborn child would become a world-renowned artist. Unfortunately, those same oracles gave her bad intelligence about the baby's gender, so she had to put aside her chosen name—Enrico Caruso—and name the infant after her grandmother Lula instead. Still, little Lula was treated like a golden child. Marguerite was convinced her future lay in music, boasting to friends that the baby could cry in key. From early childhood, she was sent for piano lessons designed to tease out the inner greatness her mother just knew was there.

At age seventeen, Carson traveled to New York City to study music at Julliard. Her family filled her pocketbook with tuition money they had raised by selling an heirloom ring. Whether by accident or simple indifference to her fate, Carson lost the pocketbook on the subway, and her musical career was over before it began. She instead enrolled in writing classes, taking odd jobs to pay her way, but they never lasted long. "I was always fired," she told an interviewer. "My record is perfect on that. I never quit a job in my life." In 1937 she married Reeves McCullers, a fellow misfit who shared her need for public adulation and lovers of both sexes. Theirs was to be a toxic coupling. Reeves wasn't nearly as good a writer as Carson, though he craved the limelight just as much as she did. The marriage lasted only three years.

In 1940, at the invitation of her friend George Davis, former *Harper's*

Bazaar fiction editor, McCullers moved into a ramshackle Brooklyn brownstone that doubled as an ad hoc artist's commune. Her flatmates included poets W. H. Auden and Louis MacNiece and the flamboyant stripper Gypsy Rose Lee, with whom she shared the third floor. A panoply of eccentric visitors floated in and out, from Paul and Jane Bowles to Leonard Bernstein to Salvador Dali. The free-spirited milieu proved invigorating, on the heels of the collapse of her stultifying marriage, and McCullers began work on *The Member of the Wedding* and *The Ballad of the Sad Café*. She also formed something of an unlikely bond with Auden, a pretentious fussbudget ten years her senior. Although they found each other's accents mutually incomprehensible—McCullers mispronounced his first name as "Winston"—a kind of teacher-student relationship developed. It didn't hurt that Auden was gay and could relate to her agonized sex life, which for the most part involved lusting after unattainable women. ("I was born a man," she said, perhaps proving her mother's prenatal prophecy after all.)

In 1945 the now world-famous author remarried her ex-husband Reeves McCullers. If anything, he was even weirder than before. He became fascinated by the idea that they should commit suicide together. When a creeped-out Carson demurred, he went ahead and offed himself without her, overdosing on barbiturates in his Paris hotel room in 1953. The sudden death of her doting mother two years later was an even harsher blow. Bereft of emotional support, the widow McCullers sank into a deep despair that she never really climbed out of. She spent most of the rest of her life battling the debilitating effects of various illnesses. Multiple strokes left her all but paralyzed on one side of her body; she was diagnosed with breast cancer in 1962; and operations on her arm, leg, hip, and fingers severely limited her literary output. By the end of her life, she could type with only one hand and produced barely one page of writing per day. She suffered her final fatal stroke and slipped into a forty-seven-day coma that ended her short life on September 29, 1967.

CARSON AND THE COUNTESS

McCullers had a special affinity for Russian writers, such as Anton Chekhov, Fyodor Dostoyevsky, Turgenev, and Leo Tolstoy. She also had a knack for bumping into their relatives on public transportation. One day she and her mother were on a bus bound for New York City when they struck up a conversation with a regal-looking Russian woman. Mama McCullers was going on and on about her daughter's literary prowess when the woman remarked that her father had also been a writer. Her name? Countess Tolstoy.

> AT ONE OF HER LEGENDARY DINNER PARTIES, CARSON MCCULLERS SUPPOSEDLY TABLE-DANCED WITH MARILYN MONROE WHILE ARTHUR MILLER AND ISAK DINESEN CHEERED THEM ON.

-------- ON MARILYN, ON BLIXEN! --------

In one of the ultimate "wish I'd been a fly-on-the-wall" dinner parties in literary history, McCullers once hosted a chowdown attended by Arthur Miller, Marilyn Monroe, and Baroness Karen Blixen-Finecke (better known as Isak Dinesen, author of *Out of Africa*). The eminent Blixen had recently arrived in the United States to deliver an address at the American Academy of Arts and Letters and was itching to meet the bombshell star of the soon-to-open movie *Some Like It Hot*. McCullers, who had compiled an impressive Rolodex through her years of literary fame, made it happen on February 5, 1959.

They made a decidedly odd-looking foursome. The erudite, bespectacled Miller was between plays, still reeling from his recent court battle with the federal government over his refusal to appear before the House Un-American Activities Committee. Monroe, his wife of nearly two years, was at the height of her fame and already showing signs of the emotional instability that would lead to her death three years later. She showed up in a black sheath dress that highlighted her ample cleavage. McCullers, as usual, was a physical and mental train wreck. Her series of strokes had left her all but paralyzed on the left side of her body. At age seventy-four, Blixen was the group's elder

stateswoman. In many ways, she was in the worst shape of all. Decades past her prime, she suffered from the debilitating effects of syphilis and anorexia. She weighed a mere eighty pounds and was chain smoking and popping amphetamines like they were going out of style.

When the dinner bell rang, Blixen ordered up just about the only thing she ever consumed: oysters and champagne. A bemused Miller asked her what doctor had put her on such a strange diet. Blixen turned to him with a withering stare. "Doctor?" she said. "The doctors are horrified, but I love champagne and I love oysters and they do me good." That ended all talk of diets for the rest of the evening. (In a side note, Baroness Blixen was rushed to the hospital a few days later with an acute case of malnutrition.)

Amazingly, the three women seemed to get along well. Perhaps they were bound together by their common dysfunction. Blixen was wowed by Marilyn's beauty, vitality, and air of innocence, which she likened to a lion cub she had encountered in Africa. For her part, McCullers rated it the best dinner party she ever gave. Reports that the evening ended with the three ladies dancing together on McCullers's marble dinner table were apparently unfounded, at least according to Arthur Miller.

THEY SHARED A BOND

Count Ian Fleming, creator of James Bond, among the unlikely fans of Carson McCullers. The spy novelist was so smitten with her novel *Reflections in a Golden Eye* that he named his Jamaican mansion Goldeneye in her honor.

THE UNBEARABLE WHITENESS OF BEING

Late in life, McCullers became obsessed with the color white. Apparently believing she was channeling the spirit of Emily Dickinson, she began to wear all-white dresses and robes and suggest to friends that they redecorate their rooms in white. She even granted interviews attired in nothing but a white nightgown and tennis shoes.

J. D. SALINGER

JANUARY 1, 1919–

NATIONALITY:
AMERICAN

ASTROLOGICAL SIGN:
CAPRICORN

MAJOR WORKS:
THE CATCHER IN THE RYE (1951),
FRANNY AND ZOOEY (1961)

CONTEMPORARIES & RIVALS:
JOHN CHEEVER, JOSEPH HELLER,
CARSON MCCULLERS

LITERARY STYLE
1950s NEW YORKERISH

*"THERE IS A MARVELOUS
PEACE IN NOT PUBLISHING."*

WORDS OF WISDOM

The Sandy Koufax of world literature, Jerome David Salinger long ago mastered the art of enhancing one's reputation by being unapproachable, unavailable, and incommunicado. (Greta Garbo and Howard Hughes also turned this nifty trick, back in their day.) In terms of volume, his contributions to the literary canon were slim. But few authors can match the mystique of the man who once called the very act of being published "a terrible invasion of my privacy." Wouldn't most writers kill for such an incursion?

His signature novel, of course, was *The Catcher in the Rye*, a masterpiece of teenage alienation that still resonates with disaffected high school students—among other unsavory types—to this day. The character of Holden Caulfield (named for actors William Holden and Joan Caulfield) was based largely on Salinger himself, with exclusive Pencey Prep standing in for the Waspy military academy he had once attended. An enemies list couched in the form of a novel, the acerbically funny book gave its sensitive, nebbishy Jewish author a forum to exact rhetorical revenge on everyone who made him feel like an outsider. After having written a few more books beloved by a growing cult of Eisenhower-era misfit toys, he went into seclusion, never to publish again.

Was his retreat from the limelight the product of a thin skin? In the years after the book's publication, such literary eminences as John Updike, Alfred Kazin, and Leslie Fiedler all expressed strong misgivings about Salinger's work. Joan Didion called it "spurious," deriding Salinger's "tendency to flatter the essential triviality within each of his readers, his predilection for giving instructions for living." Maybe these were just sour grapes. He was, after all, making a lot more money and getting a lot more attention than any of them. But some think the criticism may have gotten to Salinger. Perhaps he was just concerned that he could never match that early achievement. Whatever the reason, he became the world's most celebrated recluse.

When he surfaces, Salinger tends to create controversy. In the early 1970s, he shacked up with the eighteen-year-old memoirist Joyce Maynard and then unceremoniously kicked her out nine months later. She took revenge by auctioning off his love letters and writing a tell-all book about their relationship. In 2000, Salinger's daughter Margaret wrote her own memoir, painting a decidedly unflattering portrait of the literary icon. In her account, the man who captivated a generation of readers with his tales of adolescent anomie was in fact a scowling martinet who drank his own urine and clung to outmoded racial stereotypes drawn from old Hollywood movies. "To my father, all Spanish speakers are Puerto Rican washerwomen," she wrote, "or the toothless, grinning gypsy types in a Marx Brothers movie." When Margaret became engaged to a black man, Salinger nearly blew a gasket, cautioning his daughter about an old movie he had seen in which a white woman had married a black musician with disastrous consequences.

Sequestered in his New Hampshire hideaway, Salinger continues to write. He reportedly has several room-sized safes filled with completed or in-progress manuscripts. Every now and then he puts out word that a new novel may be forthcoming, but invariably he changes his mind. He adamantly refuses to sell the film rights to any of his works and has blocked the few unauthorized adaptations that have been made. His will reportedly contains a stipulation blocking anyone from filming his stories after his death.

He certainly doesn't need the money. *The Catcher in the Rye* continues to sell more than 250,000 copies a year, inspiring angsty teens the world over. In a sordid twist of fate, Salinger's greatest creation has also become the rune text of crazed loners and would-be assassins everywhere. When Mark David Chapman shot John Lennon in December 1980, the assassin was found clutching a thumb-worn copy of *The Catcher in the Rye*. He later cited Holden Caulfield as his inspiration for the murder. When Hollywood wants to telegraph a character as a kook, as with Mel Gibson's addled paranoiac in *Conspiracy Theory*, it puts a copy of *Catcher* on their shelf. "I'm afraid of people who like *Catcher in the Rye*," sang indie rockers Too Much Joy in a 1991 song. Can you blame them?

FUN ON THE HIGH SEAS

The world's most famous recluse was once the king of the conga line. In 1941 Salinger served as entertainment director on board the H.M.S. *Kungsholm*, a Swedish luxury liner that ferried wealthy patrons to the West Indies. He later drew on this experience for his short story "Teddy," which takes place on an ocean liner.

OONATIC

In his early twenties, Salinger dated Oona O'Neill, daughter of playwright Eugene O'Neill. Salinger thought they made a good match, but he found himself outmaneuvered by the Little Tramp. Charlie Chaplin stepped in and swept young Oona off her feet. They were soon married, despite a thirty-six-year age difference. Enraged, Salinger wrote Oona a vicious, angry letter describing in sordid detail his impression of her wedding night with Chaplin.

I MARRIED A NAZI

Talk about a self-hating Jew: Salinger was always uncomfortable with his Jewish heritage, a trait he passed on to many of his fictional offspring. But he may be one of the only Jews in history who knowingly and willingly married a Nazi. It happened in the closing months of World War II, when Salinger was serving as a counterintelligence officer in occupied Germany. Charged with interrogating some low-level Nazi officials, Salinger fell in love with one of them—a woman known only as Sylvia (or "Saliva" as Salinger called her). An outspoken anti-Semite, Sylvia was not exactly welcomed with open arms by his relatives back in America. Their union lasted only a few months before Sylvia high-tailed it back to the fatherland.

HE ALSO SAYS I SHOULD SHOOT YOU

When *The Catcher in the Rye* was selected by the Book-of-the-Month Club in 1951, the organization's eminent editorial board had a problem with the book's obscure title. Asked to change it by the club's president, Salinger coldly refused. "Holden Caulfield," he explained, "wouldn't like that."

HAVE A CUPPA PEE

According to his daughter Margaret, Salinger drank his own urine, presumably for medicinal purposes, not refreshment. Urine therapy has been practiced in India for more than five millennia and is thought to offer strong curative effects. It may also whiten teeth.

RAVING HOMEOPATH

Swilling urine was only one aspect of Salinger's alternative medicine regimen. He also dabbled in Scientology, homeopathy, acupuncture, and Christian Science. He tanned himself in a homemade lean-to, equipped with metal reflectors, until his skin was dark brown. On another occasion, his macrobiotic diet made him turn a ghoulish shade of green. According to his family, his breath reeked.

Practicing alternative medicine on himself was not enough. Whenever one of his children fell sick, Salinger flew into a rage, refusing to rest until he had found the exact homeopathic remedy to cure what ailed them. He spent hours poring through books on alternative medicine, searching for the perfect cure for a case of the sniffles.

When it came to acupuncture, "Doctor" Salinger had an even stranger way of dispensing treatment. He eschewed traditional needles in favor of stubby wooden dowels (the kind that hold together IKEA furniture). The result was pure agony. His daughter Margaret described the sensation as "like having a blunt pencil shoved into your skin." Salinger tried to cure his son Matthew's cold by jamming one of his magic dowels into the bones of the boy's pinkie finger. The tyke screamed in pain, but his father was unmoved. "You, your mother, and your sister have the lowest pain thresholds I've ever seen," he railed. "You'd think you'd caught a piece of shrapnel, for Christ's sake!" No wonder the two children took to hiding their illnesses from dear old Dad.

QUACK IN A BOX

When not tormenting his children with crackpot remedies, Salinger liked to spend a little "me time" in his own personal orgasmatron. Called an orgone box, the single-occupancy wood and sheet metal man-cave was invented in the 1930s by quack psychoanalyst Wilhelm Reich. The 5-by-2-by-2-foot box, also known as an Orgone Accumulator, purportedly absorbed "orgone," the life essence of the universe. (It was also widely believed to act as a powerful sexual stimulant for the person seated inside.) The device sold like hotcakes in the early 1950s before the U.S. government declared it a fraud and imprisoned its inventor. (For the record, Reich did spend five hours talking with Albert Einstein. When their conversation was over, he said to Einstein, "You understand now why everyone thinks I'm mad." Einstein replied: "And how.")

POWER OF BABBLE

Salinger's spiritual life was of the Baskin-Robbins variety. Born Jewish, he tried Zen Buddhism, Vedantic Hinduism, and even charismatic Christianity. Apparently, Salinger was so favorably impressed by a visit to a charismatic house of worship in New York City that he returned to his home in New Hampshire and began speaking in tongues. His daughter found him rapt in glossolallia, the ancient mystical language thought to represent the power of the Holy Spirit, inside his jury-rigged tanning parlor in the family yard.

ACCORDING TO HIS DAUGHTER MARGARET, J. D. SALINGER DRANK HIS OWN URINE—PRESUMABLY FOR MEDICINAL BENEFITS.

I'LL SEE YOU IN COURT!

Salinger is fiercely protective of his privacy, often using or threatening lawsuits to scare off would-be biographers. He successfully sued to stop author Ian Hamilton from reprinting his letters in a 1988 biography. When an Iranian filmmaker directed an unauthorized adaptation of *Franny and Zooey* in 1998, Salinger had his lawyers scuttle the screening. Even his threats of legal action have proved effective. The characters of Terrence Mann, played by James Earl Jones in *Field of Dreams*, and William Forrester, played by Sean Connery in *Finding Forrester*, were both based on Salinger but later changed to avoid litigation.

MY HERO

Salinger's son is Matthew Salinger, the actor who played Marvel Comics' superpatriot superhero Captain America in a 1990 straight-to-video feature film.

JACK KEROUAC

MARCH 12, 1922–OCTOBER 21, 1969

NATIONALITY:
AMERICAN

ASTROLOGICAL SIGN:
PISCES

MAJOR WORKS:
ON THE ROAD (1957), *THE DHARMA BUMS* (1958)

CONTEMPORARIES & RIVALS:
ALLEN GINSBERG, TRUMAN CAPOTE

LITERARY STYLE:
LOGORRHEIC RAMBLING PUNCTUATED
BY MYSTICAL INSIGHTS

WORDS OF WISDOM

"GREAT THINGS ARE NOT ACCOMPLISHED BY THOSE WHO YIELD TO TRENDS AND FADS AND POPULAR OPINION."

Asked to name some of Jack Kerouac's defining characteristics, few people would peg him as (a) French Canadian; (b) a political conservative; or (c) a prep school boy. But the sainted author of *On the Road* was all those things, not to mention a hard-core baseball fan who might have been happier being beat writer for the Red Sox than father of the Beat Generation.

Born Jean-Louis Lebris de Kerouac in Lowell, Massachusetts, in 1922, Kerouac was the son of a French Canadian printer from Quebec. He didn't speak a word of English until he was five years old and didn't master the language until he was a teenager. As a child, he amused himself by writing fictionalized accounts of sporting events. He attended the Horace Mann School in New York City, an elite preparatory academy whose famous alumni include red-baiting lawyer Roy Cohn, transsexual tennis star Renée Richards, and New York governor Eliot Spitzer.

Kerouac's football prowess won him a scholarship to Columbia University, where he once boasted of having set a record for cutting classes. He might have remained a dumb jock had he not broken a leg in his second game as a freshman. Instead he dropped out and pursued life as an itinerant writer. Years of traveling and jotting down impressions in his journal culminated, in April 1951, with the legendary marathon writing session that produced *On the Road*. Kerouac later claimed that he banged out the 175,000-word manuscript over three weeks, transcribed on one enormous roll of teletype paper. Most scholars now agree that the revered "Kerouac scroll" incorporates material from several years' worth of diary entries. Whatever the process, the episodic tale of an Eastern square and his hipster buddy traveling across America and Mexico became an instant cultural touchstone for the emerging Beat Generation.

Within a year, Kerouac was appearing on *The Steve Allen Show* reading excerpts from his magnum opus to the accompaniment of Steverino's jazzy piano. Sadly, that was one of Kerouac's more lucid public appearances during the period. More often than not, he showed up drunk or descended into gassy, incoherent ramblings about Buddhism and the true nature of genius. He earned some top-shelf literary detractors, including Truman Capote, who famously remarked of Kerouac's work, "That's not writing. It's typing." It should be noted that, while he's often associated with automatic or spontaneous composition, Kerouac in fact worked assiduously to revise his manuscripts and make them more marketable to publishers. And why not? That was the only way he could earn drinking money.

A lifelong alcoholic, Kerouac spent the last decade of his life drinking himself into a stupor. His literary output slowed to a trickle. He moved several times, always accompanied by his mother, and grew increasingly devout in his Catholicism. He died of a massive abdominal hemorrhage, with pen and pad in hand, on October 21, 1969.

!

ON THE RIGHT

The more radical Beats would have been mortified to find out that the father of their movement was a political conservative. A devout Catholic, Kerouac despised hippies and supported the Vietnam War. When someone draped an American flag over his shoulders at a party in the late sixties, he made a point of folding it up properly and putting it away. Kerouac also counted *National Review* founder and right-wing pundit William F. Buckley among his closest friends.

WHAT'S THE WORD? THUNDERBIRD!

Kerouac was a lifelong alcoholic. His drink of choice was Thunderbird, the inexpensive fortified wine that is the lifeblood of indigent winos everywhere.

THE DIAMOND BUM

On the Road may have been Kerouac's greatest novel, but his greatest creation is surely the Fantasy Baseball League. Long before online fantasy and "Rotisserie" leagues became a national craze, the father of the Beats was kicking it old school with a set of index cards and pads of multicolored paper.

He invented the league as a child growing up in Lowell, Massachusetts, in the mid-1930s and often referred to it in his journal entries as an adult, suggesting that it was a lifelong pastime. With its use of cards and statistics, the game was similar to Strat-o-Matic, which became popular in the 1960s. However, Kerouac's version was much more intricate and complex. Comprised of six imaginary teams, his league was populated with real-life figures such as Pancho Villa and Lou Gehrig, along with imaginary players, such as Homer Landry, Charley Custer, and Luis Tercerero. Kerouac made himself the manager of a team known as the Pittsburgh Plymouths.

"Games" were played in real time using marbles, toothpicks, and white-rubber erasers, which Kerouac launched at targets forty feet away. "Commissioner" Kerouac kept detailed records of each player's performance. He devised scorecards, box scores, and even salaries and team financial data. He also put out a newsletter, "Jack Lewis's Baseball Chatter," and published a broadsheet called the "The Daily Ball," for which he provided summaries of the day's games, up-to-the-minute standings, and lists of league leaders. Some of these obsessive jottings appear in *Atop an Underwood*, a collection of Kerouac's early writings. Others, sadly, have passed into baseball history.

ON THE ROAD AND OFF THE WAGON

In 1958, fresh off his greatest literary triumph, Kerouac moved with his mother into a house in Northport, a small harbor town on Long Island's North Shore. Locals there still remember him fondly—as the town drunk. Kerouac was often seen padding through town barefoot or wearing bedroom slippers, soused to the gills and pulling a metal "granny cart" behind him for groceries. Liquor was the only provision he really needed, however. He kept a bottle of Canadian Club in a briefcase just in case he ever ran dry. On the mornings after his benders, he could be found sleeping astride the abandoned trolley tracks that ran through town.

Kerouac's other haunts included the local pub and the liquor store, where he set up a cot for midday siestas. He often visited the town library but refused to go inside, demanding that librarians bring him books while he waited on the sidewalk. He became notorious for never mowing his lawn and bumming rides whenever he needed to go somewhere, which wasn't often. Most nights he stayed home and played with his deck of fantasy baseball cards or blasted selections from requiem masses on his reel-to-reel tape recorder. Every once in a while, some groupies would make the hour-long trek from New York City to meet him. Insecure about his growing fame, Kerouac liked to get them wasted and take them along on "wilding" excursions to abandoned North Shore mansions.

Kerouac left Northport for St. Petersburg, Florida, in 1964. He spent his last night in town drinking, carousing, and singing along to Mel Tormé records. He was later found sleeping it off in a field a few miles away.

THAT'S NAKED LUNCH—NOT FREE LUNCH

Kerouac and William Burroughs were longtime friends, but their relationship began to sour in the mid-1950s, due especially to Kerouac's constant freeloading. When Kerouac stayed at Burroughs's place, he never paid for anything and ate the *Naked Lunch* author out of house and home. By 1957 Burroughs broke off their friendship. The two Beat Generation icons didn't speak for more than a decade. They met only once more, in 1968, prior to Kerouac's appearance on his old pal William F. Buckley's TV chat show *Firing Line*. Kerouac was drunk, and Burroughs urged him not to go on and embarrass himself. Kerouac ignored him and proceeded to make an ass of himself on national television.

DURING HIS DAYS IN NORTHPORT, LONG ISLAND, JACK KEROUAC COULD OFTEN BE SEEN PADDING THROUGH TOWN BAREFOOT, DRUNK AS A SKUNK AND PULLING A GRANNY CART.

ON THE BALL

The first one thousand baseball fans who stepped through the turnstiles at the August 21, 2003, game between the Lowell Spinners and Williamsport Cross-cutters of the Class-A New York-Penn League received a rare treat: a Jack Kerouac bobble-head doll. Made of plastic and hard rubber, the doddering doll depicts the young Kerouac as he might have looked during his years in Lowell. Sporting a backpack, with a pen and notebook in his hands, he is standing on a copy of *On the Road*.

The unusual giveaway generated more than $10,000 for the Jack Kerouac Scholarship Fund and received extensive media coverage, including articles in *Sports Illustrated* and the *New York Times*. It was a late substitute for the club's

original plan: to roll out the original manuscript of *On the Road* on the field. That request was denied by Kerouac's estate. The Kerouac bobble-head is now enshrined at the Baseball Hall of Fame in Cooperstown, New York.

OUT OF HIS DEPP

Who knew Jack Sparrow was such a fan of Jack Kerouac? In 1991 actor Johnny Depp bought more than $50,000 worth of items from the executors of Kerouac's estate. His purchase included $15,000 for Kerouac's raincoat; $10,000 for his suitcase; $5,000 for one of his old travel bags; $2,000 for his sweatshirt (hopefully, it had been washed in the interim); $3,000 for a rain hat (can't have the raincoat without the rain hat); $10,000 for a tweed coat; $5,000 for a letter from Kerouac to Neal Cassady; and $350 for a canceled check to a liquor store.

CREDIBILITY GAP

In its eternal quest for hipster cachet, middlebrow clothing retailer The Gap launched a Beat-themed advertising campaign in the early 1990s. Print ads featured a photograph of Kerouac in twill pants and a casual shirt underneath the tagline "Kerouac Wore Khakis." Many of the writer's more radical fans were outraged at this posthumous appropriation of his likeness. (The Gap's sister chain Banana Republic was selling a $70 "Kerouac Bomber Jacket" about the same time.) To protest, a group of poets in Chicago created a spoof ad reading "Hitler Wore Khakis" and featuring a picture of the Nazi dictator. Hundreds of copies were then surreptitiously deposited inside Gap outlets in the Windy City. All those years later, the Beats were not to be messed with.

KURT VONNEGUT

NOVEMBER 11, 1922–APRIL 11, 2007

NATIONALITY:
AMERICAN

ASTROLOGICAL SIGN:
SCORPIO

MAJOR WORKS:
CAT'S CRADLE (1963), *SLAUGHTERHOUSE-FIVE* (1969), *BREAKFAST OF CHAMPIONS* (1973)

CONTEMPORARIES & RIVALS:
JOSEPH HELLER, THOMAS PYNCHON

LITERARY STYLE:
WRY, AFFECTLESS VERNACULAR PROSE, OCCASIONALLY INTERRUPTED BY DOODLES

"IF YOU REALLY WANT TO DISAPPOINT YOUR PARENTS, AND DON'T HAVE THE HEART TO BE GAY, GO INTO THE ARTS."

◀ WORDS OF WISDOM

Early in his career, Kurt Vonnegut bemoaned his status as a "sore-headed occupant of a file drawer labeled 'science fiction.'" He asked to be let out, "particularly because so many serious critics regularly mistake the drawer for a urinal."

Vonnegut did eventually escape from the file drawer, but he never totally won over the literary establishment. Some critics always saw him as nothing more than a hip "genre" writer whose shelf life ended with the 1960s. Or maybe they were just put off by the scatological doodles that adorned his later work. Undaunted, Vonnegut soldiered on—writing, drawing, and espousing his humanist gospel.

Born on Armistice Day in 1922, Vonnegut was the son and grandson of architects. (His grandfather was the first licensed architect in Indianapolis.) His parents intended to send him to a private school, along with his sisters, but then the family's fortunes bottomed out during the Great Depression. Instead, he attended public school, and his father, increasingly embittered, urged him to take up a practical profession. Determined to pursue a degree in biochemistry, he enrolled at Cornell University in the early 1940s. World War II put the kibosh on that plan, however, and he enlisted in the U.S. Army as an Infantry Battalion Scout. While he was serving overseas, his mother committed suicide by taking an overdose of sleeping pills. That was but one of two wartime traumas that haunted Vonnegut for the rest of his life.

The other was the Allied firebombing of Dresden, Germany, on February 13, 1945, which Vonnegut witnessed firsthand as a prisoner of war. The senseless slaughter of thousands of civilians shook his faith in humanity and the rationality of the universe. He later incorporated these experiences into his most famous novel, *Slaughterhouse-Five*.

After returning from the war, Vonnegut worked briefly as a police reporter and then wrote press releases for General Electric in Schenectady, New York. He tried—but failed—to earn a master's degree in anthropology from the University of Chicago. (In fact, the department's faculty unanimously rejected his final proposal for a master's thesis, titled "Fluctuations Between Good and Evil in Simple Tales.") His academic hopes dashed, Vonnegut turned to writing full-time. He supported himself penning short stories and novels throughout the 1950s while working at GE. He eventually moved to Cape Cod, Massachusetts, where he proceeded to manage a Saab dealership to supplement his income. Unfortunately that venture also failed, and the business went bankrupt in the early 1960s. Apparently his performance as a car salesman was lackluster, at best, and he felt the Swedes never forgave him for it.

Vonnegut hit his literary peak in the 1960s, publishing the novels *Cat's Cradle* (1963) and *Slaughterhouse-Five* (1969), which are considered to be his masterworks. In both, he cleverly bent the conventions of the science-fiction genre to suit his satiric and philosophical purposes. *Slaughterhouse-Five* introduced mainstream readers to Kilgore Trout, a minor character reprised from one of his earlier books who would become a recurring figure in later works. A hacked-out writer of schlock sci-fi for adult magazines, Trout may have been a stand-in for Vonnegut himself—or what the author might have become had he remained trapped in the genre.

Some critics noted a decline in the quality of Vonnegut's work during the next two decades. It's true that his novels did become increasingly self-referential, with dark undertones of the despair that eventually led him to attempt suicide in 1985. But after the cult success of *Slaughterhouse-Five* and its movie adaptation, his later works sold reasonably well, and Vonnegut stuck to his humanist guns. He bemoaned the advent of new technology, fretted about U.S. government policy and the demise of organized labor, and generally did what you would expect a crotchety left-leaning curmudgeon to do in his old age. Not even a devastating house fire, which hospitalized him in 2000, could silence his unmistakable voice. He vowed that his 2005 memoir, *A Man Without a Country*, would be his last published book, although he continued to write the occasional essay for the progressive monthly *In These Times* until his death in April 2007. Ironically, the man who had survived the devastating firebombing of Dresden and a lifetime of heavy smoking was ultimately cut down by a simple tumble down the stairs of his Manhattan apartment. He suffered brain trauma as a result of the fall and succumbed to his injuries a few weeks later.

NO SEUSS FOR YOU!

Contrary to popular belief, Vonnegut was not a fraternity brother of Dr. Seuss. In fact, he and Theodore "Seuss" Geisel did not even attend the same college. (Vonnegut went to Cornell; Geisel attended Dartmouth.) However, Vonnegut did share school ties with another famous writer. He went to Shortridge High School in Indianapolis with Madelyn Pugh, who went on to become the head writer of TV's *I Love Lucy*. Vonnegut and Pugh were both proud members of the school fiction club. Republican Senator Richard Lugar of Indiana was also a Shortridge grad.

TROUT FISHING

Vonnegut's most famous character, hack science-fiction writer Kilgore Trout, was loosely based on respected science-fiction writer Theodore Sturgeon, author of several short stories and the award-winning novel *More Than Human*. For those keeping score at home, Sturgeon's real name is Edward Hamilton Waldo.

LIGHTS, CAMERA . . . KURT!

Vonnegut appeared in the movie versions of two of his novels. He had a cameo as "Sad Man on the Street" in the 1996 adaptation of *Mother Night* and appeared as a TV commercial director in 1999's *Breakfast of Champions*. Vonnegut enjoyed a meatier big-screen role in the 1986 Rodney Dangerfield comedy *Back to School*. Appearing as himself, he helps Dangerfield's oafish Thornton Melon character write a term paper on the works of … Kurt Vonnegut.

KURT AND JERRY, PART ONE

Vonnegut once shared a joint with Grateful Dead front man Jerry Garcia, who was a big fan of the author's work. In fact, the Dead's music publishing company, Ice Nine Publishing, is named after the destructive substance at the center of Vonnegut's 1963 novel *Cat's Cradle*. Garcia was especially fond of Vonnegut's 1959 science-fiction classic *Sirens of Titan*, to which he owned the film rights until his death in 1995. For years, rumors abounded that Garcia and former *Saturday Night Live* writer Al Franken were developing a movie adaptation of *Sirens*. Sadly, it was not to be.

KURT AND JERRY, PART TWO

Vonnegut's daughter was once married to tabloid telejournalist Geraldo Rivera. The union lasted only four years and was not a happy one. By his own admission, Rivera repeatedly cheated on Edith Bucket "Pie" Vonnegut and in the process earned the everlasting enmity of her father. In interviews, whenever Vonnegut spoke about his erstwhile son-in-law, he made a point of referring to him as "Jerry," after Geraldo's real name, Jerry Rivers.

WOULD YOU BUY A CAR FROM THIS MAN?

Vonnegut was, by his own admission, "among the very first Saab dealers in the United States." In fact, until he went out of business in the early 1970s, he was the owner and manager of Saab Cape Cod in West Barnstable, Massachusetts. By all accounts, he was an extremely unhappy car salesman— although unlike Dwayne Hoover, the deranged Pontiac dealer in Vonnegut's semi-autobiographical 1973 novel *Breakfast of Champions*, he never went on a violent rampage. Instead, Vonnegut simply talked trash about the Swedish-made vehicle—which he called a "stinker" and "the ultimate yuppie canoe"— until he drove away most of his customers. Vonnegut always claimed that his public derision of Saabs was the reason the Swedes have never awarded him the Nobel Prize in Literature.

NEVER THE TWAIN SHALL MEET?

Vonnegut's idol was Mark Twain, for whom he named his firstborn son and with whom he shared a number of similarities. Both men were born in November. Both were American humorists who held a jaundiced view of their native country's politics and culture. Both served in the army and worked as journalists early in their careers. Both were heavy tobacco smokers. Both had their books banned in schools and libraries. And then, of course, there's that weird physical resemblance. Twain's hair could have almost come unstuck in time à la Billy Pilgrim and wound up on Vonnegut's noggin.

• POINTS FOR HONESTY •

During a 1990 speech at the National Air and Space Museum in Washington D.C., Vonnegut admitted that he owed his entire career to the firebombing of Dresden, which resulted in the deaths of between 25,000 and 250,000 civilians. "I got about five dollars for each corpse, counting my fee tonight," he remarked.

WHEN HE WASN'T WRITING CLASSIC NOVELS LIKE *SLAUGHTERHOUSE-FIVE*, KURT VONNEGUT MANAGED HIS OWN SAAB DEALERSHIP.

'ROID RAGE

In 1999 the asteroid formally known as 25399 was named in Vonnegut's honor.

THE FUTURE'S SO BRIGHT, I GOTTA WEAR . . . SUNSCREEN?

An outspoken computer skeptic, Vonnegut had little use for the Internet—making it all the more ironic that he once became the center of a worldwide e-mail hoax. In 1997 electronic messages began circulating that purportedly contained the text of a commencement address Vonnegut had given at the Massachusetts Institute of Technology. In the speech, "Vonnegut" extols the many benefits of sunscreen. He also dispenses a lot of platitudes about learning to love yourself and dancing the funky chicken, which anyone familiar with his work would never believe he could utter. Needless to say, Vonnegut never delivered such an address. The author was Mary Schmich, a columnist for the *Chicago Tribune*, though no one ever found out who was responsible for the false attribution. Australian movie director Baz Luhrmann later turned the faux Vonnegut address into a song, which hit #1 in the United Kingdom. Asked about the bizarre incident, Vonnegut replied laconically, "The Internet is spooky."

TONI MORRISON

FEBRUARY 18, 1931–

NATIONALITY:
AMERICAN

ASTROLOGICAL SIGN:
AQUARIUS

MAJOR WORKS:
THE BLUEST EYE (1970), *SONG OF SOLOMON* (1977), *BELOVED* (1987)

CONTEMPORARIES & RIVALS:
ALICE WALKER, MAYA ANGELOU

LITERARY STYLE:
NONLINEAR, ALLUSIVE, EMOTIONALLY POWERFUL

WORDS OF WISDOM

"IF THERE'S A BOOK YOU REALLY WANT TO READ, BUT IT HASN'T BEEN WRITTEN YET, THEN YOU MUST WRITE IT."

*T*oni Morrison's parents were perfectionists. Her father, George Wofford, was a welder who proudly burned his initials into the seams of every piece of metal he ever soldered together. When young Toni—then known as Chloe—reminded him that no one would ever see them, he replied, "Yes, but I'll know it's there." Her mother, Ramah Wofford, was no shrinking violet either. She once wrote a letter to President Franklin D. Roosevelt complaining about the quality of the flour the U.S. government was providing during the Great Depression. Eccentric? Perhaps, but the Woffords got themselves noticed, and so did their second of four children, Chloe Ardelia.

The Woffords had more to complain about than rancid flour. They were dirt poor. While George toiled in the steel mills of Lorain, Ohio, Ramah handed out towels in an amusement park restroom to help make ends meet. The family lived in at least six different apartments during Chloe's childhood. One of their landlords even burned down their home when they couldn't pay the $4-a-month rent. Being in a steel town, the Woffords always lived "below or next to white people"—circumstances that fed George Wofford's bitter hatred of Caucasians. Also around to foment racism was Chloe's crazy great-grandmother, who considered light-skinned blacks, like Chloe, "impure." "She thought that we had been 'tampered with,'" Morrison later admitted. To her credit, she never subscribed to any of these weird prejudices.

When she was twelve years old, Chloe Wofford converted to Catholicism. She selected Anthony as her baptismal name, which her friends shortened to Toni. Convinced that people would never figure out how to correctly pronounce the name Chloe, she soon began calling herself Toni. (The "Morrison" she added later, after her brief marriage to Jamaican-born architect Harold Morrison.) From an early age, she was an avid reader, devouring the works of Leo Tolstoy and Jane Austen, among others. It was no surprise when in 1949 she enrolled at Howard University, America's most prestigious black college, to study humanities.

After graduating and then earning a master's degree from Cornell University, Morrison returned to Howard to teach English. Among her students was the future black radical Stokely Carmichael, whom she described as "the kind of student you always want in a class—smart, perceptive, funny, and a bit of a rogue." Marriage and a teaching career didn't satisfy Morrison, so she ditched her husband and took an editorial job with Random

House. She would remain there for nearly twenty years while she nurtured her fledgling writing career.

Had she done nothing else besides edit other people's books, Morrison would still be a legend in the publishing industry. She discovered and developed numerous important African and African American writers, including Gayl Jones, Toni Cade Bambara, Chinua Achebe, and Athol Fugard. As her own novels began to sell, she supported her protégés financially as well. Morrison was known to send small checks to up-and-coming authors, along with a note announcing that they had been awarded a fictitious grant to subsidize their work. All the while, Morrison continued to toil away at her own novels, exploring different aspects of the African American experience. Each one seemed to earn more critical acclaim and attracted an ever-wider audience.

In 1981, Morrison made the cover of *Newsweek*, becoming the first black woman to appear on the cover of a national magazine since Zora Neale Hurston in 1943. Twelve years later, she was awarded the Nobel Prize in Literature, besting fellow Americans Thomas Pynchon and Joyce Carol Oates, who were also being considered that year. Not everyone was happy with the selection. Black novelist Charles Johnson called it "a triumph of political correctness," and Erica Jong fumed that "her prize was not motivated solely by artistic considerations." African American cultural critic Stanley Crouch, a longtime Morrison detractor (he once called her novel *Beloved* "protest pulp fiction"), would say only, "I hope this prize inspires her to write better books."

Whether it did or not is up to readers. What's not debatable is that the post-Nobel Toni Morrison has evolved into the dreadlocked éminence grise of African American letters. Often called upon by such cultural mandarins as Oprah and Charlie Rose to pontificate on the state of black America, she only occasionally makes headlines. (Her infamous reference to Bill Clinton as "America's first black president" is one such example.) Her books, which now come about twice a decade, continue to bridge the gap between high art and the best-seller list. Oprah's Book Club could not have a more worthy patron saint.

--- MY DAD THE BIGOT ---

By her own admission, Morrison's father was a virulent racist. "He disliked most whites," she observed. "He thought they were genetically corrupt." He once beat the stuffing out of a white man who appeared to be loitering around their apartment building because he was convinced the man wanted to molest his daughters. Throwing the drunken man down the stairs, George Wofford then crowned him with a children's tricycle while a "thrilled" Chloe cheered him on. "It made me know that it was possible to win," she later confessed.

THAT OLD BLACK MAGIC

Supernatural elements pervade Toni Morrison's work—and with good reason. She's a believer. "Black people believe in magic," she once told an interviewer. When someone asked Morrison if she believed in ghosts, she replied, "Yes. Do you believe in germs? It's part of our heritage." Morrison claims her family was "intimate with the supernatural" when she was a child. Her grandmother even used a special "dream book" to help her pick lucky numbers in the neighborhood lottery. Without a belief in spirits, Morrison has said, "I would have been dependent on so-called scientific data to explain hopelessly unscientific things."

PLUS I JUST THINK CHRIS NOTH IS DREAMY

Morrison is a rabid fan of the long-running TV drama *Law and Order*. She describes the criminal justice procedural as providing "mild engagement with a satisfying structure of redemption." Lennie Briscoe couldn't have put it better himself.

WHITE FRIGHT

It seems absurd now, but at one time Morrison was viewed by some as a dangerous radical, and even her friends at Random House seemed scared of her. When Morrison made plans for a book publication party at a club in Harlem, the publishing company's marketing department freaked out. Management circulated memos warning staff about the perils of convening in the largely black neighborhood. As it turned out, only two Random House publicity officials attended the event. When it was over, they declared it to be the best party they'd ever been to. Even better, the controversy attracted extensive TV news coverage, giving the book a bigger boost than Morrison could have hoped for.

Morrison also ran into resistance when she tried to arrange a book signing for heavyweight champion Muhammad Ali, whose autobiography *The Greatest* came out in 1976. All the major New York City department store chains, except one, refused to host the event out of fear of riots and looting. Morrison did manage to cajole one store, E. J. Korvette's, into hosting the signing. To ease their concerns, she hired the Nation of Islam to provide security. The evening went off without a hitch, to the delight of some two thousand autograph seekers and the amazement of nervous white people everywhere.

THE NOBEL PRIZE–WINNING TONI MORRISON IS ALSO, AMONG OTHER THINGS, A FAN OF THE TELEVISION SHOW *LAW AND ORDER*. SHE ONCE EVEN PAID A VISIT TO THE SET.

FRIENDS IN HIGH PLACES

Stanley Crouch may not dig her, but Morrison has some high-profile celebrity backers. Before his death (and perhaps after, given Morrison's belief in ghosts), Marlon Brando was known to call her on the phone and read aloud passages from her novels that he found particularly uplifting. He once called her "the best writer of the world, in my estimation."

Oprah Winfrey was so touched by Morrison's 1987 novel *Beloved* that she ordered her "people" to acquire the movie rights no matter what the cost. Unfortunately, meeting Morrison's asking price proved easier than adapting such difficult material for the big screen. The 1998 film version, starring Oprah and Danny Glover, failed to impress critics and bombed at the box office.

ONCE AN EDITOR . . .

. . . always an editor. After nineteen years with Random House, Morrison found it hard to put down her red pencil. She still reads the *New York Times* with a marker at the ready, copyediting articles as she goes along.

BLACK BUBBA

In a 1998 essay in *The New Yorker*, Morrison caused a stir when she declared Bill Clinton to be America's "first black president." His "white skin notwithstanding," Morrison wrote, Clinton was "blacker than any actual black person who could ever be elected in our children's lifetime. . . . [He] displays almost every trope of blackness: single-parent household, born poor, working-class, saxophone-playing, McDonald's-and-junk-food-loving boy from Arkansas." For the record, the notion of Clinton as a black man originated with comedian Chris Rock, who was referring to him as a "black president" in his stand-up routines more than two years before Morrison's infamous pronouncement.

NOBEL, SCHNOBEL

Forget Stockholm. For truly high honors, you get a call from Passaic. In 2007 Morrison was one of the inaugural nominees for enshrinement in the New Jersey Hall of Fame. According to Chairman Bart Oates, an offensive lineman on the 1986 Super Bowl champion New York Giants, the Hall honors New Jersey residents "who have made invaluable contributions to society and the world beyond." Morrison's fellow honorees included famed movie straight man Bud Abbott, billionaire publisher Malcolm Forbes, and Buzz Aldrin, second man on the moon.

SYLVIA PLATH

OCTOBER 27, 1932–FEBRUARY 11, 1963

NATIONALITY:
AMERICAN

ASTROLOGICAL SIGN:
SCORPIO

MAJOR WORKS:
THE COLOSSUS (1960),
THE BELL JAR (1963), *ARIEL* (1965)

CONTEMPORARIES & RIVALS:
TED HUGHES, ANNE SEXTON,
ROBERT LOWELL, W. S. MERWIN

LITERARY STYLE:
BRUTALLY HONEST, CONFESSIONAL, ACCUSATORY

*"THE WORST ENEMY
TO CREATIVITY IS
SELF-DOUBT"*

◀ WORDS OF WISDOM

*I*n the early morning hours of February 11, 1963, Sylvia Plath went up to the room where her children were sleeping and left them a plate of bread and butter and two mugs of milk. She then headed back downstairs to the kitchen. After sealing the door and window with towels, she opened the oven, stuck her head inside, and turned on the gas. A few hours later, she was found dead on the floor.

So ended the life of a great poet, and so began a legend that has inspired generations of depressive college girls to pursue their dreams of writing, wallowing, and man hating. Plath did a lot of all those things during her thirty-plus years. She also became an object lesson in self-destruction.

Plath's father was an expert on bees. His sudden death when Plath was eight years old would haunt her the rest of her life and provide powerful images for her poetry. After his demise, she vowed never to speak to God again and instead plunged herself into schoolwork. The Boston *Sunday Herald* published her first poem when she was just eight-and-a-half years old.

Plath grew up in Wellesley, Massachusetts, then, as now, a hotbed of headband-wearing women. In 1950, at a cultural turning point for angsty teenage girls everywhere, she sold her first short story to *Seventeen* magazine. She won a scholarship to Smith College in Northampton, where she was dubbed the "golden girl" and began her writing career in earnest. She began filling up notebooks with her stories, sonnets, and journal entries.

After winning a writing contest sponsored by *Mademoiselle*, Plath was awarded the chance to serve as guest editor of its June 1953 issue. That meant moving to New York, which turned out to be a big mistake. Plath was a fish out of water in the high-fashion world of Manhattan magazines. She likened the experience to pledging a sorority and soon returned home, where she suffered a nervous breakdown. She crawled into the cellar of the family home and overdosed on sleeping pills; she was institutionalized briefly and given electric shock treatments. The entire demoralizing experience formed the basis for her novel *The Bell Jar*, which was published in England under the pen name Victoria Lucas. A classic of 1950s alienation, the book was on par with J. D. Salinger's *The Catcher in the Rye*. When finally published in the United States in 1970, it attracted a whole new generation of readers, who regarded the work as an important work of proto-feminism.

Psychological fragility would become a hallmark of Plath's life. So would domineering treatment at the hands of medical professionals and men in general. When she asked despairingly for a lobotomy to alleviate her suffering, her psychiatrist laughed and told her, "You're not going to get off that easy." Scholars now generally agree that Plath must have suffered from some form of bipolar disorder. She remained a high achiever, however, and received a Fulbright fellowship to Cambridge University upon her graduation from Smith. That's when her life really spun out of control.

At Cambridge, Plath met Ted Hughes, the archetype for swaggering, macho, self-absorbed poets everywhere. Drawn in by his animal magnetism, she eagerly wed him on June 16, 1956. It turned out to be a match made in hell. With her wild mood swings and volcanic temper, Plath was ill-suited to the role of docile wife to such a philandering narcissist. Their raucous arguments often ended with Plath burning Hughes's latest work in a ritual bonfire or torching her own. Somehow the couple managed to produce two children and to avoid scorching either of them.

Plath produced her first volume of poetry, *The Colossus and Other Poems*, in 1960. Its publication marked a turning point in her literary career. Fed up with fiction, she turned to confessional poetry as a vehicle to pour out her feelings of loss and anger—at the death of her father, at the role of women in a male-dominated society, and at her own sense of marginality. Some poems deal with the troubles in her marriage or with devastating events, like her 1961 miscarriage. Many contained violent and disturbing images of the Holocaust, death, mutilation, and brutality. Her poems grew only more intense and autobiographical during the last few years of her life.

In the summer of 1962, Plath discovered that her husband was having an affair. When she confronted him, he left her. Emotionally devastated and physically ill, she holed up in a flat in London and began writing her final volume of poetry, one that would result in her greatest literary acclaim. By October, she was cranking out one poem a day, many of them powerful denunciations of her father, Hughes, or some imagined combination of the two. "Daddy, daddy, you bastard, I'm through," she wailed in "Daddy," one of her most often quoted poems. In "Lady Lazarus," she likened her father to a Nazi physician.

If the new poems seemed like kiss-offs to the world, that's because they were, for their composition preceded Plath's suicide by just a few months. As an especially cold winter deepened, Plath's depression—which always had a seasonal-affective component—worsened. Her doctor scrambled to find an open bed in one of London's psychiatric hospitals, but all were full. After her suicide, Hughes became heir to her estate as well as her literary executor. To the eternal consternation of her fans, he edited her final poetry collections with a heavy hand, reshuffling the order and removing some poems entirely. Critics accused him of suppressing those that referred to him or their fractured marriage.

Plath joins a long line of suicidal poets, stretching back to Hart Crane and Edna St. Vincent Millay and forward to John Berryman and Anne Sexton, whose poem "Sylvia's Death" morbidly commemorates their friendship. But with the possible exception of Virginia Woolf, nobody grew more in stature due to the circumstances of her demise—or, to borrow her phrase, excelled at the "art" of dying—quite like Plath. Her *Collected Poems* was finally published in 1981. The next year, she became the first poet to win a Pulitzer Prize posthumously.

!

SMARTY PANTS

No wonder Plath excelled at school—and had so much trouble fitting in. She was often the smartest person in the room. According to an IQ test she took in 1944, she had a genius-level IQ of 166.

THE FIRST TIME SYLVIA PLATH MET HER FUTURE HUSBAND, TED HUGHES, SHE WAS SO EXCITED THAT SHE BIT HIM ON THE FACE, DRAWING BLOOD. IT WAS LOVE AT FIRST SIGHT.

WHO SAYS YOU CAN'T GO HOME AGAIN?

Plath held two jobs for which she was uniquely qualified: English teacher at Smith College and receptionist in the psychiatric clinic at Massachusetts General Hospital—the same health center where she had been a patient several years earlier.

TAKES ONE TO KNOW ONE

Although she spent much time in England, Plath wasn't exactly smitten with British men. She described them in her journals as a pack of "pallid, neurotic homosexuals."

SYLVIA PLATH . . . CHILDREN'S AUTHOR?

Plath will never be confused with Dr. Seuss, but she did write a children's book. *The Bed Book*, a collection of nonsense poems about the various kinds of beds, was published after her suicide in 1963.

FOR BETTER OR WORSE

Plath and her husband, Ted Hughes, set a new standard for dysfunctional, destructive relationships. The tone was established at their first meeting, at a Cambridge University student party. As Plath records in her journal, after a few minutes of conversation, Hughes kissed her "bang smash on the mouth" and proceeded to rip off her hair band in a savage display of his desire. Not to be outdone, Plath "bit him long and hard on the cheek, and when we came out of the room, blood was running down his face."

Like many couples, they couldn't maintain this level of passion for long. After marrying the dour Hughes in 1956, Plath soon started complaining about his habits. He was moody, he picked his nose, and he dressed like a slob. Most important, he cheated on her. Amazingly, they persevered through seven years of marriage before Hughes finally pulled the plug—thereby earning the everlasting enmity of Plath's devoted fans.

DEAD POETS' SOCIETY

Plath committed suicide in a London apartment once occupied by W. B. Yeats, her favorite poet. She had considered moving into Yeats's old flat to be a positive omen.

BETTER DEAD THAN TED

For thirty-five years, until his death in 1998, Ted Hughes never lived down his role as the villain in Sylvia Plath's tragic demise. Many of her fans blamed him for her suicide, even though she had already tried to kill herself three years before she met him. People shouted "Murderer" at Hughes's poetry readings and repeatedly chiseled his name off Plath's gravestone. For his part, Hughes rarely spoke about his late wife, silently fanning the rage of those who considered him responsible for the loss of a great poetic voice.

TO BEE OR NOT TO BEE

Plath's father, Otto Emil Plath, the "Herr Doktor" whom the poet excoriates in her famous poem "Daddy," was indeed a physician, although not the vicious Nazi the verses suggest. A professor of biology and German at Boston University, Otto Plath was a respected etymologist and author of the book *Bumblebees and Their Ways*. Although he was undoubtedly imperious and emotionally distant, Herr Doktor's greatest fault may have been in the area of personal hygiene. In 1940 he refused medical treatment after his toe became infected; he contracted gangrene and died.

THOMAS PYNCHON

MAY 8, 1937–

NATIONALITY:
AMERICAN

ASTROLOGICAL SIGN:
TAURUS

MAJOR WORKS:
V (1963), *GRAVITY'S RAINBOW* (1973)

CONTEMPORARIES & RIVALS:
DON DELILLO, JORGE LUIS BORGES,
DONALD BARTHELME

LITERARY STYLE:
GNOMIC, ERUDITE, IMPENETRABLE—
LIKE THE MAN HIMSELF

WORDS OF WISDOM

*"EVERY WEIRDO IN THE
WORLD IS ON MY WAVE-
LENGTH."*

We'd love to provide some biographical background on Thomas Pynchon, but we're afraid of what might happen if we do. He is obsessive about his privacy, after all, and was thought by some to be the Unabomber. Others tried to link him to the Branch Davidians, the troubled religious sect that went down in flames in a compound near Waco, Texas, in 1993. One enterprising journalist even contended that the famously reclusive author is in fact that *other* famously reclusive author, J. D. Salinger. (Pynchon's retort? A pithy "Not bad. Keep trying.") Allegations that Pynchon is also Harper Lee have thus far gone unsubstantiated, mostly because they have been unmade.

Although he refuses to be photographed, does not grant interviews, and almost never appears in public, Pynchon insists he is not a recluse. He describes that term as "a code word generated by journalists" because "it's hard for reporters to believe that somebody doesn't want to talk to them." Most of the existing photos date back to his time in the navy, when presumably the words "I'm Thomas Pynchon and I don't want to be photographed" carried less weight. Pynchon must have had a good time in the navy because he mentions it throughout his early work. What exactly did he do? We may never know. His service records have mysteriously vanished—some say at Pynchon's request.

One place where Pynchon did leave a paper trail was Cornell University, where he maintained an atypically uninebriated undergraduate lifestyle. A college classmate described him as "a constant reader—the type who read books on mathematics for fun . . . one who started the day at 1 pm with spaghetti and a soft drink and read and worked until three the next morning." When not burning the midnight oil with Chef Boyardee, Pynchon was taking classes with *Lolita* author Vladimir Nabokov. The two didn't exactly bond. Pynchon couldn't understand a word Nabokov said because of his thick Russian accent, and Nabokov barely registered Pynchon's existence. Years later he couldn't even remember having taught him, although Nabokov's wife did recall Pynchon's distinctive half-printed, half-cursive handwriting style.

After college, Pynchon worked briefly as a technical writer for the Boeing Corporation, compiling articles on surface-to-air missile safety for company newsletters. It was a waste of his talent but good grist for his fiction, which is filled with paranoid screeds about military-corporate conspiracies. In his free time, he wrote *V*, his first novel. With its success came unwanted attention. Pynchon moved to Mexico, where he grew a bushy moustache and tried to lose himself among the locals, who dubbed him "Pancho Villa." Since returning to the United States, Pynchon has divided his time between California and New York (if anecdotal sightings are to be trusted). About once a decade, he drops some science on his avid cult of admirers, who argue endlessly about whether this or that novel marks a return to the form established by his masterpiece, *Gravity's Rainbow*.

Pynchon isn't completely incommunicado. He's made two guest appearances on the animated series *The Simpsons*. On both occasions, he played a scarily insane caricature of himself, complete with a bag over his head. In 1996 he emerged from his bunker to write the liner notes for an album by the alternative rock band Lotion. Apparently enamored with the band, Pynchon reportedly turned up backstage at one of their shows wearing a Godzilla T-shirt and pledging his undying appreciation for their songcraft. Though initially weirded out by this apparition, band members quickly took a liking to their new groupie and benefited enormously from the attendant PR buzz. Where or in what manner Pynchon will turn up next is anybody's guess.

"Why should things be easy to understand?" Pynchon once asked, an imponderable he must silently cackle over every time he drops another maddeningly opaque thousand-page novel on an unsuspecting public. So here's to you, Tom, for making the work of journalists and biographers—not to mention English majors—just a little bit harder through your lifelong commitment to avoidance and obfuscation.

GRAMPA THE HERETIC

Centuries before *Gravity's Rainbow*, a Pynchon was stirring up trouble with the local censors. William Pynchon, Thomas Pynchon's ancestor, was one of the earliest Americans of European descent. He emigrated from England in 1630, just ten years after the *Mayflower* landing, arriving in the same fleet as William Hathorne, the great-great-great-grandfather of novelist Nathaniel Hawthorne. William Pynchon later served as an aide to the Massachusetts

Bay colony's colonial governor, John Winthrop. However, he had to flee to England in 1650 after one of his religious tracts was denounced as heretical by the Puritan authorities.

GRAVITY'S DILDO

Pynchon's niece is adult filmmaker Tristan Taormino, the director of such hardcore porn classics as *House of Ass* and *The Ultimate Guide to Anal Sex for Women*, parts one and two. The Wesleyan graduate and *Village Voice* sex columnist is considered a pioneer in her use of handheld "perv cams" that allow adult-movie stars to film one another without directorial interference. She runs an online sex-toys store and has big plans to include her uncle on upcoming DVDs. "I think it would be fascinating for him to do commentary on the next one," Taormino told the *New York Post* in 2006. Pynchon scholars waiting with bated breath for that appearance will have to hold off until he actually watches one of his niece's previous films. "He hasn't asked me for any, and I haven't sent him any," Taormino admits, although she is quick to point out the similarities that could foster future collaboration. "We're both writers, and I think he's intrigued in general by pop culture."

OVERWRITTEN, YES. UNREADABLE, POSSIBLY. BUT *OBSCENE?*

Despite overwhelming sentiment in Pynchon's favor, in 1974 the Pulitzer Prize committee passed him over when it elected to award no prize at all rather than honor *Gravity's Rainbow*. In defiance of the recommendation of its nominating jury, the Pulitzer editorial board spurned the novel, deeming it "overwritten," "turgid," "obscene," and "unreadable." Pynchon had to console himself with a National Book Award instead.

PYNCH HITTER

The early 1970s were the heyday of sending other people to accept your awards for you. In 1973 Marlon Brando dispatched Sacheen Littlefeather (real name: Maria Cruz), a phony Indian, to pick up his Academy Award for *The Godfather*. The next year, Pynchon bettered that stunt when he had pretend academic "Professor" Irwin Corey accept the National Book Award for

Gravity's Rainbow. In his acceptance speech, the Brooklyn-born stand-up comic, who bills himself as "the world's foremost authority," referred to Pynchon as "Richard Python" and thanked Truman Capote, Soviet premier Leonid Breshnev, and "acting president of the United States" Henry Kissinger. Toward the end of the rambling address, that other fixture of early 1970s awards ceremonies—a streaker—ran through New York's Alice Tully Hall. The next day, the *New York Times* noted that the bizarre scene "left some people roaring with laughter and others perplexed." Hmm, not unlike Pynchon's last three novels.

> THOMAS PYNCHON HASN'T BEEN PHOTOGRAPHED IN MORE THAN FORTY YEARS—BUT THIS DESIRE FOR PRIVACY HASN'T KEPT FANS FROM STALKING HIM.

NEXT WEEK: J. D. SALINGER ON SCRUBS!

For a guy who refuses to make public appearances, Pynchon sure is vigilant when it comes to policing his image in the media. Not even lousy sitcoms escape his notice. In 1994 he received word that NBC's *John Laroquette Show* planned to feature him in an episode. Smelling a lawsuit, the producers sent the script to Pynchon for his approval. His agent called back with the novelist's suggested changes: "First, you call him Tom, and no one ever calls him Tom," she said. In addition, the script had Pynchon giving a friend a Willy DeVille T-shirt as a gift. The agent reported that although Pynchon "likes Willy DeVille, he would prefer if it were a T-shirt with Roky Erickson of the 13th Floor Elevators." Finally, Pynchon vetoed a scene that called for the actor playing him to be filmed from behind. The larger issue of why one of America's most acclaimed novelists would be ambling through the ramshackle St. Louis bus depot where this train wreck of a show was set did not seem to have troubled him at all.

APPENDIX

ODD JOBS

When you're a writer, you have to do whatever it takes to pay the bills. Here's what some of the world's literary giants did *before* they hit the big time.

Henry David Thoreau worked in his father's pencil factory.

Arthur Conan Doyle was an ophthalmologist.

William Faulkner was a bank teller, a bookstore clerk, and a postmaster.

Wallace Stevens was an insurance executive. He even kept the gig long after he became one of America's greatest poets.

Richard Wright was a mailman.

Kurt Vonnegut ran a Saab dealership and wrote press releases for General Electric.

Jack London was an oyster pirate. (It sounds more exciting than it actually is.)

Charles Dickens worked in a shoe polish factory.

Langston Hughes was a busboy. In fact, he got his break one night when he was bussing poet Vachel Lindsay's table. He left some of his poems on the table with the soup course, Lindsay liked them, and the rest is history.

Henry Miller was an employment manager for the Western Union Telegraph Company.

Jack Kerouac, the man who inspired a generation to take off "on the road," once did so literally. He was a gas station attendant.

Ernest Hemingway, Dashiell Hammett, E. E. Cummings, W. Somerset Maugham, John Dos Passos, and Archibald MacLeish all drove ambulances during World War I. So did Walt Disney, for that matter.

LITERARY CRITTERS

Every writer needs a muse. Many have turned to pets for inspiration, consolation, or as a means to strike a really eccentric figure in the history books.

Virgil, the ancient Greek poet, had a pet housefly, on whose lavish funeral he spent the equivalent of almost one million dollars. The memorial service entailed hiring an orchestra and constructing a tiny mausoleum.

Gérard de Nerval, the French symbolist poet, had a pet lobster, which he often took for walks through the streets of Paris. Lobsters make great pets, he wrote, because they're "peaceful, serious creatures who know the secrets of the sea, and don't bark." Nerval went insane in 1841.

Elizabeth Barrett Browning had a red cocker spaniel named Flush, who was later the subject of a "biography" by Virginia Woolf. Browning wrote the poem "To Flush" in the canine's honor and even tried to teach it to play board games to help her pass the time during her long bouts with illness.

Dog lover George Eliot once spent an entire book advance on a pug.

It seems out of character, but Ernest Hemingway was a cat person. He owned more than 30, and many had six toes (the origin of the term *Hemingway cats*). Keeping them straight involved coming up with a variety of colorful names, including Alley Cat, Boise, Crazy Christian, Dillinger, Ecstasy, F. Puss, Fats, Friendless Brother, Furhouse, Pilar, Skunk, Thruster, Whitehead, and Willy.

Mark Twain could have given Papa a run for his money in the cat-naming department. At various times, his menagerie included Appolinaris, Beelzebub, Blatherskite, Buffalo Bill, Satan, Sin, Sour Mash, Tammany, and Zoroaster.

The greatest literary cat lover of all, of course, was T. S. Eliot, who wrote an entire book of light verse about felines, the basis for the love-it-or-loathe-it Broadway musical *Cats*. Eliot didn't have a Rum Tum Tugger in his brood, but he did have a Tantomile, a Noilly Prat, a Wiscus, a Pettipaws, and a George Pushdragon.

Dorothy Parker once received a gift of two baby alligators. Not knowing what to do with them, she simply dropped them in her bathtub and left them there. The next day she found a note from her maid: "Dear Madam," it read. "I am leaving, as I cannot work in a house with alligators. I would have told you this before, but I never thought the subject would come up."

LITERARY FEUDS

Can't we all just get along? Apparently some great writers can't. So they pick fights with their fellow authors. Expect to see these epic rivals still slugging it out till the crack of doom in some corner of Literary Heaven.

Thomas Carlyle **vs.** John Stuart Mill

The great Victorian essayist and his philosopher protégé were close friends. But then Mill began to chafe under his mentor's yoke. When Carlyle lent him the manuscript for his massive history of the French Revolution, Mill had his cleaning lady throw it in the fireplace. It was Carlyle's only copy. Undaunted, the Scotsman simply sat down and wrote the entire thing all over again. But he never forgave Mill for the insult.

Lillian Hellman **vs.** Mary McCarthy

"Every word she writes is a lie, including *and* and *the*," novelist Mary McCarthy quipped of her bête noire, playwright Lillian Hellman, during a 1980 appearance on *The Dick Cavett Show*. In retaliation, Hellman promptly sued her for libel, seeking $2.2 million in damages. The writers' bitter feud originated more than 30 years earlier, when they clashed publicly at a poetry seminar at Sarah Lawrence College.

Gertrude Stein vs. Ernest Hemingway

Theirs was another case of the mentor/student relationship gone awry. Stein had nothing but praise for Hemingway until his literary star began to eclipse hers. Then she wrote a catty review of one of his books, and the gloves were off. "Papa" even dished about her sex life with Alice B. Toklas in his memoir, *A Moveable Feast*.

Gore Vidal vs. Norman Mailer

The long-simmering feud between the two egotistical novelists—both of whom wanted to be considered America's preeminent wordsmith—came to a head one evening at a tony New York dinner party, where Mailer challenged Vidal to a fight and threw a drink in his face when Vidal ignored him. Unperturbed, Vidal remarked, "Once again words have failed Norman." The two also came to blows before a scheduled appearance on *The Dick Cavett Show*, trading slaps and head butts backstage before engaging in a memorable war of words on the air. Mailer to Vidal: "You pollute the intellectual rivers"; Vidal to Mailer: "What I detest in you [is] your love of murder."

Vladimir Nabokov vs. Edmund Wilson

The *Lolita* author and the esteemed critic were once as thick as thieves. They used to write letters in which they called each other by the pet names "Volodya," and "Bunny," respectively. But the friendship soured when Wilson panned Nabokov's translation of Pushkin's *Eugene Onegin*. Word on the street was he hadn't much cared for *Lolita* either, which really pushed Volodya's buttons.

Mario Vargas Llosa vs. Gabriel García Márquez

Peru took on Colombia in a Mexico City movie theater one night in 1976, as Vargas Llosa sucker punched García Márquez in front of dozens of witnesses at a film premiere. The right hook left García Márquez's eye gushing with blood—and onlookers clucking about the possible cause. A squabble over politics? More likely it was a fight over a woman. Vargas Llosa apparently felt Colombia's greatest author had gotten a little too cozy with his wife, whom García Márquez had recently consoled through a difficult period in their marriage.

Tom Wolfe vs. Norman Mailer, John Irving, and John Updike

When Wolfe's novel *A Man in Full* was published in 1998, the three contemporary fiction masters unanimously agreed that it was rubbish. That ground the gears of the white-suited New Journalism pioneer. He slagged the trio on a Canadian TV show as "the Three Stooges" and claimed their criticism was motivated by jealousy. "It must gall them a bit that everyone—even them—is talking about me," Wolfe said.

LIVE BY THE PEN, DIE BY THE PEN

Nothing cuts a writer down to size quite like a rejection letter. Even the greatest authors have found themselves on the receiving end of some stinging rebukes from publishers.

When Emily Dickinson finally mustered up the courage to submit her poems for publication, she was informed that they were "as remarkable for defects as for beauties and ... generally devoid of true poetical qualities."

Herman Melville labored for months over *Moby-Dick*, only to have it dismissed by one publisher as "very long [and] rather old-fashioned."

H. G. Wells must have taken it personally when one publisher called his *War of the Worlds* "an endless nightmare." (Perhaps he was envisioning the Tom Cruise movie version.) The rejection letter went on to say: "I do not believe it would 'take' ... I think the verdict would be, 'Oh, don't read that horrid book.'" Ouch.

An American publisher apparently missed the point of George Orwell's *Animal Farm*. He sent back the manuscript with the note: "It is impossible to sell animal stories in the USA."

Ayn Rand got off relatively easy. Her massive novel *Atlas Shrugged* was merely deemed "unsalable and unpublishable." For William Faulkner, the rejection was more pointed. An editor passed on his 1931 novel *Sanctuary*—a sensational tale in which a young woman is raped with a corncob—writing to the author: "I can't publish this. We'd both be in jail!"

Almost as bad as the rejections are the nasty reviews. *The New York Times Book Review* almost wore out the thesaurus excoriating Thomas Pynchon's *Gravity's Rainbow*. The reviewer called it "bonecrushingly dense, compulsively elaborate, silly, obscene, funny, tragic, pastoral, historical, philosophical, poetic, grindingly dull, inspired, horrific, cold, bloated, beached, and blasted." Of Walt Whitman, now recognized as America's most beloved poet, the critic for the *Boston Intelligencer* wrote: "He must be some escaped lunatic raving in pitiable delirium."

Of course, writers often have unkind words to say about each other's work as well. Sometimes very unkind things. Robert Graves, the author of *I, Claudius*, once called Dylan Thomas "a demagogic Welsh masturbator who failed to pay his bills." Henry James railed that "H. G. Wells throws information at the reader as if emptying his mind like a perpetual chamber pot from a window." To William Faulkner, Mark Twain was "a hack writer who would have been considered fourth rate in Europe." Ambrose Bierce labeled Oscar Wilde an "ineffable dunce," "an impostor," "a blockhead," and "a crank"—all in the course of two sentences.

Even the greatest writer in the English language wasn't immune from criticism. Voltaire dismissed Shakespeare's entire oeuvre as "a vast dunghill," calling him "a drunken savage." Charles Dickens tried to read the Bard's work, but "found it so intolerably dull that it nauseated me." Tolstoy merely found it "rude, immoral, vulgar, and senseless." It seems with great literary power comes great power to harm—not to mention a great big target to wear on your backside.

FAMOUS LAST WORDS

Great writers build their lives around expressing themselves verbally, and some of them save the best for last. Here's a selection of the wise, witty, and downright bizarre things legendary authors have said on their way out the door of life.

Lord Byron: "Now I shall go to sleep. Good night."

Edgar Allen Poe: "Lord, help my poor soul."

Anne Brontë: "Take courage, Charlotte, take courage."

Henry David Thoreau: "Moose, Indian."
Walt Whitman: "Hold me up, I want to shit."

Leo Tolstoy: "But the peasants. . . . How do the peasants die?"

Emily Dickinson: "The fog is rising."

Louisa May Alcott: "Is it not meningitis?"

Oscar Wilde: "My wallpaper and I are fighting a duel to the death. One or the other of us has to go."

L. Frank Baum: "Now I can cross the Shifting Sands."

Arthur Conan Doyle (to his wife): "You are wonderful."

H. G. Wells: "Go away. I'm all right."

Gertrude Stein: "What is the answer? [no response] In that case, what is the question?"

James Joyce: "Does nobody understand?"

Franz Kafka: "Kill me, or else you are a murderer!"

Eugene O'Neill: "Born in a hotel room—and God damn it—died in a hotel room."

Dylan Thomas: "I just had eighteen straight scotches. I think that's the record. . . . After thirty-nine years, this is all I've done."

INDEX